Much has [...]
American War and [...]
intervention in Cuba. The military administration of General Leonard Wood has been a favorite subject of both Cuban and American orators and writers. In vivid contrast is the story of the second intervention and the civil administration of Provisional Governor Charles E. Magoon. Cubans have praised Wood and denounced Magoon, and writers of United States history have ignored or only briefly mentioned the government's role in Cuban affairs from 1906 to 1909.

Dr. Lockmiller has not attempted to write a detailed account of Cuban history prior to the elections of 1905; nor does he concern himself with the particulars of the period following the withdrawal of the provisional government in 1909. Rather, this volume presents as background the events of the first intervention and Estrada Palma's administration. Consideration of the elections of 1905, the August Revolution of 1906 (as a result of which the United States civil authorities were requested to take over the government of Cuba), the Taft and Bacon Peace Mission,

(continued on back flap)

(continued from front flap)

and the Platt Amendment introduce the more original phases of the study.

The second intervention was the Platt Amendment in operation, and Magoon was the constitutional executive of Cuba as well as the agent of President Roosevelt. In this connection there is a detailed discussion of the personality of Magoon—his training and experience, and the factors which contributed to his selection as Provisional Governor. The complex political and economic problems resulting from the August Revolution and the Panic of 1907, the extensive public works program, the war against yellow fever and other diseases, and the granting of government aid to agriculture and municipalities (some of these emergency and relief measures have a striking similarity to New Deal legislation), find a place in this volume. The author gives an analysis of the laws drafted by the Advisory Law Commission, discusses the election campaign of 1908 and the inauguration of President Gómez, and concludes with an evaluation of Governor Magoon and his administration.

MAGOON IN CUBA

CHARLES E. MAGOON

Magoon in Cuba: *A History of the Second Intervention,* 1906-1909

By

David A. Lockmiller

1938

Chapel Hill: The University of North Carolina Press

F
1787
L81M

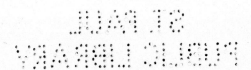

MANUFACTURED IN THE UNITED STATES OF AMERICA
BY THE STRATFORD PRESS, INC., NEW YORK

To
My Mother and Father

Preface

IT IS THE PURPOSE of this study to write the history of the second United States intervention in Cuba, 1906–1909, with special emphasis on the administration of Provisional Governor Charles E. Magoon. The word "second" is not strictly accurate. It is used to distinguish United States intervention in the Spanish colony of Cuba in 1898, which is generally known as the first intervention, from United States intervention in the Republic of Cuba in 1906.

Writers of United States history have ignored or only briefly mentioned the second intervention. Much has been written about the Spanish-American War, the Wood administration, and Section Three of the Platt Amendment; but the formal application of Section Three, the Taft and Bacon Peace Mission, and the Magoon administration have apparently been forgotten in the United States. The silence of United States historians has been more than offset by a generation of Cuban writers and orators who have praised Wood, denounced the Platt Amendment, and condemned Magoon. Professors Charles E. Chapman, Leland H. Jenks, and Russell H. Fitzgibbon in their studies on Cuba, which are listed in the bibliography, have devoted chapters to the second intervention and have done much to make that phase of history less obscure.

However, no detailed study of the second intervention has previously been made and the author ventures the hope that this work will supply that need.

Brief chapters by way of introduction are given on the first intervention and Estrada Palma's administration. The August Revolution of 1906, the Taft and Bacon Peace Mission, the Platt Amendment, and the accomplishments and criticisms of the Magoon administration are discussed. No attempt has been made to write a detailed account of Cuban history prior to the elections of 1905 or after the withdrawal of the provisional government in 1909. Reference is necessarily made to the Gómez period and to later administrations but only in so far as they relate to this special work. Those interested in the early history of the Republic or in events since the second intervention should consult the pertinent studies or bibliographical guides listed in the bibliography.

This work is subject to the advantages and disadvantages which confront the writer of contemporary history. It is difficult when working at close range to give isolated facts their proper weight and to deal with details in their true perspective. There is a natural reluctance on the part of some living witnesses to furnish evidence. A vast amount of material varying in quality is available on many points, but due to restrictions on public and private records and papers some phases of the second intervention will necessarily remain obscure.

In securing material for this work the writer was fortunate. Government documents and reports, both Cuban and United States, are abundant. There are some excellent studies and pamphlets, especially by Cubans, dealing with special phases of this subject. The Magoon, Crowder, Roosevelt, Root, and Taft papers were helpful. Newspapers and magazines constituted valuable sources, and correspondence with persons who participated in the second intervention cleared up many points. Living witnesses in Cuba and the United States who kindly granted the writer interviews contributed much information not to be found in print and added their encouragement to the completion of this study.

It would be difficult to name and thank all who have helped in the preparation of this work. However, special thanks are due to Dr. W. W. Pierson, Jr., of the University of North Carolina, under whose direction this study was first undertaken and completed, and to Dr. C. B. Robson, Professor K. C. Frazer, and Dr. W. E. Caldwell of the University of North Carolina for their help and many valuable criticisms. I am indebted to the Institute for Research in Social Science of the University of North Carolina for financial aid and stenographic help. I am under great obligations to the officials and staffs of the Library of the University of North Carolina, the D. H. Hill Library of North Carolina State College, the Library of Congress, the Biblioteca Nacional de Cuba, and the Biblioteca de Sociedad Económica de Amigos del País of Havana. I want to acknowledge the courtesy and assistance of Robert J. Flick, H. K. Beale, the late Elihu Root, Sr., and John D. Langston for making it possible for me to use private collections which otherwise would not have been available. I also want to acknowledge the assistance of Don Antonio San Miguel, Dr. Francisco Carrera Jústiz, Dr. Francisco de P. Coronado, Dr. Fernando Ortiz, Dr. Emilio Roig de Leuchsenring, Dr. Carlos M. Trelles, General Mario G. Menocal, General Faustino Guerra, General Ernesto Asbert, Colonel Aurelio Hevia, and Señorita Adda Anderson, citizens of the Republic of Cuba; and Frank Steinhart, John T. Dorgan, Judge Otto Schoenrich, Dr. Charles E. Magoun, William Franklin Sands, General Mason M. Patrick, General J. A. Ryan, Colonel Harold C. Fiske, John F. Stevens, Archibald Runner, J. D. Clark, and Dr. W. A. Brown, citizens of the United States. I am grateful to my wife, Alma Russell Lockmiller, for her helpful suggestions and aid in proof reading and typing.

The author is solely responsible for this work and for all opinions except quoted passages and statements of individuals as cited in the footnotes.

DAVID A. LOCKMILLER

Raleigh, N. C.
November 15, 1937

CONTENTS

CONTENTS

xii

CONTENTS

CHAPTER VIII

The Restoration of the Cuban Government   174

CHAPTER IX

An Evaluation of the Second Intervention   197

MAGOON IN CUBA

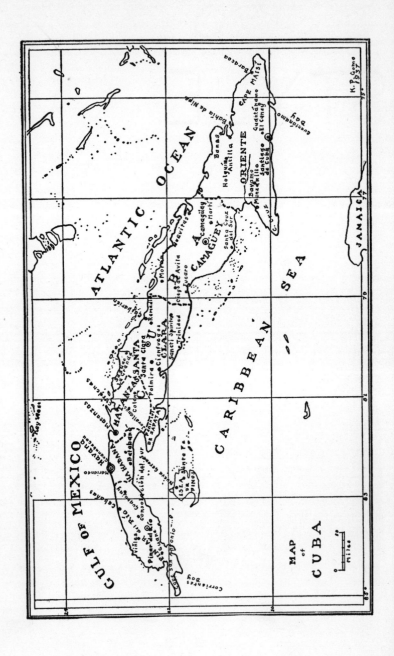

MAP
of
CUBA

miles

K. P. Gomo
1937

II

The First Intervention, 1898-1902

O<small>N</small> A<small>PRIL</small> 11, 1898, President William McKinley sent a message to Congress requesting authority to end the war existing in Cuba and to secure the establishment on the island of a stable government capable of maintaining order and observing its international obligations.[1] On April 19, in response to this message, Congress, after setting forth the deplorable state of affairs in Cuba and the grievances of this country, resolved in part as follows:

That the People of the island of Cuba, are, and of right ought to be, free and independent.

That it is the duty of the United States to demand, and the government of the United States does hereby demand, that the government of Spain at once relinquish its authority and government in the island of Cuba and withdraw its land and naval forces from Cuba and Cuban waters.

That the President of the United States be, and he hereby is, directed and empowered to use the entire land and naval forces of the United States, and to call into the actual service of the

---

[1] J. D. Richardson, *A Compilation of the Messages and Papers of the Presidents,* VIII, 6281-92.

United States the militia of the several states, to such extent as may be necessary to carry these resolutions into effect.[2]

These resolutions were tantamount to a declaration of war and were followed by a chain of events of far-reaching consequences.

The first United States intervention in Cuba began on April 22, 1898, with the issuance of a blockade proclamation by President McKinley. The following day the President issued a proclamation calling for 125,000 volunteers, which number was later increased to 200,000.[3] Congress, by a formal declaration approved by the President on April 25, announced that war with Spain had existed since April 21. On the day following the passage of this declaration, Commodore Dewey and his squadron captured or destroyed the ships of the Spanish fleet in Manila Bay.

United States troops sailed from Port Tampa, Florida, on June 14, for Santiago de Cuba. On July 1 and 2, the United States forces in engagements at San Juan, Lawton, and El Caney, defeated the Spanish troops. The following day the Spanish fleet under Admiral Cervera while attempting to escape from Santiago harbor was destroyed by the United States squadron. This victory practically ended the war.[4]

On August 12, 1898, at Washington, William R. Day, Secretary of State of the United States, and Jules Cambon, the French ambassador, who was the authorized agent of Spain, signed a protocol which provided for the cessation of hostilities. After negotiations, a peace treaty was signed at

---

[2] *Compilation of the Acts of Congress, Treaties, and Proclamations, Relating to Insular and Military Affairs, from March 4, 1897 to March 3, 1903, Senate Document No. 105* (Fifty-eighth Congress, second session), p. 254. Hereafter cited as *Senate Document No. 105* (Fifty-eighth Congress, second session).

[3] *Ibid.*, pp. 384-87.

[4] For accounts of the Spanish-American War see F. E. Chadwick, *The Relations of the United States and Spain: Diplomacy*, and José Antonio Medel, *The Spanish-American War and Its Results*.

Paris, December 10, 1898. It was ratified by the Senate of the United States on February 6, and by Spain, March 19, 1899. Exactly one year after McKinley's war message, the treaty was proclaimed in Washington.[5] Thus ended a dramatic war which announced to the world that the United States was of age and ready to enter the race for empire.

Article One of the Treaty of Paris provided as follows:

Spain relinquishes all claim of sovereignty over and title to Cuba. And as the island is, upon its evacuation by Spain, to be occupied by the United States, the United States will, so long as such occupation shall last, assume and discharge the obligations that may under international law result from the fact of its occupation, for the protection of life and property.[6]

Upon the withdrawal of the Spanish General, Adolfo Jiménez Castellanos, the government of Cuba devolved upon the army of the United States. General John R. Brooke was appointed military governor and entered upon his duties January 1, 1899.[7]

Aside from treating with Tomás Estrada Palma as minister, the United States did not recognize the insurgent Cuban government. All claims made by Cuban leaders to the effect that Cuba was an independent nation were ignored, and when General Brooke took charge a new revolt was feared. All such fears were allayed and United States control was firmly established when General Máximo Gómez agreed to have his troops lay down their arms and accept three million dollars from the United States in payment for their services. This agreement so provoked the insurgent assembly that it de-

---

[5] *Senate Document No. 105* (Fifty-eighth Congress, second session), pp. 345 and 388.

[6] *Ibid.,* p. 345.

[7] Charles E. Chapman, *A History of the Cuban Republic: A Study in Hispanic American Politics,* p. 97.

posed Gómez as commander-in-chief and disbanded on April 4, 1899.[8]

Upon assuming office General Brooke issued a proclamation to the Cuban people stating that the object of the present government was,

. . . to give protection to the people, security to the person and property, to restore confidence, to encourage the people to resume the pursuits of peace, to build up waste plantations, to resume commercial traffic, and to afford full protection in the exercise of all civil and religious rights.[9]

To carry out this program General Brooke organized a cabinet of four departments, vesting the administration of civil government in a Department of State and Government; a Finance Department; a Department of Justice and Public Instruction; and a Department of Commerce, Agriculture, Industries, and Public Works. He utilized Cubans and tried to lay the foundation for a stable government.[10]

According to a conservative estimate, the war in Cuba from 1895 until the United States took charge caused a 12 per cent decrease in population and reduced the wealth of the island by two-thirds.[11] As a result of the war many children wandered homeless and lived almost like wild animals. Thousands of persons were without food and many lay dying in homes and public institutions. Famine and disease were everywhere and agriculture was prostrate.[12] The Spaniards left Cuba in an appalling condition and gave the island a final

---

[8] *Ibid.*, p. 102.

[9] Victor H. Olmsted and Henry Gannett, Compilers, *Cuba: Population, History, and Resources, 1907*, p. 40.

[10] W. F. Johnson, *The History of Cuba*, IV, 146; Chapman, *op cit.*, p. 100, states that under Brooke 97 per cent of the officials were Cubans.

[11] Olmsted and Gannett, *op. cit.*, p. 40.

[12] Albert G. Robinson, *Cuba and the Intervention*, p. 88. See also Rafael Martínez Ortiz, *Cuba: los primeros años de independencia*, I, 19 *et seq.* Hereafter cited as *Cuba.*

shakedown by way of farewell. They looted public buildings, destroyed plumbing and lighting fixtures, and choked up drains. The manner of their departure provoked just criticisms from Cubans and officials of the United States.[13]

Under Brooke the hungry were fed and law and order were restored. Municipal governments and local finance systems were reorganized and a thorough census of the island was taken. The marriage laws were reformed and the fee required for that ceremony was reduced. Under the able direction of Major E. F. Ladd tax laws were revised and the empty treasury of Cuba could show $10,000,000 of collected revenue by September, 1899. Alexis E. Frye drafted a new school law for Cuba which marked the beginning of popular education in that country. The Brooke administration was honest and efficient and has been justly praised by historians of Cuba and the United States.[14]

United States business interests, disappointed at the failure of their country to annex Cuba outright, determined to make their economic interests and control dominant on the island. Merchants, real estate agents, stock speculators, and promoters of a host of get-rich schemes flocked to Cuba. The War Department had at its disposal franchises, grants, and all kinds of concessions. To prevent irregularity at the expense of the Cubans, Congress passed the Foraker Amendment to the military appropriation bill of March, 1899. This amendment prohibited the granting of franchises or concessions of any nature during the occupation of Cuba by the United States.[15] It was voted over the objection of many administration leaders, including Mark Hanna. It relieved the officials in charge of the intervention from many temptations and cut short

---

[13] Johnson, *op. cit.*, IV, 133.

[14] Martínez Ortiz, *Cuba*, I, 107; Carlos M. Trelles, *El Progreso (1902 a 1905) y el retroceso (1906 a 1922) de la república de Cuba*, p. 5; Chapman, *op. cit.*, p. 105; Robinson, *op. cit.*, pp. 134 *et seq.*; and Johnson, *op. cit.*, IV, 145 *et seq.*

[15] L. H. Jenks, *Our Cuban Colony*, pp. 67-68.

many well-laid plans for great wealth. While the amendment did a great deal of good, it was often loosely construed. The military government held that mining claims were not concessions, and that there was no objection to a person or company buying land and building a railroad. The amendment prevented neither the cancellation of a dock franchise granted by the Spanish government, nor the grant of a ten-year monopoly to the Jai Alai Company.[16] However, United States activities in Cuba during the first intervention compare favorably with those of other imperialistic nations during the corresponding era.

General Leonard E. Wood, who had served under Brooke as commander of the province of Oriente, replaced the latter on December 20, 1899, as military governor. In Oriente General Wood had made an enviable record as an administrator. There he had instituted a thorough clean-up campaign, stamped out epidemic after epidemic, reëstablished municipal government, and opened the courts. He had also started public works, founded schools, created rural guards, and run Cuban newspaper critics out of town.[17]

As military governor, Wood carried on and extended the work of his predecessor. Capital was attracted to the island, Havana and other cities were modernized, yellow fever was suppressed, the university was reorganized, judicial reforms were introduced, and public works and sanitary campaigns were pushed with vigor.[18] Also, taxes were honestly collected, and justice was scrupulously administered. Although General Wood was unable, as have been all his successors, to remedy the ills resulting from a one-crop system of agriculture and to train the Cuban people in the art of self-government, it is gen-

---

[16] *Ibid.*, pp. 69-70.

[17] Johnson, *op. cit.*, IV, 140 *et seq.*

[18] Leonard Wood, "The Military Government of Cuba," *Annals of the American Academy of Political and Social Science*, XXI (March, 1903), 153-82.

erally conceded that he gave Cuba the best government the island had ever had.[19]

Before establishing military government in Cuba the United States Congress, on April 19, 1898, had adopted Section Four of the joint resolutions which was an amendment that had been introduced by Senator H. M. Teller, of Colorado. It is known in history as the Teller Amendment, and reads as follows:

That the United States hereby disclaims any disposition or intention to exercise sovereignty, jurisdiction, or control, over said island except for the pacification thereof, and asserts its determination when that is accomplished to leave the government and the control of the island to its people.[20]

Just why Congress passed this amendment is still a matter of dispute. Horatio S. Rubens, United States business man and formerly attorney for the Cuban *Junta* in New York City, asserts that Senator Teller, who was a staunch friend of Cuba, asked him if there was anything he could do to aid the Cubans in their struggle for freedom. Rubens states that he suggested the Teller Amendment which was hurriedly passed by Congress along with the other resolutions during the excitement prevailing at the time.[21] The Cuban leaders wanted the United States to recognize the independence of their country, opposed intervention, and did not want to lose the fruits of long sacrifice. General Máximo Gómez opposed in-

---

[19] For high praise of Wood's work by Cuban historians see Martínez Ortiz, *Cuba*, I, 427-38; Trelles, *op. cit.*, p. 5; and Juan M. Leiscea, *Historia de Cuba*, pp. 448-49. Chapman, *op. cit.*, pp. 105 *et seq.* gives a critical but favorable account of Wood's activities in Cuba. Robinson, *op. cit.*, *passim*, gives Wood's achievements, but is biased in favor of Brooke. Hermann Hagedorn, *Leonard Wood: A Biography*, I, *passim*, gives a favorable account of Wood's services as military governor.

[20] *Senate Document No. 105* (Fifty-eighth Congress, second session), p. 254.

[21] Horatio S. Rubens, *Liberty: The Story of Cuba*, pp. 341-42.

tervention, but desired artillery and ammunition.[22] When the United States finally decided to join intervention with recognition, the Cubans tried to secure the best possible terms, and these they obtained by the adoption of the Teller Amendment.

In agreement with the pledge made by the United States in the Teller Amendment, and in the first article of the Treaty of Paris, the military government, under General Wood, took steps to prepare the Cubans for independence and self-government. A census of the island was taken, and a basis for suffrage determined. Regulations were drawn up for the holding of municipal elections and for the establishment of local governments, and a general election was held September 15, 1900, for the selection of delegates to attend a constitutional convention in Havana.[23]

The convention was called to order by Governor Wood on November 5, 1900. The purpose of the convention was,

. . . to frame and adopt a constitution for the people of Cuba, and, as a part thereof, to provide for and agree with the Government of the United States upon the relations to exist between that Government and the Government of Cuba, and to provide for the election by the people of officers under such constitution and the transfer of government to the officers so elected.[24]

General Wood, in his opening address, reminded the delegates of their duty to consider the relations which "ought to exist between Cuba and the United States," and added that the United States would "doubtless take such action on its part as shall lead to a final and authoritative agreement between the people of the two countries." [25]

---

[22] Johnson, *op. cit.*, IV, 109.
[23] Howard C. Hill, *Roosevelt and the Caribbean*, p. 70.
[24] *House Document No. 1* (Fifty-seventh Congress, second session), I, 359.
[25] *Ibid.*, p. 359 *et seq.* For the Cuban view of the duty of the convention see

The government of the United States did not long delay in making more perfect the "ties of singular intimacy" mentioned by President McKinley in his message to Congress, December 5, 1899, and indirectly referred to by Governor Wood in his address to the constitutional convention. Early in February, 1901, the delegates had drawn up a constitution based in part on that of the United States.[26] However, the committee appointed to determine the future relations with the United States failed to agree because some members were afraid that that country desired to establish a protectorate. The Cubans were jealous of their newly won freedom, and while grateful to the United States for its assistance, were suspicious of its good intentions.

In the opinion of the McKinley administration, the settlement of Cuban-United States relations should be completed before the new republic was established. An independent Cuba might not agree to ties which would please "big business" senators. Furthermore, it was felt that the "War Congress" elected in 1898 should have the right to pass on such an important matter before its term expired. Thus, it happened that the relations between two foreign states were to be determined for some thirty-three years by an amendment to the military appropriations bill for 1901–1902.

Although the amendment was introduced by and named after Senator Orville H. Platt of Connecticut, its origin is a matter of controversy. The research of various scholars indicates that no one person drafted the amendment, but that it evolved from the ideas of General Wood, Secretary Root, General James H. Wilson, and Senator Platt. Also, practically all the proposals which were later included in the Platt

Luis Machado y Ortega, *La enmienda Platt: estudio de su alcance e interpretación y doctrina sobre su aplicación*, p. 32 *et seq.*; Luis Suárez Vera, *General Emilio Núñez, su historia revolucionaria y su actuacion en la vida publica*, pp. 119-23.

[26] Secretary of War, *Annual Report*, 1902, I, Pt. I, 84.

Amendment had been discussed by members of the Cuban constitutional convention and by the Havana press.[27]

Introduced in the United States Senate on February 25, 1901, the Platt Amendment was passed by that body February 27, after a debate of two hours. The bill as amended, after being debated for only an hour, passed the House on March 1, and became a part of the law of the land on March 2, when it was signed by President McKinley.[28]

The amendment authorized the President of the United States to turn the government and control of Cuba over to its people as soon as they should establish a government under a constitution which would contain the following provisions:

1. That the government of Cuba shall never enter into any treaty or other compact with any foreign power or powers which will impair or tend to impair the independence of Cuba, nor in any manner authorize or permit any foreign power or powers to obtain by colonization or for military or naval purposes or otherwise, a lodgement in or control over any portion of said island.

2. That said government shall not assume or contract any public debt to pay the interest upon which, and to make reasonable sinking fund provision for the ultimate discharge of which the ordinary revenues of the island, after defraying the current expenses and government, shall be inadequate.

3. That the government of Cuba consents that the United States may exercise the right to intervene for the preservation of Cuban independence, the maintenance of a government adequate for the protection of life, property, and individual liberty, and for

---

[27] For brief accounts of the origin of the Platt Amendment see Jenks, *op. cit.*, pp. 73-78; Hill, *op. cit.*, pp. 73-76; Chapman, *op. cit.*, pp. 135-43; Harry F. Guggenheim, *The United States and Cuba: A Study in International Relations*, pp. 47-109; and Russell H. Fitzgibbon, *Cuba and the United States*, pp. 78 *et seq.* For accounts by Cubans see Machado y Ortega, *op. cit.*, pp. 17-88; and Emilio Roig de Leuchsenring, *La enmienda Platt: su interpretación primitiva y sus aplicaciones posteriores* (Anuario de 1922, Sociedad Cubana de Derecho Internacional), pp. 323-86.

[28] Jenks, *op. cit.*, p. 77.

discharging the obligations with respect to Cuba imposed by the Treaty of Paris on the United States, now to be assumed and undertaken by the government of Cuba.

4. That all acts of the United States in Cuba during its military occupancy thereof are ratified and validated, and all lawful rights acquired thereunder shall be maintained and protected.

5. That the government of Cuba will execute, and as far as necessary, extend the plans already devised or other plans to be mutually agreed upon, for the sanitation of the cities of the island, to the end that a recurrence of epidemic and infectious diseases may be prevented, thereby assuring protection to the people and commerce of Cuba, as well as to the commerce of the southern ports of the United States and the people residing therein.

6. That the Isle of Pines shall be omitted from the proposed constitutional boundaries of Cuba, the title thereto being left to future adjustment by treaty.

7. That to enable the United States to maintain the independence of Cuba, and to protect the people thereof, as well as for its own defense, the government of Cuba will sell or lease to the United States lands necessary for coaling or naval stations at certain specified points, to be agreed upon with the President of the United States.

8. That by way of further assurance the government of Cuba will embody the foregoing provisions in a permanent treaty with the United States.[29]

The Cuban convention could either accept or reject these provisions as it saw fit, but until they were accepted, Cuba would continue "unpacified," and the United States military government supported by its troops would remain. After delay and many attempts at compromise, the convention sent Domingo Méndez Capote, Pedro González Llorente, Diego Tamayo, Rafael Portuondo, and Pedro Betancourt to Washington to secure modifications. The commissioners were courteously received by administration leaders and although modi-

---

[29] *Senate Document No. 105* (Fifty-eighth Congress, second session), pp. 118-19.

fications were refused, explanations were made and assurances of a favorable commercial treaty freely given.[30] The commissioners reported these assurances and as a result the constitutional convention added the Platt Amendment as an appendix to the Cuban constitution. Some two years later the Platt Amendment was embodied in a permanent treaty between the United States and Cuba, in accordance with Article Eight of that amendment.[31] Thus, the tie was triple in its nature. The amendment was the law of the land in the United States, the constitutional law of Cuba, and as a part of the permanent treaty was binding on Cuba and the United States until they abrogated it by mutual consent.

The chief Cuban criticisms were directed at Article Three. Referring to this clause, Secretary Root said:

That clause does not impair the sovereignty of Cuba; it leaves Cuba independent and sovereign under her own flag. It only will help the United States in extreme cases to assist Cuba in preserving her absolute independence; and pray God that case may never arise . . . The spirit, the tendency, the substance of the Platt Amendment is to establish in Cuba an independent and sovereign nation. But the United States goes beyond that in favor of Cuba; they seek to guarantee the subsistence of Cuba *as a free and independent* republic.[32]

Senator Platt, in writing to Secretary Root, April 26, 1901, concerning the amendment stated that:

The Amendment was carefully worded with the purpose of avoiding all possible thought that on accepting it the Constitutional Convention would produce the establishment of a protectorate or

---

[30] Aurelio Hevia, *Colección de artículos y documentos referentes a la condición actual de Cuba,* p. 52.

[31] W. M. Malloy, *Treaties, Conventions, International Acts, Protocols, and Agreements,* I, 362-64.

[32] *Senado. Memoria de los trabajos realizados,* p. 471, quoted in Jenks, *op. cit.,* p. 82.

in any way would get mixed up with the independence or sovereignty of Cuba; and speaking for myself, it seems impossible that such interpretation could be given to that clause. I think that the amendment should be considered as a whole, and it ought to be evident, on reading it, that its well defined purpose is to assure and protect Cuba's independence, and establish, of course, a definite understanding about the friendly relations of the United States to the people of Cuba, and a declared intention of the fact to help them if necessary to maintain their independence.[33]

Charles E. Magoon did not consider the Platt Amendment dangerous to Cuban liberty. In writing of that amendment, he said:

This relation between Cuba and the United States is not a limitation upon its sovereignty and independence; it is the buttress by which sovereignty and independence are protected and sustained; it is the guaranty by which the Cuban Republic is assured of equality of right and privilege in the Assembly of Nations.[34]

Much opposition was allayed when President McKinley's interpretation of Section Three was presented to the convention by General Wood. The President held that the intervention mentioned in the Platt Amendment was not synonymous with intermeddling and that the United States government would only act upon just and substantial grounds.[35] However, it was not long until officials of the United States were doing many of the things which President McKinley and Secretary Root had promised would not be done under cover of the Platt Amendment. By virtue of that amendment, Cuba was

---

[33] Roig de Leuchsenring, *op. cit.,* p. 360.

[34] Charles E. Magoon, *Report of Provisional Administration from October 13th, 1906 to December 1st, 1907,* p. 4. This work also contains the reports of the acting heads of the several executive departments to the provisional governor. Hereafter cited as Magoon, *Report,* I.

[35] Jenks, *op. cit.,* p. 81.

15

for several years practically a protectorate of the United States.[36]

In accordance with the newly adopted Cuban Constitution, presidential electors were selected by the people on December 31, 1901. Tomás Estrada Palma was joint candidate of the Nationalists and Republicans and was backed by General Máximo Gómez. The opposing candidate was former provisional president, Bartolomé Masó, who ran on an anti-Platt Amendment platform. Masó was easily defeated, but not until General Wood had refused to alter the membership of the election board of scrutiny; all members of which were supporters of Estrada Palma.[37] No doubt the elections were honest, but Wood's inflexibility created a bad precedent of partisan control. The friends of Masó seized the excuse, and in true Hispanic American style refused to go to the polls.[38] On February 24, 1902, the electoral college met and selected Estrada Palma, without opposition, as the first president of the Republic of Cuba. On May 20, 1902, amid scenes of great rejoicing, the newly elected president was inaugurated. Governor Wood handed over the government of the island to its new officials. As the Cuban flag was raised, the United States flag was hauled down. On the same day, Governor Wood and the military forces embarked for the United States.[39] The first intervention was ended.

---

[36] *Ibid.*, p. 84. Also see Francisco Figueras, *La Intervencion y su política*, pp. 43-51. It seems that United States officials frequently believed in prevention, whereas the Cubans claimed that no action should be taken until the damage was done. These different views made the Platt Amendment a lively topic of debate from the date of its enactment until its repeal on June 9, 1934.

[37] Martínez Ortiz, *Cuba*, I, 373.

[38] Chapman, *op. cit.*, p. 146.

[39] Irene A. Wright, *Cuba*, p. 170.

II

The Administration of Estrada Palma

Tomás Estrada Palma, a Cuban patriot of the first order, was born in Bayamo, Oriente, in 1835, studied law at the University of Seville in Spain, lived several years in France, and upon his return to Cuba in 1868 became active in the revolutionary movement. He took a prominent part in the Ten Years' War against Spain and in 1877 the revolutionary Cuban congress named him president, but he was soon captured and sent to Spain in chains. He was released in 1878 following the peace of Zanjón, and went to Honduras where he taught school and later served as Postmaster General. While in that country he married the daughter of Santos Guardiola, then President of Honduras. After his wife's father was assassinated, Estrada Palma went to the United States and made his home there for some twenty years.[1] He

---

[1] Emeterio S. Santovenia, *Los presidentes de Cuba libre,* pp. 49-56; Charles E. Magoon, *Report of Provisional Administration from December 1st, 1907 to December 1st, 1908,* pp. 112-13. This work also contains the reports of the acting heads of the several executive departments to the provisional governor. Hereafter cited as Magoon, *Report,* II. For summary opinions of Estrada Palma see Chapman, *op. cit.,* pp. 152-54. For collection of articles and addresses relating to Estrada Palma and the early history of the republic, see Carlos De Velasco, *Estrada Palma: contribución histórica.*

was a keen observer of the political system of that country, and later stated that he acquired his knowledge of democracy while living in the United States.[2] For a number of years he taught in a boys' school at Central Valley, New York, and while there continued to work for Cuban liberty. When his fellow patriots started the final struggle for independence in 1895, he did much to secure sympathy, money, and munitions in the United States. As head of the Cuban *Junta* in this country he served as the revolutionary government's delegate during the Spanish-American War.[3] The United States had confidence in him, and many thought him the logical successor of the great Cuban intellectual and patriot, José Martí.

"Don Tomás," as Estrada Palma was affectionately called by his people, was a man of courage, and of unimpeached integrity. He was slow in reaching conclusions, but having made up his mind he seldom changed it. He distinguished himself by guarding the nation's resources, and above all things, he loved Cuba and its people. He would have been spared much bitterness during the closing years of his life had he died before the elections of 1905.

While a patriot against Spanish tyranny, Estrada Palma was not an advocate of unrestrained liberty. He was a champion of law and order, and if his fellow Cubans could not exercise their freedom within the bounds imposed by reasonable laws, he favored annexation to the United States. His ideas on this subject are best stated in a letter written by him to a personal friend on October 10, 1906. This was just a few days after Secretary of War William H. Taft had proclaimed the establishment of provisional government by the United States. After commenting at length on the events leading up

---

[2] William H. Taft and Robert Bacon, *Cuban Pacification* (excerpt from the Report of the Secretary of War, 1906), p. 449. This work includes valuable appendixes. Hereafter cited as Taft and Bacon, *Report*.

[3] Magoon, *Report*, II, 113.

to the second intervention and his acts in connection there-
with, Estrada Palma said:

> I have always believed, since the time I took active part in the
> Ten Years war that independence was not the final goal of all
> our noble and patriotic aspirations—the aim was to possess a stable
> Government capable of protecting lives and property and of
> guaranteeing to all residents of the country, natives and foreigners,
> the exercise of natural and civil rights, without permitting liberty
> ever to become pernicious license or violent agitation, to say noth-
> ing of armed disturbances of public order. I have never feared to
> admit, nor am I afraid to say aloud, that a political dependence
> which assures us the fecund boons of liberty is a hundred times
> preferable for our beloved Cuba to a sovereign and independent
> republic discredited and made miserable by the baneful action of
> periodic civil wars.[4]

The first years of Estrada Palma's administration have been
described as the "best years of the republic." [5] No other president has succeeded in discharging the duties of that high office
as well as he did during his first term.[6]

During Estrada Palma's first administration, only three
matters of consequence arose between Cuba and the United
States. The first concerned the reciprocity treaty between
the two countries, the second was the dispute over the Isle of
Pines, and the third was the demand made by the United
States that Cuba fulfill her obligations under Section Five of
the Platt Amendment with reference to health and sanitary
conditions.

Cuban opposition to the Platt Amendment had been less-
ened to a large extent by promises of a favorable commercial

---

[4] Magoon, *Report*, I, 15.

[5] Chapman, *op. cit.*, pp. 152-75.

[6] For a comparison of Estrada Palma's administration with the later periods see
Trelles, *op. cit., passim.* For favorable accounts of Estrada Palma's first three years
as president see R. Iznaga, *Tres años de república, 1902–1905, passim.* Also see
Tres años de Cuba libre: paz, prosperidad, y progreso, passim.

treaty. McKinley, Root, Platt, and other leading figures gave the Cuban commission which visited the United States to understand that a trade agreement would be drawn up which would give Cuba special economic advantages over other countries.[7] The prosperity of Cuba depends on its ability to find a profitable market for its chief crops—sugar and tobacco. The United States was the logical market for Cuban products, and a favorable commercial treaty would guarantee the economic independence of the island because more than half of the population of Cuba depended directly or indirectly on sugar and tobacco.[8] Consequently, the new Cuban government was very anxious to secure the fulfillment of promises beneficial to Cuba.

President Roosevelt was not unmindful of the benefits to the United States which would be derived from low tariffs and easy exchange. He also recognized the obligations of the United States to Cuba and appreciated the fact that a prosperous neighbor would be of greater value than an impoverished island. Accordingly, in his first message to Congress on December 3, 1901, he advised a substantial reduction in tariff rates on Cuban products sent to the United States. The House passed a bill providing for reciprocal trade relations, but it failed in the Senate because of the opposition of powerful United States sugar interests. Finally, the President and administration leaders secured the ratification of a reciprocity treaty on December 16, 1903.[9]

The reciprocity treaty granted to United States shippers reductions which ranged from 25 to 40 per cent of the normal Cuban tariff rates. Cubans secured a reduction of 20 per cent on agricultural and industrial products sent to the United States. It was agreed that the advantages thus secured would

---

[7] Hevia, *op. cit.*, p. 52.

[8] *House Document No. 2* (Fifty-seventh Congress, first session), II, 51.

[9] J. B. Bishop, *Theodore Roosevelt and his Time*, I, 188; Hill, *op. cit.*, p. 82.

apply to the Dingley tariff or to any other tariff law there-after enacted.[10]

This treaty greatly fostered economic exchange between the two countries. Cuba practically cornered the United States sugar market and this fact proved a great boon to Americans who had purchased extensive sugar plantations on the island. The chief advantages, however, were with the United States. The closer Cuba came to supplying the entire sugar demand of the United States, the more it had to meet world prices, and as a result the profits from the treaty grew less and less. The world price of sugar with the Cuban duty added tended to become the New York price, and thus Cuba with a pre-ferred market did not necessarily receive a preferred price.[11] On the other hand, the United States by virtue of lower tariff rates and its geographical position, could easily outdistance all foreign competitors in flooding Cuba with manufactured goods. The treaty greatly improved economic conditions on the island during the Estrada Palma administration, but its chief defects, as far as Cuba was concerned, did not appear until later.

The next problem which caused considerable trouble at the time and which was not finally settled until 1925 was the dispute over the Isle of Pines. For more than four hundred years this island had been administered as a part of Cuba and Cubans considered the territory rightfully theirs. Following the Spanish-American War, United States real estate specula-tors established themselves on the Isle of Pines and claimed that its nine hundred thousand acres belonged to the United States under and by virtue of the Treaty of Paris.[12] Techni-

---

[10] For text of the convention see *Senate Document No. 105* (Fifty-eighth Con-gress, second session), pp. 369-80.

[11] Guggenheim, *op. cit.*, p. 109; Philip G. Wright, *The Cuban Situation and Our Treaty Relations, passim.* The commercial convention of 1903 should not be con-fused with the United States-Cuban reciprocity agreement of 1934.

[12] Irene A. Wright, *op. cit.*, p. 320.

21

cally, this contention was correct, as Spain ceded to the United States all its islands in the Caribbean, with the exception of Cuba. Regardless of governmental control, the Isle of Pines is and was, in fact, a separate island some fifty miles south of Cuba. The dispute took on such proportions and so interested United States citizens who had a great deal of influence among those in high office in their country that Section Six was inserted in the Platt Amendment. This section omitted the Isle of Pines from the constitutional boundaries of Cuba, and provided that the title of the island should be determined at some future date by a treaty to be entered into by the two countries. Many Cubans considered this an unwarranted breach of the Teller Amendment.[13]

While these disputes were going on, the Isle of Pines was practically without government. The United States refused to assume control, and citizens of that country on the island would not recognize Cuban authority. Finally, on March 2, 1904, a treaty was entered into between Cuba and the United States. This agreement recognized the Cuban claim and provided for Cuban control until ratifications were exchanged. Although this treaty was submitted to the United States Senate for approval on numerous occasions, it was not finally ratified and proclaimed until the Coolidge administration twenty-one years later.[14] However, with the signing of the treaty in 1904, much of the clamor died down, and Estrada Palma was credited with another victory.[15]

The third major problem between Cuba and the United States during the Estrada Palma administration concerned

---

[13] Machado y Ortega, *op. cit.*, p. 45.

[14] Chapman, *op. cit.*, p. 158.

[15] Cubans spoke of this island as *"nuestro territorio irredento,"* and as late as 1924 writers were still discussing the question. See Fernando Ortiz, "Cuba's Title to the Isle of Pines," *Cuba Review*, XXIII (December, 1924), 14-20. Just after the second intervention was started, some Cubans feared that the United States would annex the Isle of Pines, but the provisional government soon declared that the Isle of Pines would remain under the Cuban flag. *Havana Post*, October 12, 1906.

health and sanitary conditions. The United States was justly proud of the record made by the Army Medical Corps during the first intervention in instituting sanitation measures and in stamping out yellow fever and other tropical diseases. Yellow fever not only menaced the inhabitants of Cuba, but endangered the health and lives of persons living in the southeastern part of the United States. Many sanitation works started by the first intervention had not been completed when the United States turned the government of Cuba over to its duly elected officials. To promote further the welfare of the Cubans, and to protect citizens of the United States, Section Five was inserted in the Platt Amendment. This required the Cuban government to complete the sanitation measures already started in order that a recurrence of epidemic and infectious diseases might thereby be prevented.

Estrada Palma briefly mentioned the need of appropriations for sanitation purposes in his first message to the Cuban congress.[16] Because of disagreements among Cuban congressmen and financial difficulties confronting the new nation, this and other recommendations of the president were disregarded. In 1904 the island witnessed the outbreak of new epidemics. Secretary of State John Hay at once directed the United States minister to notify the Cuban government that the United States would be required to declare a quarantine against Cuban ports unless necessary sanitation measures were carried out.[17] Following this admonition, the Cuban congress voted small funds for sanitation purposes, but the amounts were not sufficient, and during 1905 it again became necessary for the United States to remind Cuba of its duty under Section Five

---

[16] *Cámara de representantes. Mensajes presidenciales remitidos al congreso, durante les siete períodos al congresionales, transcurridos desde el veinte de mayo de mil novecientos dos, hasta el primero de abril de mil novencientos deiz y siete, e indice correlative y por materias de los mismos,* I, 6. Hereafter cited as *Mensajes presidenciales.*

[17] *House Document No. 1* (Fifty-eighth Congress, third session), p. 250 *et seq.*

of the Platt Amendment. The Cubans were reluctant to spend money fighting mosquitoes and digging drainage ditches, and again the United States, through its Secretary of State, Elihu Root, sent a vigorous message to the Cuban government on this subject.[18] This communication brought about the desired result, and on January 12, 1906, Estrada Palma issued a decree establishing a sanitation organization for Cuba.[19] Later in the same year, a house-cleaning program, similar to that introduced by the United States during the first intervention, was instituted. Sanitation squads made rigid inspections and trash and rubbish were dumped into the sea. Funds were advanced to be used in localities where yellow fever had broken out, and in general, health and sanitary conditions were greatly improved. No doubt Estrada Palma would have fulfilled Cuba's sanitation and health obligations without any friction with the United States had sufficient money been available for expensive sanitation projects, and had he been able to secure the coöperation of Cuban politicians.

Another matter of concern between the two nations was the establishment of the coaling or naval stations provided for in Section Seven of the Platt Amendment. A lease was drawn up which granted to the United States Guantánamo in the eastern part of Cuba, and Bahía Honda in the northwestern part of the island. This lease was signed at Havana, July 2, and ratifications were exchanged at Washington, October 6, 1903.[20] This agreement recognized Cuban sovereignty over land leased and provided that the Cuban flag should be raised by the side of the United States flag. By a later contract the United States agreed to pay the extremely low rental of $2,000 per year.[21]

---

[18] *Papers Relating to the Foreign Relations of the United States,* 1907, p. 506.
[19] Hill, *op. cit.,* p. 85.
[20] *Senate Document No. 105* (Fifty-eighth Congress, second session), pp. 380-84.
[21] Machado y Ortega, *op. cit.,* p. 48. By the treaty of December 27, 1912, the

Aside from foreign relations, the Estrada Palma administration was confronted with domestic problems of importance and with all the routine matters of government. Wood was hardly out of sight when the "outs" began to demand jobs with unseemly greed and the "ins" exerted every power to retain the positions they held.[22] The government, in addition to being harassed by job seekers and politicians vying for favors, was faced by a military problem of magnitude. For three million dollars the United States had prevailed upon General Máximo Gómez to demobilize the Cuban army. This was only the beginning of a problem from which Cuba still suffers. From that day to this the veterans have played a leading role in public affairs and have thwarted the ambitions of younger men who because of their youth could not fight for Cuban liberty. The veteran problem was held in check by the United States military government, but three years could not destroy the rebellion habit. Estrada Palma's first administration was fairly quiet because he opened the treasury to the veterans—contracting a foreign loan in order to pay them large sums.

During Estrada Palma's first administration the United States made little attempt to meddle in Cuba's internal affairs. In fact, the United States carefully heeded Cuba's objections concerning the landing of marines, and her criticism of United States consular activities. In 1905 the United States did not oppose the proposed Cuban-Great Britain commercial treaty which seemed to grant British warships special privileges in Havana harbor.[23] In fact the Cuban leaders were given a free hand to manage their own affairs and considering the training and experience of the people in self-government

---

United States relinquished its rights at Bahía Honda for greater control at Guantánamo.

[22] Irene A. Wright, *op. cit.*, p. 172.
[23] *Havana Post*, October 25, 1905.

the accomplishments of Estrada Palma's first administration were all the more remarkable.

Roosevelt was well pleased with his country's efforts at state-making, and in his message to Congress, December 6, 1904, he said:

If every country washed by the Caribbean Sea would show the progress in stable and just civilization which with the aid of the Platt Amendment Cuba has shown since our troops left the island, and which so many of the republics in both Americas are constantly and brilliantly showing, all questions of interference by this Nation with their affairs would be at an end.[24]

Events were shortly to prove Roosevelt wrong. Forces were already at work which were to overturn Estrada Palma's ideals of liberty with law and order and bring about the second intervention.

Upon assuming office Estrada Palma gave his country a non-partisan administration. He refused to join any of the various political groups and selected the members of his cabinet irrespective of their political affiliations.[25] Congress, on the other hand, was divided into partisan groups. These factions not only blocked the president, but prevented congress from enacting legislation required to give effect to the constitution. That document provided that municipal officers should be elected, but when congress refused to act the municipal officials elected during the first intervention became subject, under Spanish law, to removal by the president. The same situation came to pass with reference to judges. The executive could appoint or remove them at will because congress had failed to give effect to the constitution, which called for a judiciary independent of and irremovable by the executive. Congress also failed to pass an election law which would

---

[24] Theodore Roosevelt, *State Papers as Governor and President*, p. 257.
[25] Taft and Bacon, *Report*, p. 451.

adequately comply with the provision in the constitution providing for minority representation in both houses. The continued concentration of power seemed to indicate that the party in power was determined to retain control regardless of law. To make matters worse the electoral law was amended so that the control of elections would rest largely in the hands of municipal chiefs. This, of course, placed the municipalities and indirectly the control of elections in the hands of the president.

Estrada Palma cannot be charged with responsibility for this situation because in his first message to congress on May 26, 1902, he advised that body to pass a municipal law which would conform to the constitution.[26] However, he did make the mistake of allowing the leaders of the new Moderate party to influence him from his non-partisan course. The Moderates wanted to make a partisan of Estrada Palma, and decided that all officials not in sympathy with them should be removed in order that their followers might secure more jobs and be in a position to assure victory at the polls in the coming elections.

By the spring of 1905, Estrada Palma, having failed to secure the legislation he desired, cast in his lot with the Moderates. He thought that through party loyalty and discipline he could secure the legislation required by the constitution. He dismissed his cabinet and appointed a group of Moderates who became known as the *Cabinete de Combate*. They were given this name because most of them were war veterans. However, the Liberals claimed it was because they were selected to carry the next elections by force.[27] The president had the right to change his cabinet, but he made the mistake of appointing unsuitable men. The prominent figure in the new cabinet was General Fernando Freyre de Andrade, who

[26] *Mensajes presidenciales,* I, 6.
[27] Taft and Bacon, *Report,* p. 452.

served as Secretary of Government. He was a man of ability and because of his forceful orders and zealous activity in the elections of 1905 was referred to as the "Czar of Russia." [28] General Rafael Montalvo was Secretary of Public Works and also provisional Secretary of Agriculture. Juan F. O'Farrill y Chappotin was Secretary of State and Justice; Juan Ríus Rivera, Secretary of Treasury; and Eduardo Yero Buduén, Secretary of Public Instruction.[29] This new cabinet was highly acclaimed by the Moderates, but its selection was unfortunate for the welfare of Cuba.

Political factions were present during Estrada Palma's first administration, but well defined parties advocating special issues or platforms could hardly be said to have existed. The leading groups were the Moderates and the Liberals. Groups calling themselves Nationalists usually acted with the Moderates.[30] The Liberals declared for the immediate abrogation of the Platt Amendment. The Moderates pointed with pride to the achievements of Estrada Palma's administration. Especially did they mention the prosperous condition of the country and the surplus in the treasury. They also advocated repeal of the Platt Amendment, but at some future date. Issues were mentioned, but the election turned on personalities, fraud, and force.

Estrada Palma, having been convinced that his services were indispensable to the welfare of Cuba, allowed himself to be nominated by the Moderates for president to succeed himself.[31] The candidate for vice-president was Domingo Méndez Capote, the leader of the Moderate party. The Lib-

---

[28] Amado Randín, *Cuba: reivindicada*, p. 5.

[29] Martínez Ortiz, *Cuba*, II, 114. Martínez Ortiz states that this cabinet change brought on the August Revolution and the second intervention. *Ibid.*, p. 112.

[30] Vicente Pardo Suárez, *La electión presidencial en Cuba*, p. 90.

[31] Practically all writers and the many living witnesses interviewed agree that Estrada Palma did not desire a second term. Politicians and officeholders looking out for themselves convinced the old gentleman that Cuba needed his services.

eral candidate for president was General José Miguel Gómez, governor of the Province of Santa Clara. For vice-president, the Liberals backed Alfredo Zayas.

In addition to selecting a president and vice-president in 1905 the people were to elect half the house for a term of four years and half the senate for a term of eight years. Also all six provinces were to elect governors for four-year terms. The political plums were worth a fight and both Liberals and Moderates prepared for the contest.

Under the new cabinet practically all the national officers were members of the Moderate party. The president controlled the police, the rural guards, the municipal alcaldes, and pressure was placed on all to insure victory in the coming elections. The Secretary of Government, General Freyre de Andrade, just before the September elections ousted opposition officials in some twenty municipalities.[32] Those removed were charged with violation of duty, but it was enough for the followers of Gómez that the removals were made in Liberal provinces. The officials who were removed had been elected by popular vote during the first intervention and their summary dismissal by the Estrada Palma government aroused intense opposition among the common people.

The Liberal party was not free from blame—

. . . in Santa Clara, and possibly in Pinar de Rio, there were organizations of the Liberal party that did not stop at peaceful means to influence voters before the elections were held, and threats of force were not wanting to justify the Moderates in possession of the Government in preparing to meet them.[33]

All during the summer of 1905 the Liberals excited the island with their speech-making. They prevented a quorum of congress and thereby defeated the budget bill. Estrada

---

[32] Taft and Bacon, *Report*, p. 453.
[33] *Loc. cit.*

Palma, by executive decree, extended the budget law then in force for another year only to be blamed for his usurpation of legislative powers. On July 22, 1905, the Liberals burned the government building at San Antonio de las Vueltas.[34]

Gómez, the Liberal candidate for president, accused the administration of trampling on the rights of the people and corrupting the judiciary. Later during the campaign a resolution was adopted by the Liberals to impeach Estrada Palma for alleged violations of the constitution. By September the Liberals were calling the Moderates "Cossacks" and the Moderates called their opponents "Tartars." Parades were held, manifestoes were issued, and a battle to the finish was waged with the winner taking all.[35]

The Cuban electoral law of 1903 provided that a preliminary election should be held in September to select the ward registration boards. These boards prepared the registration lists and also acted as election boards for the definitive election which was held in December. The preliminary elections were held on September 23, 1905, with the aid of the government's rural guards and police. The Liberals, in many instances denied the right to vote and being convinced that a fair election was not being held, withdrew from the polls. "In some places where the Liberals were known to be in a majority, only a few Liberal votes were recorded, and more votes were registered for the Moderate candidates than there were inhabitants in the ward." [36] In addition to fraud the elections were marked by bloodshed and disorders in various parts of the island. The murder of Enrique Villuendas, Liberal Leader of Cienfuegos, was a notable case. He had publicly accused the Moderates of all manner of crimes and on September 22, a few hours before his death, had written General

---

[34] *Havana Post*, July 5, 1905; Chapman, *op. cit.*, p. 185.

[35] *Havana Post*, June 27, 1905; *ibid.*, August 11, 1905; *La Discusión*, Havana, September 14, 1905.

[36] Taft and Bacon, *Report*, pp. 453-54.

Gómez that his life was in danger. At the time Villuendas was shot a Moderate chief of police was killed. The Moderates were greatly stirred by the murder of an officer who was making an authorized search, and Liberals listed Villuendas as a martyr to their cause.[37] General Freyre de Andrade's policies produced results—the Moderates carried all provinces and every important town.

The Moderate victory did not go without protest. On September 27, 1905, the Liberals published a vigorous statement which denounced the Moderates and made specific charges of fraud and violence.[38] On the same date Gómez resigned as chief of the Liberal party and on October 4, sailed for New York stating that he feared assassination if he remained in Cuba. In New York Gómez stated that the United States should intervene in Cuba since the Moderate government was nothing short of despotism.[39]

Conditions became worse in October when the voters were required to register. At least 150,000 fictitious names were added to the rolls by the recently elected Moderate election boards. Many of the Liberals refused to register because they felt they could not get fair treatment under any conditions. A leading Moderate journal, *La Discusión*, criticized the high-handed methods of the Moderates, stating that:

The figures furnished by the provincial board of scrutiny to the department of government leave a most painful impression upon the spirits of those who really love their country and take an interest in its future. It shows most clearly our very poor moral conditions, evident in unscrupulous and reckless acts manifested in the worst of forms—that is, to consider unnecessary the veil of decorum with which even the most shaky of society hides its bad acts.[40]

---

[37] Martínez Ortiz, *Cuba*, II, 154; Enrique Collazo, *Cuba: intervenida*, pp. 29-85.
[38] *El Liberal*, Havana, September 27, 1905.
[39] *Havana Post*, October 5, 1906; *ibid.*, October 7, 1905.
[40] *La Discusión*, Havana, November 11, 1905.

A year later the United States peace commissioners questioned General Freyre de Andrade concerning the use of force to carry the 1905 elections and the 150,000 fraudulent names on the rolls. He answered that force had only been used to meet force and that it was possibly true that many were enrolled who were not entitled to register, but that it was impossible to hold a fair election in Cuba.[41]

The campaign conducted by the president's advisers was a thorough success. The *Cabinete de Combate* had left nothing undone to insure victory. Defeated by force and fraud in September and disgusted by the fictitious names placed on the registration books by the electoral boards in October, the Liberals withdrew from the final December election. Estrada Palma was unanimously reëlected president and not a single Liberal candidate was successful on the entire island.[42]

The fact that the Liberals did not vote did not mean that they had decided to yield to the Moderates without a fight. Their absence from the polls was a typical Hispanic American procedure and Cubans recognized it as the beginning of a revolt.[43] The Liberals promptly formed a revolutionary committee to secure by force the justice denied them at the polls. Soon insurrection flared forth, and the August Revolution was under way.[44]

---

[41] Taft and Bacon, *Report,* pp. 454-55.

[42] *Havana Post,* December 2, 1905; Taft and Bacon, *Report,* p. 455.

[43] Chapman, *op. cit.,* p. 189.

[44] Perhaps the best and most detailed account of the elections of 1905 is in Martínez Ortiz, *Cuba,* II, 113-227; Chapman, *op. cit.,* pp. 177-94, has an accurate and readable chapter on the reëlection of Estrada Palma. The best summary of the period is the Taft and Bacon *Report.*

III

The August Revolution and the Second Intervention

THE LIBERALS, thwarted at the polls, resorted to armed rebellion, and uprisings occurred in Havana and Pinar del Río provinces in November, 1905.[1] Following the December election, discontent became more widespread. During the night of February 24, 1906, an attack on the Guanabacoa barracks just outside Havana resulted in the killing of several guards and the taking of horses and arms by the rebels. Just prior to the inauguration of the new government an insurrection was quickly suppressed by General Freyre de Andrade and the rural guards. There were rumors of plots against the government and the leaders of conspiracies were known, but the Estrada Palma government, not fearing a general uprising, took no special action to put down the rebels or to protect itself.[2]

In April, 1906, at the opening of congress the Liberals remaining in that body tried to secure redress by having the elections declared illegal and void. Failing in that they walked

---

[1] *Havana Post*, November 24, 1905.
[2] Velasco, *op. cit.*, p. 18; *Diario de la Marina*, Havana, August 2, 1906.

out in a body following the lead of General Faustino "Pino" Guerra.[3] Following the second inauguration of Estrada Palma, May 20, 1906, General Freyre de Andrade resigned from the cabinet and became speaker of the house of representatives.[4] On the surface all danger of revolution appeared to be past, but discontent continued and the Liberals, bitter in defeat and hungry for jobs, broke into open rebellion on August 16, 1906.

The standard of revolt was raised in Pinar del Río by "Pino" Guerra. "It consisted—of a Cuban flag draped in crepe." [5] Other bands quickly took the field and by the end of the month armed forces were active in every province. The "Little War of August" came so suddenly and spread so fast that the government, which had been pursuing the arts of peace, was caught unprepared. The local *Havana Telegraph* "whooped up" the disturbance, hoping for intervention and annexation.[6]

One writer in discussing the revolt makes the point that the sole object of the uprising was to oust those who occupied certain desirable posts in order to secure places for other men.[7] The United States Peace Commission gave the cause of the revolution as follows:

The cause for the insurrection is to be found primarily in the election and the methods which were pursued in carrying it for the Moderate party. Of course it could not have occurred in a country in which the common and ignorant people are not as easily aroused by personal appeals of local leaders as they are in Cuba. It could not have occurred in a country where such a thing as an insurrection and "Going to the field," as it is called, does

---

[3] Chapman, *op. cit.*, p. 191.

[4] *Cámara de representantes. Memoria de los trabajos realizados* (tercer periodo congressional, 1906–1908), III, 84.

[5] Irene A. Wright, p. 173.

[6] *Ibid.*, p. 175; Martínez Ortiz, *Cuba*, II, 229.

[7] Irene A. Wright, p. 174.

not offer relief from daily labor, the pleasures of a picnic, and the opportunity to live on the country and the earnings and prosperity of other people; but with all this and with the natural tendency to insurrection that has been cultivated by a long history of insurrection in Cuba, no such formidable force could have been organized, had there not been some real feeling of injustice and outrage on the part of the less educated and poorer classes, who seemed more or less dimly to understand that the victory of the Moderates at the polls was the beginning of the end of power which they might exercise in the government.[8]

General Guerra declared that the purpose of the insurgents was "to re-establish a reign of law." [9]

The government forces, when the insurrection began, were limited to 600 artillery and 3000 rural guards. The rural guards were distributed in small detachments in the various towns of the island, and were thus unable to cope with the insurrectos where they were organized in any numbers at all. This weakness of the Government left it naked to its enemies and critics.[10]

On August 20, Estrada Palma ordered an increase of two thousand in the rural guards. However, only inefficient men could be secured and they cost the government $2.50 per day in gold.[11]

On August 17, the rural guards engaged in a skirmish with the men under the rebel leader, Mesa. On the same date the government troops in Havana revolted because of alleged bad food. The government was alarmed by the spread of the revolt and ordered the arrest of all leaders. General José Monteagudo, revolutionary commander in Santa Clara, General Castillo Duany and Juan Gualberto Gómez, leaders in

---

[8] Taft and Bacon, *Report*, p. 456.
[9] *Havana Post*, August 23, 1906.
[10] Taft and Bacon, *Report*, p. 456.
[11] Martínez Ortiz, *Cuba*, II, 237.

Oriente province, and General José Miguel Gómez were arrested and taken to Havana. Other leaders escaped the government agents. Some, like Zayas, went into hiding, and others raised bands and appeared in the field in open opposition to the government.[12]

Many citizens of the United States and Cuban annexationists were in sympathy with the revolt. It has occasionally been charged that United States capitalists financed the uprising with the hope that the United States would secure control of the island. However, a confidential report from a government investigation shows that most of the funds for the revolution came from wealthy Cubans who in many instances hoped that their contributions would insure the safety of their property.[13] There were rumors that United States citizens on the Isle of Pines contributed to the insurgent cause, that the United States minister delivered large sums to General Gómez, and that the tobacco trust purchased the protection of its property; but these charges have never been proved.[14] Evidence is also lacking to support the charges that United States politicians and business men gave financial aid to the revolt.

The Peace Commission in its report describes the progress of the August Revolution as follows:

It spread from Pinar del Rio to Havana. In Pinar del Rio Faustino Guerra, making himself a major-general, marched from Pinar del Rio eastward into the province of Habana and there joined Loynaz Castillo, also a major-general, so that their joint forces amounted to from 8,000 to 10,000 men. Probably not more than 40 per cent of these men had rifles and ammunition, and not more than half of the men who were armed had really serviceable weapons. The rest were armed with machetes and revolvers. They were all mounted with horses of their own or

---

[12] *Ibid.*, p. 232.

[13] Memorandum of a United States Secret Service agent sent in a letter from Taft to Roosevelt, September 22, 1906. *Roosevelt Papers.*

[14] *Havana Post*, January 3, 1907.

with horses which they had appropriated. In Santa Clara, under Generals Guzman, Ferrara, and other leaders, a force of 6,000 or 8,000 men was organized. They were not so well armed even as the forces of Guerra and Castillo. In Camaguey there were only a few hundred insurrectos, and in Santiago a still smaller number, although if the insurrection had continued it is quite likely that in Santiago, which has heretofore been the home of insurrection, a large force would have been raised. The province of Matanzas was loyal to the Palma government, and there were substantially no insurrectos in it. Had the insurrection proceeded, this would have been important, because Matanzas divides Santa Clara from Habana and Pinar del Rio.[15]

In the province of Havana generals Ernesto Asbert and Enrique Loinaz del Castillo were especially active. On August 27, Estrada Palma promised a pardon to all rebels who would accept it. Few took advantage of this generous offer and by September the rebels were in control of the greater part of the island.[16] The insurgent forces were poorly organized and their campaigns consisted largely of skirmishes and property raids. British-owned railway companies had some of their engines wrecked and their bridges blown up to the end that the Court of St. James might urge intervention upon the United States. Foreign legations were also aroused by reports of the burning of large sugar mills. Such reports would often be sent from distant parts of the island and then the rebels would cut the wires. As the messages could not be checked for several days the insurgents were credited with much property destruction which in fact did not take place.[17] The United States Department of State kept in touch with events in Cuba and the Estrada Palma government was warned that it would have to protect life and property. The Cuban government found itself faced with the choice of

---

[15] Taft and Bacon, *Report*, p. 457.

[16] Randín, *op. cit.*, pp. 8-9; *La Lucha*, Havana, August 28, 1906.

[17] Irene A. Wright, p. 179; Jenks, *op. cit.*, p. 82.

either making terms with the rebels or organizing an army and defeating them. Aside from the cities and the province of Matanzas, Estrada Palma had little support. To have negotiated with the insurgents would have strengthened their cause. It was beyond the president's power to put them down by force, and even though this had been possible, it would have required time and occasioned great loss of life and destruction of property. Then too it would have wiped out the surplus in the treasury of which Estrada Palma was so proud.

On the first of September the Central Revolutionary Committee issued a manifesto to the government and the Cuban people. This proposed that the government should enter into a pact with the Liberals and make changes which would have done much to justify their complaints. The basic idea of the Liberals or Constitutionalists, as they now called themselves, was to have the elections of 1905 declared void. They also wanted the ousted municipal officials and government employees restored.[18] Estrada Palma refused to discuss compromise with the rebels and affairs soon reached a crisis.

The veterans of the War of Independence offered their aid and authorized some of their leaders to effect a compromise between the rebels and the government. General Mario G. Menocal, chief among the leaders selected, had an excellent record as a soldier and at the time was manager of the great sugar estate of Chaparra. On September 1, he had a conference with Estrada Palma in Havana and outlined plans for a compromise. The plan suggested by the veterans required the resignation of all officials elected in 1905, with the exception of the president and vice-president, and stipulated that Estrada Palma should see that the necessary electoral and municipal laws should be enacted and that those Liberals unjustly removed from office should be restored.[19] The presi-

---

[18] Manuel Secades, *Patriotas y traidores,* II, 24-25.
[19] *Ibid.,* p. 23 *et seq.;* Enrique Collazo, *La revolución de agosto de 1906,* p. 18.

dent took the matter of compromise under advisement and a truce was entered into between the rebels and the government. On September 8, Estrada Palma rejected the compromise proposals and stated that he would not treat with the rebels until they had laid down their arms. The insurgents refused to do this and the truce, by order of the president, came to an end. On the same day Estrada Palma issued a decree calling congress into extraordinary session, and on the following day he suspended the Cuban constitution and ordered the arrest of all Liberal leaders not already in custody.[20]

The consul-general of the United States in Havana, Frank Steinhart, was keeping the government in Washington informed of developments in Cuba. On September 8, he sent the following message to the Secretary of State:

Absolutely confidential. Secretary of State, Cuba, has requested me, in name of President Palma, to ask President Roosevelt send immediately two vessels; one to Habana, other to Cienfuegos; they must come at once. Government forces are unable to quell rebellion. The Government is unable to protect life and property. President Palma will convene Congress next Friday, and Congress will ask for our forcible intervention. It must be kept secret and confidential that Palma asked for vessels. No one here except President, Secretary of State, and myself know about it. Very anxiously awaiting reply.[21]

Section Three of the Platt Amendment, which was thus invoked by Estrada Palma and the Moderates, provided that the United States could intervene to protect Cuban independence and to maintain a government adequate for the pro-

---

[20] *La Lucha,* Havana, September 10, 1906. Liberal pamphleteers accuse Estrada Palma of stalling for time in order to secure United States intervention. General Mario G. Menocal, in an interview granted the writer, stated that the president agreed to the veteran's proposals, but that he was later persuaded by advisers who desired intervention to change his mind.

[21] Taft and Bacon, *Report,* pp. 444-45.

tection of life, property, and individual liberty. The Moderates preferred intervention to civil war, and government by the United States to Liberal officers. The United States was slow to act on this rush invitation and Steinhart, not having any answer by September 10, cabled Washington for a reply and stated that Estrada Palma wanted war vessels to be sent at once. On September 10, Assistant Secretary of State Robert Bacon sent the following wire to Steinhart:

Your cable received. Two ships have been sent; due to arrive Wednesday. The President directs me to state that perhaps you do not yourself appreciate the reluctance with which this country would intervene. President Palma should be informed that in the public opinion here it would have a most damaging effect for intervention to be undertaken until the Cuban Government has exhausted every effort in a serious attempt to put down the insurrection and has made this fact evident to the world. At present the impression certainly would be that there was no real popular support of the Cuban Government or else that the Government was hopelessly weak. As conditions are at this moment we are not prepared to say what shape the intervention should take. It is, of course, a very serious thing to undertake forcible intervention, and before going into it we should have to be absolutely certain of the equities of the case and of the needs of the situation. Meanwhile we assume that every effort is being made by the Government to come to a working agreement which will secure peace with the insurrectos, provided they are unable to hold their own with them in the field. Until such efforts have been made, we are not prepared to consider the question of intervention at all.[22]

At this time, Secretary of State Elihu Root was making a good-will tour of South America. The Platt Amendment, the seizure of Panama, and our Caribbean policies were causing alarm. President Roosevelt was especially anxious to avoid anything which might cause resentment in the minds of our

---

[22] *Ibid.*, p. 445.

neighboring republics to the south. On September 11, Bacon cabled Steinhart in part that Roosevelt "believes actual, immediate intervention to be out of the question." [23] Events quickly forced Roosevelt's hand and made intervention inevitable. On September 12, the Cuban Secretary of State handed to Steinhart the following memorandum which he promptly forwarded to Washington:

Secretary of State the Republic of Cuba at 3:40 to-day delivered to me memorandum in his own handwriting, a translation of which follows and is transmitted notwithstanding previous secret instructions on the subject: "The rebellion has increased in the provinces of Santa Clara, Habana, and Pinar del Rio, and the Cuban Government has no elements to contend it, to defend the towns and prevent the rebels from destroying property. President Estrada Palma asks for American intervention and begs that President Roosevelt send to Habana with the greatest secrecy and rapidity 2,000 or 3,000 men to avoid any catastrophe in the capital. The intervention asked for should not be made public until the American troops are in Habana. The situation is grave and any delay may produce a massacre of citizens in Habana." [24]

On the twelfth, the United States cruiser "Denver" arrived in Havana harbor. Her decks were cleared for action, and her guns commanded O'Reilly and Obispo streets.[25] This ship was the answer to the urgent requests of Estrada Palma. There were rumors that the rebel General Loinaz del Castillo would invade Havana and that the police would mutiny and join him. On September 13, the United States Department of State received the following cable:

President Palma, the Republic of Cuba, through me officially asks for American Intervention because he cannot prevent rebels from entering cities and burning property.

[23] *Ibid.*
[24] *Ibid.*, p. 446.
[25] Irene A. Wright, p. 179.

It is doubtful whether quorum when Congress assembles next Friday, to-morrow. President Palma has irrevocably resolved to resign and to deliver the Government of Cuba to the representative whom the president of the United States will designate as soon as sufficient American troops are landed in Cuba. This act on the part of President Palma to save his country from complete anarchy, and imperative intervention come immediately. It may be necessary to land force of *Denver* to protect American property.

Probably about 8,000 rebels outside Habana. Cienfuegos also at mercy of rebels. Three sugar plantations destroyed.

Foregoing all resolved in palace. Present, the President, secretary of state, secretary of war, and

Steinhart, *Consul-General*.[26]

Also, on the thirteenth an agent of Zayas and General Loinaz del Castillo stated to Captain Colwell of the "Denver" that those Liberal leaders were ready to surrender to the United States, but that they would not consider surrender to the Moderate Estrada Palma government.[27]

During the evening of September 13, the United States chargé d'affaires, Jacob Sleeper, and Captain Colwell, after a conference with Estrada Palma and with his approval, landed one hundred and twenty-five marines from the "Denver" for the protection of life and property. Some of the marines camped in front of the palace and others patrolled the quiet Havana streets.[28] These troops were landed without any authority from the United States government and when the news reached Washington Roosevelt had the State Department wire Sleeper that he should not have directed the landing of the troops and that they should not be used in the future without express authority.[29] On the fourteenth Sleeper

---

[26] Taft and Bacon, *Report*, p. 446.
[27] *Havana Post*, September 14, 1906.
[28] Taft and Bacon, *Report*, p. 458.
[29] Robert Bacon to Sleeper, September 13, 1906. *Roosevelt Papers*.

cabled Washington that he had ordered Captain Colwell to withdraw his force.[30]

While the above events were taking place in Havana, Roosevelt at Oyster Bay was busy with Cuban affairs. On September 14, the following cable from Steinhart to the State Department was communicated to him:

President Palma has resolved not to continue at the head of the Government, and is ready to present his resignation, even though the present disturbances should cease at once. The vice-president has resolved not to accept the office. Cabinet ministers have declared that they will previously resign. Under these conditions it is impossible that Congress will meet, for the lack of a proper person to convoke same to designate a new president. The consequences will be absence of legal power, and therefore the prevailing state of anarchy will continue unless the Government of the United States will adopt the measures necessary to avoid the danger.[31]

Roosevelt did not await the return of Secretary Root but, after consulting with Taft and Bacon, reluctantly announced to the world the United States policy towards Cuba in an open letter to the Cuban minister, Gonzalo de Quesada. While intervention was not formally declared until later, it really began with the publication of the following letter:

OYSTER BAY, N. Y., *September 14, 1906*

MY DEAR SEÑOR QUESADA:

In this crisis in the affairs of the Republic of Cuba, I write you, not merely because you are the minister of Cuba accredited to this Government, but because you and I were intimately drawn to-

---

[30] Sleeper to William Loeb, Jr., Secretary to the President, September 14, 1906. *Roosevelt Papers*. Sleeper was soon superseded by Frank Steinhart as the chief diplomatic official of the United States in Cuba. The United States minister Edwin V. Morgan was away on his vacation at this time.

[31] Taft and Bacon, *Report*, pp. 446-47.

gether at the time when the United States intervened in the affairs of Cuba, with the result of making her an independent nation. You know how sincere my affectionate admiration and regard for Cuba are. You know that I never have done and never shall do anything in reference to Cuba save with such sincere regard for her welfare. You also know the pride I felt because it came to me as President to withdraw the American troops from the island of Cuba, and officially to proclaim her independence and to wish her Godspeed in her career as a free republic. I desire now, through you, to say a word of solemn warning to your people, whose earnest well-wisher I am. For seven years Cuba has been in a condition of profound peace obtained under her own independent government. Her peace, prosperity, and independence are now menaced; for of all possible evils that can befall Cuba the worst is the evil of anarchy, into which civil war and revolutionary disturbances will assuredly throw her. Whoever is responsible for armed revolt and outrage, whoever is responsible in any way for the condition of affairs that now obtain, is an enemy of Cuba; and doubly heavy is the responsibility of the man who, affecting to be the especial champion of Cuban independence, takes any step which will jeopardize that independence. For there is just one way in which Cuban independence can be jeoparded, and that is for the Cuban people to show their inability to continue in their path of peaceful and orderly progress. This nation asks nothing of Cuba, save that it shall continue to develop as it has developed during these past seven years; that it shall know and practice the orderly liberty which will assuredly bring an ever-increasing measure of peace and prosperity to the beautiful Queen of the Antilles. Our intervention in Cuban affairs will only come if Cuba herself shows that she has fallen into the insurrectionary habit, that she lacks self-restraint necessary to secure peaceful self-government, and that her contending factions have plunged the country into anarchy.

I solemnly adjure all Cuban patriots to band together, to sink all differences and personal ambitions, and to remember that the only way that they can preserve the independence of their republic is to prevent the necessity of outside interference, by rescuing it from the anarchy of civil war. I earnestly hope that this word of adjuration of mine, given in the name of the American people, the stanchest friends and well-wishers of Cuba that there are in all the world, will be taken as it is meant, will be seriously considered, and will be acted upon; and if so acted upon, Cuba's permanent independence, her permanent success as a republic are assured.

Under the treaty with your Government, I, as president of the United States, have a duty in this matter which I cannot shirk. The third article of that treaty explicitly confers upon the United States the right to intervene for the maintenance in Cuba of a government adequate for the protection of life, property, and individual liberty. The treaty conferring the right is the supreme law of the land and furnishes me with the right and the means of fulfilling the obligation that I am under to protect American interests. The information at hand shows that the social bonds throughout the island have been so relaxed that life, property, and individual liberty are no longer safe. I have received authentic information of injury to, and destruction of, American property. It is in my judgment imperative for the sake of Cuba that there shall be an immediate cessation of hostilities and some arrangement which will secure the permanent pacification of the island.

I am sending to Habana the Secretary of War, Mr. Taft, and the Assistant Secretary of State, Mr. Bacon, as the special representatives of this Government, who will render such aid as is possible towards these ends. I had hoped that Mr. Root, the Secretary of State, could have stopped in Habana on his return from South America, but the seeming imminence of the crisis forbids further delay.

Through you I desire in this way to communicate with the Cuban Government, and with the Cuban people, and accordingly I am sending you a copy of this letter to be presented to President Palma, and have also directed its immediate publication.

Sincerely yours,
THEODORE ROOSEVELT [32]

---

[32] *Ibid.*, pp. 491-92.

This friendly warning letter was well received and much discussed in Cuba. *La Discusión,* a leading Havana paper, in an editorial expressed the view that Roosevelt did not want to take advantage of the Platt Amendment, but that he would order intervention if the Cubans did not behave.[33] *La Lucha* praised Roosevelt highly as a man and complimented him on his attitude toward Cuba.[34] The *Havana Post,* owned by citizens of the United States and printed in English, stated that Roosevelt's letter had been much discussed and that it was approved by all.[35]

The fact that Taft and Bacon were being sent to Cuba caused both factions to rest and await their arrival. Since no rules were adopted to regulate the insurgents pending the arrival of the Peace Commission, the situation remained tense.

Taft and Bacon left Oyster Bay for Cuba the evening of September 14. They stopped in Washington where Taft consulted generals Bell and Ainsworth concerning "what could be done by the army in case it was thought necessary to enforce peace in the island." [36] Taft reported to Roosevelt that the army was fit, and that a force of 5,500 or 6,000 men could be in Havana, ready for action, within ten days. In Washington, Taft also conferred with George B. Davis, Judge-Advocate-General, relative to the right of Roosevelt to intervene without authority from Congress. Taft wrote Roosevelt that he thought that under the permanent treaty between the United States and Cuba, and because of the President's obligations under the law to enforce the treaty, the executive had the right to intervene. In this view Taft was supported by Davis, who wrote an opinion to the effect that Article Three of the treaty, permitting intervention, was

---

[33] *La Discusión,* Havana, September 16, 1906.
[34] *La Lucha,* Havana, September 15, 1906.
[35] *Havana Post,* September 16, 1906.
[36] Taft and Bacon, *Report,* p. 492.

a part of the "supreme law of the land," and that as such it was the duty of the President to enforce it.[37]

Roosevelt entertained similar views, and no congressional speech-making or legal technicalities delayed United States intervention. Answering Taft's letter, Roosevelt said:

> that treaty is the law of the land and I shall execute it. I most earnestly hope that there will be no necessity for intervention; and I have profound faith that you will be able to settle things, for I think that the Cubans of both sides have been a good deal impressed by the notice of what will come of them if they do not quit quarreling.[38]

Roosevelt was given cause for thought when he received the following wire from Senator J. B. Foraker, of Ohio. Referring to the President's Cuban policy, the Senator said,

> . . . notwithstanding I fear it may be unwelcome, [I] . . . call your attention to the fact that, under our treaty with Cuba, consent is given to the United States, not to the President, to intervene on certain specified grounds, among them for the maintenance of a government adequate, etc., not civilly, as an intermediary, or with force of arms to overthrow established government or compel it to make peace with lawless bands of insurgents, who have no complaint except charge of fraud at the elections for which there should be found ample remedy in the courts. Only the United States, acting as the treaty contemplated, by the Congress and the President, representing the political departments of the Government, can determine that ground exists for intervention under the treaty, and no one I imagine would claim that intervention according to the principles of international law could be otherwise authorized. Pardon me for saying this is an awfully serious matter, with far-reaching serious consequences to follow to this country, as well as to that, if more be intended than the preservation of law and order until the Congress can act.[39]

---

[37] *Ibid.*, pp. 492-93.

[38] *Ibid.*, p. 448.

[39] J. B. Foraker, *Notes on a Busy Life*, II, 56.

In 1901 when the Platt Amendment was up for brief discussion in the Senate, Senator Foraker, an able and farseeing man, had suggested that Section Three be amended. On this point he said:

If we adopt this amendment as reported by the Committee, it seems to me that it is likely to lead to conditions down there, that would seem to invite intervention. Suppose they have an election. One party or the other will be defeated. The party that is out is apt to complain, and with this kind of a provision, it seems to me, it might very naturally be done; it would be thought that, by making objection, by making trouble and creating difficulties, they would make a condition that would lead to an intervention of the United States to put the successful party out. It seems to me that, instead of having a restraining influence, it would have an exciting influence, and that the very result the Committee evidently sought to accomplish would be defeated, and the opposite would be the result . . . We are not to intervene when they have a government, on the ground that their government does not protect life, liberty, and property; but we are to be allowed to intervene, according to this, only when they do not have a government capable of it. . . . [40]

Foraker closed his argument by stating that his proposed amendment would remove the invitation to intervene which, in his opinion, was a standing menace to both Cuba and the United States.[41]

Replying to the Senator's telegram regarding the existing crisis, Roosevelt immediately telegraphed him:

Your communication will have my most careful consideration. . . . Let me, for your private information only, explain that there is not the slightest intention, and never has been, of acting against

[40] Quoted in Rubens, *op. cit.*, p. 433.
[41] *Loc. cit.*

the established government, but only as acting in view of the established government abdicating its powers. I sent Bacon and Taft down into Cuba, only on receipt of a statement from President Palma that he intended to resign, and that neither the Vice President nor the members of the Cabinet would consent to go on with the government, and, therefore, that chaos would come. I should be derelict to my duty if chaos came and I hesitated to land troops to protect our interests and fulfill our obligations.[42]

In addition to this wire which was sent September 26, 1906, Roosevelt the next day wrote Foraker as follows:

Palma sent us a series of appeals asking for immediate armed intervention, saying that if it was delayed his government would fall and chaos would ensue; and then another telegram, reiterating the statement that he was going to resign at once, that the Vice President and Cabinet would refuse to go on with the government, and that he did not believe a quorum of Congress would assemble, so that absolute chaos would come, and we must land troops to protect property . . . I . . . realize now, as a matter of course, that anything I do must be of a tentative nature, and that as soon as Congress comes together, it must decide as to what policy we shall permanently follow . . . I accordingly had to act, understanding of course that I could inaugurate no permanent policy, but simply handle affairs until Congress met . . .

The Palma Government has been utterly unreasonable and has evidently been bent to forcing us to an armed intervention in their support . . . When Taft gets the insurgents to agree to what under the circumstances and having in view the utter military incapacity of the Palma Government, is a very good compromise, namely, that Palma shall continue in office for his term, and that a new election shall be held for Senators and Congressmen to take the place of those who were undoubtedly put into office by glaring frauds last December, Palma bluntly repudiates the agreement, and says he will not go into it . . . Taft's last dispatch to me is that Palma insists upon resigning, and upon the

---

[42] Foraker, *op. cit.*, II, 56.

United States taking control, because his resignation cannot be accepted, inasmuch as there is not a quorum of Congress present, and so there will be no government at all.[43]

On September 27, Roosevelt wrote Senator Henry Cabot Lodge that the situation demanded immediate action, and added:

. . . just imagine my following the Buchanan-like course of summoning Congress for a six weeks' debate by Bacon, John Sharp Williams, and Tillman as to whether I ought to land the marines to protect American life and property!—the fighting would have gone on without break and the whole Island would now be a welter of blood.[44]

Aside from thinking that the United States Constitution and the permanent treaty with Cuba gave him full power to act, Roosevelt did not wish to stir up criticism in Congress prior to the November elections. Accordingly, the United States intervened in Cuba under the Platt Amendment by executive order and not by act of Congress. Citizens of Cuba and the United States acquiesced in Roosevelt's leadership.[45]

In response to Estrada Palma's special decree the Cuban congress met in extraordinary session September 14, 1906. The president addressed the body and gave a brief account of the rebellion and the steps his government had taken to restore order. The congress gave Estrada Palma a vote of confidence by approving the actions taken by him to suppress the revolt.[46]

---

[43] *Ibid.*, II, 57-59.

[44] Roosevelt to Lodge, September 26, 1906. *Roosevelt Papers.* See also Bishop, *op. cit.*, II, 26.

[45] Senator Foraker acquiesced in Roosevelt's actions, but contended that the President acted under his general powers and not under the Platt amendment. Foraker, *op. cit.*, II, 59-60. Horatio S. Rubens, one-time attorney for the Cuban Revolutionary *Junta* in New York City, agrees with the Foraker view. Rubens, *op. cit.*, pp. 435-36.

[46] *Mensajes presidenciales*, I, 175-76; *Cámara de representantes. Memoria de les trabajos realizados* (tercer período congressional), III, 288 *et seq.*

On September 16, knowing that Taft and Bacon were on their way to Cuba, the president issued a decree suspending hostilities. Some of the political prisoners were released; Zayas was allowed to come out of hiding to represent the revolutionists. The representatives of the veterans made a final attempt to bring about a compromise before the United States commissioners arrived, but all such efforts were in vain.[47]

Taft and Bacon, with the United States minister to Cuba, Edwin V. Morgan, Judge Otto Schoenrich, and Captain Frank R. McCoy left Washington September 16, by train and arrived in Tampa, Florida, the next day. There they boarded the United States S. S. "Des Moines" and reached Havana the morning of the nineteenth. For the next several days the commissioners, under the guidance of the United States consul-general, Frank Steinhart, interviewed Liberal and Moderate leaders and listened to all who could throw any light on the situation or offer a solution.[48]

Frank Steinhart has played an important and interesting role in Cuba. Born in Germany, May 12, 1864, he came in his youth to America, and became a citizen of the United States. He distributed newspapers, and later served as a private in the regular army. At the request of General Philip Sheridan, who had taken a friendly interest in him, he was transferred from a western military post to Chicago prior to the Spanish-American War. While stenographer for General Sheridan he went to a night law school and became an expert military adviser. During the Spanish-American War he saw service at Camp Chickamauga and in Puerto Rico. He went to Cuba in 1899 as chief clerk of the first army and helped General Brooke feed the hungry and clean up the island. He remained in Cuba after Wood became military governor, and

---

[47] *Havana Post*, September 17-19, 1906.
[48] Taft and Bacon, *Report*, pp. 448-50.

was placed in charge of civil and military affairs at the palace. During the Estrada Palma administration and at the time of the "Little War of August," he was United States consul-general. Steinhart was a close friend of Estrada Palma and according to Taft and Bacon "was better acquainted with the conditions and public men than any other American whom we could have consulted. He was with us constantly, and greatly aided us." [49]

The peace commissioners, desiring a friendly solution of the controversy, were careful not to mention intervention. The Moderates had requested intervention, but for political reasons they wished to avoid all responsibility for bringing it about. The Liberal leaders preferred intervention to the Estrada Palma government, but also wished to avoid all responsibility. Estrada Palma would not consider compromise until the rebels laid down their arms and the latter refused to give in until assured that their demands would be met. As the commissioners, above all, desired compromise without bloodshed, they were confronted with defeat from the first.

Taft and Bacon, fearing at any time an outbreak resulting from breach of the truce, suggested rules, "which both sides acquiesced in, to insure peace during the truce, and to avoid charges of unfair advantages." [50] On September 20, United States sailors were landed at Cienfuegos to protect property. Meanwhile conferences were being held, assistants were collecting data, and compromise plans were being formulated.

The insurgent forces lacked cohesiveness and therefore were difficult to deal with. Finally, after a secret meeting of the rebel chiefs held in Marianao the night of September 22, Liberal leaders held by the government in Havana as politi-

---

[49] *Ibid.,* p. 450. Today (1937) although past seventy, Steinhart is still a leading figure in Cuba. He is the active president and general manager of the Havana Electric Company. He is the honorary life president of the United States Chamber of Commerce of Cuba.

[50] *Ibid.,* p. 459.

cal prisoners were given full power by their rebel companions to act as a committee and to treat with the American commissioners.[51] The prisoners were allowed to attend the conferences and were then returned to jail. Estrada Palma as head of the government and Méndez Capote as chief of the Moderate party were always available to the commissioners, but these leaders were obstinate and progress was slow.

As a result of many conferences, Taft and Bacon were soon convinced that the elections of 1905 were dishonest. They were also convinced that the compromise proposals submitted by General Menocal in behalf of the veterans were "with some modifications . . . a fair basis for settlement." [52] Accordingly the peace commissioners submitted to the warring groups compromise proposals calling for the resignation of all officers elected in 1905, except the president and vice-president, and for new municipal, electoral, and judiciary laws; and demanding a civil service law, redress for Liberals ousted from office, and also a date for the holding of new elections.[53]

The Liberals accepted these terms, but the Moderates, insisting that the dignity of the government would not allow it to treat with armed rebels, refused. Estrada Palma said that:

. . . it was inconsistent with his dignity and honor to acquiesce in the resignation of members of his party who had been elected on the same ticket with him; that he did not think the compromise, if entered into, would last three months; that it was useless and that he would not lend himself to it.[54]

The United States commissioners "deemed it important, in order to maintain the good name of Cuba, and in order to

---

[51] *Ibid.*, p. 460; Martínez Ortiz, *Cuba*, II, 311-12.
[52] Taft and Bacon, *Report*, p. 460.
[53] *Ibid.*, p. 462.
[54] *Loc. cit.*

show that a conservative man was retained in power, to have Mr. Palma remain as President." They "thought it would preserve the continuity of the Government under the Constitution, and perhaps prevent the injury to the credit of the island which a violent or abrupt change in chief executive would be likely to effect." [55]

Estrada Palma appeared to the commissioners as "the most disinterested patriot in the island," and they even proposed a modification of the Menocal compromise if he would remain in office. According to this plan a fair election would be held in three months, a commission with an equal number of Moderates and Liberals and with a member from the United States would draw up needed laws to be adopted by congress, and meanwhile the municipal officers would remain. [56]

On September 24, the proposals were explained to the representatives of the Liberal party. The proposals were discussed at length, and although,

. . . there was much objection to the failure to provide for an immediate restoration of the municipal governments and to an absence of a restriction upon the President's power to appoint such a cabinet as he saw fit, they indicated the probability of their acquiescence. [57]

The proposition was next submitted informally to Méndez Capote and he replied that:

. . . he did not think the compromise proposed was a practical suggestion; that the Government thus organized would not stand for three months, and that it was a mere patched-up affair which simply postponed the evil day. [58]

---

[55] Taft and Bacon, *Report*, p. 460.
[56] *El Liberal*, Havana, September 23, 1906.
[57] Taft and Bacon, *Report*, p. 461.
[58] *Loc. cit.*

On the evening of September 24, the commissioners sought and had an interview with Estrada Palma. After an extended discussion the president flatly refused the compromise. With expressions of regret at the failure to reach an agreement the commissioners on the same night wrote the president a lengthy letter explaining the situation in detail; they concluded by asking him to remain in office and to make another sacrifice for Cuba. On the following day the old patriot, no doubt deeply moved, in replying to the commissioners stated that:

... the conditions which you deem are absolutely necessary to get the rebels to lay down their arms are against my personal decorum and the dignity of the Government over which I preside, therefore, my decision to present before Congress the resignation of the official position to which I was elected by the will of the Cuban people at the last presidential election, is irrevocable.[59]

Following this communication from the chief executive, the peace commissioners made an effort to secure an agreement between a part of the Moderate party and the Liberals, but all such efforts were now hopeless.

On September 25, Roosevelt telegraphed Estrada Palma and requested him to sacrifice his own feelings for the good of Cuba and to remain in office. He suggested that Estrada Palma accept the Taft and Bacon compromise or "any practicable modification which he could suggest." [60] The Cuban president was no doubt displeased by this wire and *La Lucha* seemed to think that he construed Roosevelt's note as an invitation to get out.[61] This was hardly the case, because the press reported as early as September 21 that the president and his cabinet would probably resign. Also Steinhart in his cable

---

[59] Taft and Bacon, *Report*, p. 512.
[60] *Ibid.*, pp. 473-74.
[61] *La Lucha*, Havana, September 26, 1906.

to Washington on the fourteenth stated that Estrada Palma had resolved not to continue at the head of the government.[62]

Estrada Palma's dignity, his concept of his duty, and his academic principles of right and wrong would not allow him to compromise for the sake of political expediency. He did not think the Liberals, legally or otherwise, were entitled to govern Cuba, but he felt that all loyal citizens should have supported the government. He expected the United States to uphold law and order and not to treat with rebels in arms. Being unable to restore order and anxious to avoid civil war, it was only natural for him to resign his high office and turn the government of his beloved Cuba over to the United States.

On September 28, 1906, Estrada Palma convened congress to receive his resignation. He accepted the resignations of his cabinet, and submitted them to congress along with that of the vice-president, Méndez Capote. As the Moderate members of that body wished to avoid the responsibility of bringing about intervention they asked Estrada Palma to withdraw his resignation. A committee was appointed to confer with the president, and congress adjourned at 4:30 P.M. to meet again at nine that night to hear the report of the committee.[63] That evening at eight o'clock a letter arrived for the congress from Ricardo Dolz, a member of the committee. The message stated that the committee had seen Estrada Palma and that he refused to withdraw his resignation. It further stated that the Moderate members would not attend the session at nine o'clock that evening. The Moderates, true to their word, refused to attend, and as a quorum could not be obtained, Cuba was without a government.[64]

[62] *Havana Post*, September 22, 1906; Taft and Bacon, *Report*, pp. 446-47.

[63] Pardo Suárez, *op. cit.*, pp. 97-99.

[64] *Cámara de representantes. Memoria de los trabajos realizados* (tercer período congressional), III, 331 *et seq.* Alfredo Zayas vainly tried to persuade Taft and Bacon to name him president, "arguing that 'some of his friends' thought such a

In vain the United States commissioners waited all night for a quorum of the Cuban congress to gather and select a new president. Estrada Palma, having no successor and considering his resignation irrevocable, on the night of the twenty-eighth directed a letter to Taft and Bacon and turned his authority and the national treasury over to them. The peace commissioners took charge for the United States and a small guard of marines was ordered to protect the treasury. On the following day, September 29, 1906, with the approval of President Roosevelt, Taft proclaimed himself provisional governor of Cuba.[65]

The second intervention began formally with the publication of the following proclamation: [66]

To the People of Cuba:

The failure of Congress to act on the irrevocable resignation of the President of the Republic of Cuba, or to elect a successor, leaves this country without a Government at a time when great disorder prevails, and requires that pursuant to a request of President Palma, the necessary steps be taken in the name and by the authority of the President of the United States, to restore order, protect life and property in the Island of Cuba and islands and keys adjacent thereto, and for this purpose, to establish therein a provisional government.

The provisional government hereby established by direction and

---

measure would be the best solution." Judge Otto Schoenrich to the author, July 13, 1936.

[65] Taft and Bacon, *Report,* p. 463. This report is the best source for the work of the peace commissioners and the events in Cuba which led to the second United States intervention. The best account of this period by a Cuban is Martínez Ortiz, *Cuba,* II, 294-363. This is the work of a Liberal and it is based largely on newspaper accounts and the Taft and Bacon *Report.* See also *Papers Relating to the Foreign Relations of the United States, 1906–1907,* Pt. I, pp. 454-94, and David A. Lockmiller, "La base legal de la intervención de los Estados Unidos en Cuba en 1906," *Revista bimestre cubana,* XXXVIII (Septiembre-Deciembre, 1936), 268-81.

[66] As stated in the preface, this was the first and only formal intervention that has been made by the United States in the Republic of Cuba.

in the name of the President of the United States will be maintained only long enough to restore order and peace and public confidence, and then to hold such elections as may be necessary to determine those persons upon whom the permanent Government of the Republic should be devolved.

In so far as is consistent with the nature of a provisional government established under the authority of the United States, this will be a Cuban Government conforming, as far as may be, to the constitution of Cuba. The Cuban flag will be hoisted, as usual, over the government buildings of the island. All the executive departments and the provincial and municipal governments, including that of the city of Habana, will continue to be administered as under the Cuban Republic. The Courts will continue to administer justice, and all laws not in their nature inapplicable by reason of the temporary and emergent character of the government will be in force.

President Roosevelt has been most anxious to bring about peace under the Constitutional Government of Cuba, and has made every endeavor to avoid the present step. Longer delay, however, would be dangerous.

In view of the resignation of the Cabinet, until further notice the heads of all departments of the central government will report to me for instructions, including Maj. Gen. Alejandro Rodriguez, in command of the Rural Guard and other regular government forces, and Gen. Carlos Roloff, treasurer of Cuba.

Until further notice the civil governors and alcaldes will also report to me for instructions.

I ask all citizens and residents of Cuba to assist in the work of restoring order, tranquillity, and public confidence.

WM. H. TAFT
Secretary of War of the United States,
Provisional Governor of Cuba.[67]

The Cubans "scuttled" their government. Estrada Palma's cherished ideals of independence with law and order gave way

[67] Taft and Bacon, *Report,* pp. 463-64; *Cámara de representantes. Memoria de los trabajos realizados* (tercer período congressional), III, 332-33.

to anarchy. Estrada Palma requested intervention, and Roosevelt was forced by circumstances, against his wishes, to comply. The United States intervened not because it was invited, but because Cuba was without government. The Cubans, generally speaking, were pleased with intervention and astonished at the generous terms of Taft's proclamation. This is indicated by the fact that, although thousands of men were under arms, a simple proclamation and a small squad of marines to protect the national treasury were sufficient to establish the provisional government.

The *Havana Post,* glad to have law and order restored, welcomed intervention and stated that Cuba had a great opportunity for progress and development under the United States.[68] *El Mundo,* no doubt thinking of United States military rule in Cuba, stated that military occupation of Cuba had started.[69] The editor of *La Discusión,* evidently having read Taft's proclamation carefully, stated that intervention did not mean annexation.[70] As the intervention was a foregone conclusion the event failed to receive the newspaper comments that one might expect.

However, questions concerning the justice of the August Revolution and the necessity of the second intervention were not neglected by Cuban writers. On the question of the justice of the August Revolution, *Cuba y América* stated that the elections of 1905 were a disgrace to Cuban democracy, but that the present rebellion was a greater disgrace.[71] The historian Martínez Ortiz disposes of this question in short order by asking, "Was the war just?" and by answering "Surely not." [72] Enrique José Varona, writing a few months after the intervention had been declared, said: "The more I study the

---

[68] *Havana Post,* September 29, 1906.
[69] *El Mundo,* Havana, September 29, 1906.
[70] *La Discusión,* Havana, September 29, 1906.
[71] *Cuba y América,* September 8, 1906, p. 386.
[72] Martínez Ortiz, *Cuba,* II, 366.

August Revolution and its causes, the more I censure it, and the more disastrous I find its consequences." [73] Both Moderates and Liberals were to blame for the revolution and Cuba was the chief loser.

Was intervention necessary? The majority of those who have covered this period agree that it was. There can be no doubt that intervention was the only solution after the Cuban government quit. However, should not the United States have stood by Estrada Palma and aided him in putting down the rebels? Probably this could have been accomplished with little or no bloodshed. Generals Guerra, Asbert, and other Cubans interviewed on this point are emphatic that the Constitutional forces would not have fought against the Americans had the United States backed Estrada Palma. They stated that reasons of sentiment and a certain knowledge of the outcome would have prevented Liberals from fighting United States troops. One able observer who was on the ground at the time states that Estrada Palma had expected the United States to support his government; that Taft and Bacon "trafficked" with rebel forces because they were afraid of the "ragamuffins" assembled before Havana; and that Taft as a presidential candidate "temporized" when he should have used force, if necessary, to support the government. [74]

Bacon was in favor of upholding the Estrada Palma government and felt that electoral mistakes should be corrected by the courts and ballots and not by revolution. The day before he left Havana he stated that he was not satisfied and added that intervention was contrary to what Secretary Root had been preaching on his South American tour. [75] It was Taft who made the decision which forced intervention. He seems

---

[73] Enrique José Varona, "Proofs," *El Figaro*, February 3, 1907.

[74] Irene A. Wright, *op. cit.*, pp. 181-82. Herbert S. Duffy in his book *William Howard Taft*, pp. 183 *et seq.* mentions Taft's trip to Cuba, but aside from general praise he throws no light on this point.

[75] James Brown Scott, *Robert Bacon: Life and Letters*, p. 118.

to have had rather definite ideas concerning the Cuban government before he and Bacon arrived in Havana. On September 15, 1906, in writing to Root about the Cuban situation and his proposed trip he spoke of the Estrada Palma government as a "house of cards." [76]

The historian, W. F. Johnson, severely criticizes the Peace Commission for yielding to the threats of the rebels. He closes his criticism by listing the virtues of Estrada Palma.[77] Professor Chapman in discussing the commission and the intervention states that the stable elements in Cuba were opposed to the August Revolution, but that after it started they hoped the United States would support the Estrada Palma government. He adds that these elements still criticize the Peace Commission for not supporting the existing order.[78]

No one can say, but firm support of Estrada Palma by the United States on August 16, 1906, might have made Cuba's history brighter from that day to this. It is the writer's opinion that if the United States had supported Estrada Palma during the August Revolution of 1906 as it later supported President Menocal during the February Revolution of 1917, the second intervention would not have been necessary. However, it should be stated that some of the Liberals might have resisted force with force. Undoubtedly this would have led to bloodshed, and Americans and Cubans would have been killed. Much property would probably have been destroyed, for in the cane fields one match would go far. There is no accurate way to tell what might have happened had force been applied. As it turned out, not one life was lost and no property was destroyed.

Don Tomás accepted his downfall without bitterness, approved the Taft proclamation, and was happy that law and

---

[76] Taft to Root, September 15, 1906. *Root Papers*.

[77] Johnson, *op. cit.*, IV, 281-82.

[78] Chapman, *op. cit.*, p. 218.

order would be restored under the Cuban flag. When he and his family were ready to leave the palace, Taft offered him a battleship, but this offer he graciously declined. On October 2, the ex-president with his family left by train for Matanzas. After a short stay there he returned to his old home at Bayamo in Oriente. Liberal hatred pursued the old man, but he did not complain. He lived in poverty until his death, on November 4, 1908, at Santiago de Cuba.[79] Many say that he died from a broken heart. The governor of Oriente, Rafael Manduley del Río, speaking at the grave said:

The man whom we leave here, like every human being, had defects and virtues; like every human being, he made mistakes. But his defects and mistakes were as nothing compared with those virtues which he demonstrated as a loving son, faithful husband, affectionate father, and exemplary citizen. If he was a model in his private life, he was a model also in his honored public life; that is the mirror in which all Cubans ought to look, those that hear me and all the generations of those to come.[80]

Roosevelt should be praised for his conduct in dealing with Cuban affairs in 1906. He sent able commissioners to Cuba to represent him, and he followed their advice. He wanted Cuba to solve her own problems without United States "intermeddling." When Steinhart cabled for warships and intervention he received no encouragement from the State Department and on September 17, 1906, Roosevelt wrote Taft, "I most earnestly hope that there will be no necessity for intervention." [81] When it became necessary to land troops, Roosevelt gave his reluctant permission, but stated: "I desire, if possible, that you communicate with me before taking such final steps as will irrevocably commit us to intervention." [82] The dis-

---

[79] Velasco, *Estrada Palma,* p. 19.
[80] *Ibid.,* p. 201.
[81] Taft and Bacon, *Report,* p. 448.
[82] *Ibid.,* p. 471.

patches are full of similar statements. In his annual message to Congress, December 3, 1906, Roosevelt, after giving an account of his acts in connection with the August Revolution and the establishment of provisional government, stated that:

The United States wishes nothing of Cuba except that it shall prosper morally and materially, and wishes nothing of the Cubans save that they shall be able to preserve order among themselves and therefore to preserve their independence. If the elections became a farce, and if the insurrectionary habit becomes confirmed in the island, it is absolutely out of the question that the island should continue independent; and the United States, which has assumed the sponsorship before the civilized world for Cuba's career as a nation, would again have to intervene and to see that the government was managed in such orderly fashion as to secure the safety of life and property. The path to be trodden by those who exercise self-government is always hard and we should have every charity and patience with the Cubans as they tread this difficult path. I have the utmost sympathy with, and regard for, them; but I most earnestly adjure them solemnly to weigh their responsibilities and to see that when their new government is started it shall run smoothly, and with freedom from flagrant denial of right on the one hand, and from insurrectionary disturbances on the other.[83]

Intervention having been formally proclaimed, the Americans lost no time in taking full charge and in restoring peace and order. United States officials remained in Cuba until January 28, 1909, at which time the government of the island was returned to its people.

---

[83] Roosevelt, *op. cit.*, p. 390. Roosevelt reported to Congress but he and not Congress established provisional government in Cuba. Roosevelt and Taft without the aid of Congress determined the policies and directed the activities of the provisional government. Roosevelt alone was "the United States" as far as Section Three of the Platt Amendment was concerned.

IV

Governor Magoon Takes Charge

TAFT REMAINED IN CUBA as provisional governor until
October 13, 1906. His first task was to restore order and
to secure the disarming and disbandment of the insurgent
forces. On the same date the provisional government was established, the revolutionary committee of the Liberal party
sent the following letter to Taft:

With the understanding that the provisional government this
day established in Cuba intends to carry out, in so far as the same
may be applicable to the changed conditions, the bases of settlement which the peace commissioners recommended to both the
Moderate and Liberal parties, including a general amnesty for
political offenses, the undersigned, representing the insurgent forces
in the field by proper delegation, hereby agree on behalf of such
insurgent forces that they will at once lay down their arms, return
to their homes, restore the property which was taken by them for
military purposes, and which is now in their possession. We request the appointment of a commission by the provisional governor
to meet a similar commission appointed by us to arrange the details for the surrender of arms and property and the return of the
men to their homes.[1]

[1] Taft and Bacon, *Report*, p. 464.

The provisional governor immediately expressed gratification at the action of the Liberal committee and named General Fredrick Funston, General Mario G. Menocal, General E. Sánchez Agramonte, Colonel Carlos Hernández, and Major E. F. Ladd as commissioners, with Burton J. Mitchell as recorder, to meet with the revolutionary commission to arrange the details of the surrender. General Menocal declined to serve and General Tomás Padró Griñán was named to fill the vacancy. The revolutionists were represented by generals Francisco de Paula Valiente, Lope Recio Loinaz, José de J. Monteagudo, Enrique Loinaz del Castillo, and Faustino Guerra.[2]

When it appeared that a government would have to be established in Cuba, six thousand United States troops were sent there as an army of pacification. Twelve thousand more were ready to join the expeditionary force, but were not needed. In Cuba the troops were stationed at Camp Columbia near Havana and their presence was decisive in bringing about a prompt surrender of the insurgents. Also, the United States fleet in Havana Bay presented a formidable force and aided the provisional governor in effecting a peaceful surrender. Marines were landed from the ships and sent to various parts of the island to aid in dispersing the raw militia. All forces exhibited courage and self-restraint and coöperated in bringing about a speedy peace.[3]

The commissions appointed to arrange the details for the surrender of the insurgents met in the municipal building at Marianao, September 30, with all members present. The terms agreed upon required the rebel forces to deliver up their arms and all property in their possession which had been unlawfully seized for military purposes.[4] Horses were about

---

[2] Martínez Ortiz, *Cuba*, II, 382.
[3] Taft and Bacon, *Report*, p. 468.
[4] *Ibid.*, p. 465.

the only property wrongfully taken by the rebels which could be returned. These, in most cases, had been seized without notice or compensation and no receipts were given. The insurgents kept no record of the owners of the horses in their possession, and it was a common practice for a rebel to ride a horse until it was tired or had a sore back and then to exchange it for a fresh mount from the nearest pasture. Also, the insurgents frequently traded horses among themselves and occasionally they stole them from each other.

The rebels desired to retain the horses in their possession and by docking the tails of their mounts and otherwise disguising them made it almost impossible for anyone to prove ownership. Under these conditions it was out of the question to return the horses to their lawful owners. It was finally decided that each insurgent could take the horse he had back home with a certificate describing the animal and showing his right to keep it until the true owner should establish his claim.[5] However, in Spanish these certificates vested title in the holder, and the insurgent forces so understood them. In reporting to Roosevelt, Taft blamed General Funston for this error, but added that he should have exercised closer supervision.[6]

Funston stated that the American members of the commission agreed to this settlement because they felt that the rebels would keep the horses anyhow and that if they were given permission to do so, they would at once surrender their arms and return to their homes.[7] Taft recommended that the insurgents be allowed to keep the horses and that the government indemnify any owner who could produce a registered title. Roosevelt agreed to this procedure and a decree was issued by Taft on October 10, 1906, which provided that law-

---

[5] Irene A. Wright, *op. cit.*, p. 184.
[6] Taft and Bacon, *Report*, p. 488.
[7] Irene A. Wright, *op. cit.*, p. 184.

ful owners upon making proper claim could secure compensation from the government. The decree further provided that no rebel could claim more than one horse.[8] Subsequently a claims commission restricted the scope of this decree by holding that it did not cover horses which the rebels had taken from other insurgents. The solution made may have been the only workable one, but to Cubans it appeared that the United States was giving official approval to horse-stealing.[9]

All obstacles considered, disarmament proceeded at a rapid pace, and by October 8, practically all rebels were disarmed and disbanded except those in the province of Santa Clara where the Liberals were afraid of ill-treatment by Moderate officials. Although the insurgents were poorly armed and not one gun in ten was of any value, they did not want to march home without their arms. It was finally agreed that the forces would "proceed to the vicinity of their homes under the command of the several brigade commanders who were all members of the commission, and these commanders would deliver the arms to the provisional government." [10] To prevent the rebels from living off the country on their way home the government issued rations for the men and their horses.

A summary of all disarmament reports shows that the revolutionary forces in the island totaled 24,479, and turned in 3,153 arms. A total of 8,312 horse certificates were issued and men and horses were issued rations to the value of $44,-080.55. In less than two weeks the members of the Constitu-

---

[8] *Republic of Cuba under the Provisional Government of the United States, Decrees, 1906*, Decree no. 9. Hereafter cited as *Decrees*. The government decrees and official notices were published in the *Gaceta Oficial*. The decrees were later published in English and Spanish in nine large volumes.

[9] Irene A. Wright, *op. cit.*, p. 185.

[10] Taft and Bacon, *Report*, p. 530. General Ernesto Asbert, one of the insurgent chieftains, in an interview granted the writer stated that the arms given up were worthless, and that the good arms, especially when in the possession of the lawful owners, were usually kept.

tional Army were back home and reported to be engaged in lawful pursuits.[11]

The matter of discharging the militia proved to be almost as difficult as the dispersal of the rebels. The former were poorly disciplined and in some places were more unruly than the insurgents. The greater part of Taft's time during his stay as provisional governor was devoted to the disarmament and disbandment of these two forces.

Taft released all political prisoners on the same day provisional government was declared and on October 10, 1906, he issued an amnesty proclamation covering crimes committed in connection with the revolt. All factions had desired a general amnesty, except the Liberal friends of Villuendas who wished to exclude those responsible for his death and those Moderates who were not willing to pardon those implicated in the killing of certain rural guards at Guanabacoa. However, Taft made no exceptions in these cases for he believed that those arrested had been engaged in political crimes and were entitled to be included in the amnesty.[12]

Soon after the United States took charge the Liberals began to intimate that the Moderates held too many offices. When they requested that Moderate officials be replaced with Liberals Taft let it be known "that it was not the intention of the Provisional Government to oust faithful public servants to make places for Liberals, however deserving." He did recognize the greater preponderance of Moderates, however, and told the Liberals that when vacancies occurred they would be preferred until an equality was restored.[13]

In keeping with time-honored custom Taft, as head of the government, was invited to attend the opening exercises of the National University in Havana on October 1, 1906. He

---

[11] *Ibid.*, p. 531.
[12] *La Discusión*, Havana, October 11, 1906; Martínez Ortiz, *Cuba*, II, 383.
[13] Taft and Bacon, *Report*, p. 466.

accepted the invitation and in his address made a fuller statement than his proclamation could give of the purpose of the
United States in Cuba. He assured his audience that the
United States was in Cuba to help, not to exploit the Cubans.[14] This address was translated into Spanish and received
with great interest throughout the island. It was accepted as
a semi-official statement of the attitude of the United States
towards Cuba.

During the August Revolution and the stay of the Peace
Commission in Cuba much was said and written about the
annexation of Cuba to the United States. Citizens of the
United States in Cuba wanted annexation and the Northern
press in the United States favored permanent occupation.
Southern sugar planters, fearing annexation, made plans to
visit Cuba with the view of investing their money there.[15]
Brokers dealing in stocks and bonds were recommending
securities to their clients with annexation in mind.[16] The
Temps of Paris, France, expressed the view that the Cubans
were not worthy of liberty and that ultimate annexation to
the United States was certain.[17] Cuban leaders held widely
divergent opinions on the subject of annexation. Many favored annexation but refrained from expressing this opinion
because they feared political opposition if the idea was not
carried out. Estrada Palma preferred a political dependence
which would assure the blessings of liberty to an independence
"discredited and made miserable by the baneful action of
periodic civil wars." [18] Enrique José Varona, who spoke for
the majority of his countrymen, was violently opposed to annexation and criticized his people for bringing upon them-

---

[14] *El Mundo,* Havana, October 2, 1906.
[15] *Havana Post,* November 26, 1906.
[16] Jenks, *op. cit.,* p. 93.
[17] Quoted in the *Havana Post,* October 2, 1906.
[18] Magoon, *Report,* I, 15.

selves United States intervention.[19] Taft had been approached by prominent Cubans who desired annexation, but he gave them no encouragement. Roosevelt ignored all discussion of annexation and was determined to give the Cuban people another chance at self-government. As he saw it, his duty was to guard and protect Cuban liberty, not to destroy it. All discussion of annexation soon subsided, but subsequent events were to prove that the issue was not dead.

Taft, who had been designated provisional governor in an emergency, was needed back in Washington to look after his duties as Secretary of War. There was much interest and speculation in Cuba concerning his successor. The names most frequently mentioned were those of General Leonard Wood, former military governor of Cuba; Charles E. Magoon, late member of the Panama Canal Commission, governor of the Canal Zone, and minister to Panama; and Governor Beekman Winthrop of Puerto Rico.[20] The military situation was well in hand and since a civil and not a military government was to be administered, General Wood, to the regret of many Cubans, did not receive the appointment.

Magoon, having finished his task in Panama, was called to Washington early in September, 1906. The administration had selected him to go to the Philippines as vice-governor to aid the governor-general in solving legal problems which had arisen there. Magoon left Panama September 25, just as matters were breaking in Cuba to force United States intervention. His knowledge of law and of United States insular possessions was well known to the State Department; his mission in Panama was a success, and the national assembly of that country, on September 19, 1906, passed resolutions praising his services and voted a sum of money to present him a gold

---

[19] Enrique José Varona, "Aquiles Heel," *El Fígaro*, September 26, 1906.
[20] Martínez Ortiz, *Cuba*, II, 384.

medal.[21] His departure from Panama which "was attended with manifestations of esteem and regard on the part of the Government and people" of the Republic called him to the attention of administration leaders as a fit man to succeed Taft in Cuba.[22]

When Magoon reached Washington early in October, it appeared that Roosevelt had definitely decided to send Winthrop to Cuba. Secretary of State Root, just back from his South American tour, was familiar with Magoon's services in Panama and knew the worth of the man from his work as Law Officer in the Bureau of Insular Affairs. Root was keenly interested in Cuba and Pan-American relations and urged Roosevelt to appoint Magoon provisional governor. The President, relying on Root's judgment and thinking that the Cuban situation was more pressing than Philippine problems, decided to send Magoon and not Winthrop to Cuba.[23] On October 6, 1906, Roosevelt commissioned Charles E. Magoon provisional governor of Cuba and directed him to leave at once to assume the duties of that office.[24]

The new provisional governor arrived in Havana October 9, 1906. He spent the next few days in familiarizing himself

---

[21] *Star and Herald,* September 21, 1906.

[22] W. F. Sands of the United States Legation in Panama to Alvey A. Adee, Acting Secretary of State, September 28, 1906. *Magoon Papers.*

[23] Roosevelt's appointment of Magoon after he had decided on Winthrop surprised many. Martínez Ortiz, *Cuba,* II, 387, stated that Taft persuaded Roosevelt to name Magoon. It appears, however, that Root secured Magoon's appointment. On September 15, 1906, Taft wrote Root that Magoon was going to the Philippines as vice-governor. *Root Papers.* On September 29, Taft requested Roosevelt to send Winthrop to Cuba in two weeks. On October 2, Taft cabled Roosevelt that Magoon was a good man for Cuba, but argued that he was badly needed in the Philippines and that Winthrop had already been notified of his appointment. Root immediately answered this wire for the President by strongly recommending Magoon to Taft, and on October 3, Taft telegraphed Root that he would withdraw his recommendation of Winthrop. *Roosevelt Papers.* On October 4, 1906, after Magoon had been selected the *Havana Post* quoted Taft as stating that Winthrop was too much needed in Puerto Rico to be transferred to Cuba and thus the matter was closed.

[24] Magoon, *Report,* I, 8.

71

with the Cuban situation and in discussing and formulating future policies with Taft, Bacon, and various Cuban leaders. On October 13, 1906, at noon, Magoon was inducted into office by Taft. He immediately issued the following proclamation:

To the People of Cuba:

Acting under the authority conferred upon him by the appendix to the constitution of Cuba, by the treaty between the United States and Cuba, ratified July 1, 1904, and by the act of Congress of the United States approved March 2, 1901, the President of the United States has appointed me provisional governor of Cuba, to succeed the Hon. Wm. H. Taft, and I hereby assume that office.

The policy declared and the assurances given by my predecessor, Secretary Taft, will be strictly adhered to and carried out.

As provisional governor I shall exercise the powers and perform the duties contemplated and provided for by the third article of the appendix to the constitution of Cuba, for the preservation of Cuban independence, and for the protection of life, property, and individual liberty.

As soon as it shall prove to be consistent with the attainment of these ends I shall seek to bring about the restoration of the ordinary agencies and methods of government under the other and general provisions of the Cuban constitution.

All provisions of the constitution and laws, the application of which for the time being would be inconsistent with the exercise of the powers provided for by the third article of the appendix, must be deemed to be in abeyance. All other provisions of the constitution and laws continue in full force and effect.

CHARLES E. MAGOON, *Provisional Governor.*

Following the inauguration of Magoon, Taft and Bacon embarked for the United States. All kinds of water craft escorted them to the mouth of the harbor, salutes were fired from the forts, and the people who thronged the shore manifested their good will by loud cheers.[25] A mass meeting of American citizens in Havana adopted resolutions thanking the peace commissioners for their great services "to them and to all the people of Cuba." [26] Taft and Bacon failed to bring about a compromise, but they did end armed conflict and give the island peace.

Magoon went to Cuba well recommended and ruled there until the second intervention ended on January 28, 1909. He has been so praised, condemned, and abused that it is difficult to give a fair and accurate account of the man and his work.[27]

Charles Edward Magoon was born in Steele County, Minnesota, December 5, 1861.[28] His parents, Henry C. and Mehitable (Clement) Magoon, were not people of wealth but they worked hard and strove to give their children a chance in the world. Charles Magoon was the youngest by many years of six children, an older brother having fought in the Civil War with distinction. Soon after the war the Magoon family moved to a homestead in Platte County, Nebraska. Charles later attended the preparatory department and the college of arts of the University of Nebraska at Lincoln. He did not graduate, but after a year in college studied law in the offices of O. P. Mason and C. O. Whedon. In 1882 he was admitted to the bar and engaged in the practice of his profession in Lincoln, the capital of Nebraska, where he became an intimate friend of John J. Pershing, Charles G. Dawes, Robert J. Flick, Frank Zehrung, John T. Dorgan and other promising young men of that city. He was a member of

---

[25] *Havana Post*, October 14, 1906.

[26] Magoon, *Report*, I, 10-11.

[27] For summary sketches of Magoon by various writers see Chapman, *op. cit.*, pp. 230-32. Also see *Dictionary of American Biography*, XII, 201-2. The author's account of Magoon is based chiefly on interviews and correspondence with citizens of the United States and Cuba who knew Magoon during the various periods of his life.

[28] Some of the family spell the name Magoun. Dr. Charles E. Magoun to the author, February 20, 1934. Dr. Magoun resides in Sioux City, Iowa, and is a cousin of the late Charles E. Magoon.

the Volunteer Fire Department, which was considered quite an honor by the young men of his time, the Elks Club, the Pleasant Hour Social Club, and the Congregational Church.

Magoon was a successful lawyer. In addition to his courtroom duties he found time to engage in legal research and to participate in the civic life of his community. The *Daily Nebraska State Journal* of the early 1890's carried many articles by him involving legal questions, such as reviews of supreme court decisions, the trial and sentence of Jesus Christ, Sunday laws, municipal government, and capital punishment.[29] His interest in civic affairs is shown by his efforts to secure a new city charter and paved streets for Lincoln. In 1889 he compiled and published *The Municipal Code of Lincoln.*[30] For a few years he was associated in the practice of law with his teachers Mason and Whedon and after the death of Mason the firm became Whedon and Magoon and so remained until 1899. During this period Magoon served as Major and Judge-Advocate of the Nebraska National Guard and acted as attorney for and engaged in many real estate transactions with J. W. McDonald of Lincoln. When Magoon moved to Washington in 1899 he was estimated to have been worth about one hundred thousand dollars.[31]

In 1899 Magoon was in Washington on legal business and while there his friend George D. Meiklejohn, Assistant Secretary of War, introduced him to President McKinley who took a liking to the man. McKinley was much in need of someone to advise him and various government officials on legal questions arising out of the United States military occupation of Cuba and those territories ceded to the United States by the Treaty of Paris. He offered the job to Magoon. The salary was small, but the work appealed to Magoon and

[29] Scrap Book, *passim. Magoon Papers.*
[30] *Ibid., passim.*
[31] John T. Dorgan to the author, September 6, 1934. Also see Chapman, *op. cit.,* p. 233.

he became Law Officer of the Bureau of Insular Affairs under the direction of the Secretary of War. Magoon's efficient work and excellent opinions soon commanded the attention of Elihu Root, Secretary of War. Magoon passed on many Philippine and Cuban questions, and at Root's insistence published his findings in 1902 in a volume entitled *Report on the Law of Civil Government in Territory Subject to Military Occupation by the Military Forces of the United States.* Also, his *Report on the Legal Status of the Territory . . . Acquired by the United States During the War with Spain* is an exhaustive study of that subject.

His success as Law Officer seemed to fit Magoon for higher service in the relations of the United States with Hispanic America; so in 1904 he was sent to Panama as general counsel of the Isthmian Canal Commission and the following year was named a member of that commission. The United States minister to the new republic at that time was John Barrett and the governor of the Canal zone was Major-General George Davis. These two officials were deadlocked in the preliminaries of organizing the Canal Zone so that actual construction of the canal was being delayed. The governor maintained that he must have direct access to the authorities of Panama to avoid delay and to get all preliminary questions settled. The minister pointed out that the governor should approach the government of Panama through the accredited diplomatic envoy. Both officials were right, but Roosevelt and Taft agreed that there was no time for argument.

Taft knew Magoon from his work in connection with the Philippine Friars' Lands negotiations and on the recommendation of W. F. Sands, member of the United States Legation in Panama, suggested that Roosevelt solve the dispute by recalling Barrett and Davis and appointing Magoon to the dual office of minister and governor. The appointment was made on May 25, 1905, and from that date until September, 1906,

Magoon served his country well in Panama. When Magoon was appointed governor and minister,[32] the feeling between Americans and Panamanians was bitter. Up until this time Panama had been the "graveyard of American reputations." In a little over a year the situation, because of Magoon's ability, judgment, and tact, was completely changed. Mention has been made of the resolutions adopted by the national assembly and the gold medal presented him by Panama. In an editorial concerning Magoon's work on the Isthmus the *Star and Herald* said:

His tact and good judgment and genial personality won the confidence and sympathy of all with whom he came in contact. His advice and counsel were unhesitatingly accepted by both Panamanians and Americans and to him, more than any one else, is due the feeling of confidence and friendliness which now exists on the Isthmus, officially and personally, between the people of the United States and the people of Panama.[33]

Magoon, by virtue of his knowledge of the Spanish colonial legal system and his experience in Panama was well qualified for the post of provisional governor. However, he was handicapped to an extent by the fact that he did not speak Spanish and had never resided in Cuba. Then, too, he had to harmonize warring Cuban factions, and contend with rival big business interests from the United States. His was the difficult task of pleasing Washington and governing under the Cuban constitution. All things considered, Magoon was probably the best man available to administer a civil government in Cuba in 1906.

The new governor, a bachelor forty-five years of age, was well over six feet tall and weighed about two hundred and

---

[32] W. F. Sands to the author, February 22, 1934. This version of Magoon's appointment to Panama is supported by Robert J. Flick of Beverly Hills, California, a lifelong friend of Magoon and executor of his estate.

[33] *Star and Herald*, Panama, September 28, 1906.

thirty pounds. He had thick black hair, a short mustache, an agreeable disposition, and a pleasant smile. His bulk and manner made an impression on all whom he met. Once a countryman catching sight of him exclaimed *"Ave Maria, que hombronazo."* Easy-going, kind, and courteous, Magoon enjoyed smoking black cigars and always set a good table for his friends. He was inclined to trust people, was a good diplomat, and perhaps knew more about Cuban law than any other United States citizen. Unlike Wood, Magoon was not a military man, but a civilian sent to administer a civil government.

Taft's proclamation made it clear that the United States was administering Cuba for the Cubans and the Cuban flag was hoisted over government buildings as usual. In theory, at least, Cuba continued to be a sovereign state. On October 3, 1906, Taft issued a decree which confirmed Cuban diplomatic representatives in foreign countries in their respective positions and recognized foreign representatives accredited to the government of the Republic of Cuba.[34] Magoon in his proclamation stated that the policy declared by Taft would "be strictly adhered to and carried out." All provisions of the Cuban constitution and laws which were inconsistent with the powers claimed and exercised by the United States under the third article of the Platt Amendment were suspended. Magoon ruled by decree and his power was limited only by his sound discretion and instructions from Washington.

Taft, following the veterans' compromise proposals, had largely determined the United States policy in Cuba before Magoon arrived. After the rebel army was disbanded and sent home and the militia was discharged it was thought intervention would soon end. Magoon was to draw up electoral and municipal laws, hold a fair election, and then get out as quickly as possible. He was bound to Taft's policy not only because of the statement in his proclamation that he would

---

[34] *Decrees, 1906,* no. 5.

follow it, but also because of an executive order issued by Roosevelt on October 23, 1906, in which the provisional governor was made subject to the supervision of the Secretary of War.[35] Taft continued as Secretary of War until just before the second intervention ended and was chiefly responsible for the policy of the United States in Cuba from 1906 to 1909.

New laws to meet Cuba's needs could not be written in a short time. Meanwhile Magoon had to govern Cuba, and, to the disappointment of many Cuban politicians, he used chief clerks for cabinet officers.[36] He quickly directed his attention to the principal cause of the revolution, namely, the interference by the government with the municipalities. The Liberal committee was requested to submit proof concerning each town alleged to have been illegally interfered with by the Moderates. Each case was carefully considered on its merits and Liberal governments were, in whole or in part, reëstablished in the following municipalities: Guane, San Juan y Martínez, Consolación del Sur, and Guanajay in the province of Pinar del Río; Güines, Aguacate, Alquízar, and Guanabacoa in the province of Havana; and Camajuaní, Vueltas, Placetas, Yaguajay, Calabazar, Trinidad, Cienfuegos, Rodas, Lajas, Ranchuelo, Cruces, Palmira, Rancho Vélez, and Sanctí Spiritus in the province of Santa Clara. This action by the provisional government was generally approved throughout the island.[37]

One of the most troublesome matters confronting Magoon was the ever-present demand by the Liberals that they be appointed to government positions. Party lines were not drawn tightly in Cuba and individuals at various times belonged to different parties and were governed largely by the personality

---

[35] Taft and Bacon, *Report*, p. 543.

[36] *La Discusión*, Havana, October 16, 1906.

[37] Magoon, *Report*, I, 15-16.

of some candidate or party leader. The provisional governor was a stranger in Cuba and because he had no cabinet to advise him it was difficult to know just who was entitled to be considered for a job. The chief clerks who were serving as cabinet officers were all Moderates and the Liberals were not willing to allow these political opponents to pass on their applications for employment. Taft had made it clear from the start that Moderates would not be replaced just to give the Liberals jobs. However, he had promised that Liberals would be given a preference, when vacancies occurred, until an equality was restored. It was proposed that a committee of leading Liberals representing all excluded and opposition factions should nominate suitable persons to the provisional governor for jobs when vacancies occurred. The plan was accepted and the following men were named on the committee: Faustino Guerra, president; Eduardo Guzmán, vice-president; Ernesto Asbert, secretary; Alfredo Zayas, José Miguel Gómez, Juan Gualberto Gómez, Tomás Recio, Demetrio Castillo Duany, José de J. Monteagudo, and Carlos García Vélez.[38]

The committee on jobs saved the provisional government much time and trouble, but it did not entirely solve the patronage question. The Liberals wanted every vacancy filled with a member of their group and any appointment of a Moderate to office was met with a storm of protest.[39] Then, too, the Liberals soon split into Miguelistas and Zayistas and each faction pulled wires to secure favors from the provisional governor. Both sides claimed to be the regular Liberal party. This caused the provisional government much trouble because each faction admitted that the other was entitled to share in the patronage, yet each accused Magoon of favoring the other side. These quarrels split the committee on jobs.[40]

---

[38] Magoon, *Report*, I, 16-17.
[39] *El Liberal*, November 9, 1906.
[40] Martínez Ortiz, *Cuba*, II, 401.

Magoon listened patiently to the claims and demands of both sides and then awarded positions to all factions as he deemed expedient and best. In this instance the governor's good nature, fairness, and diplomacy were valuable assets.

The split in the Liberal party caused the remnants of the old Moderate party to draw together. They were encouraged by Magoon who hoped that strong opposition would force the Liberal factions to reunite. Ríus Rivera, leader of the conservative movement, tried to organize a strong party under a new name but failed to the disappointment of the provisional governor.[41] Later during the second intervention the strong Conservative party was organized and the Miguelistas and Zayistas were forced to unite to win the elections of 1908.

The Magoon administration was not favored by nature. The provisional governor had hardly taken charge when on October 17, 1906, a violent cyclone and storm passed through the island. Crops were ruined, trees destroyed, and several lives were lost. The damage ran into the millions. The most serious losses occurred in Havana Province where the power lines were blown down and in the city of Batabanó on the southern coast which was almost entirely destroyed. The provisional government lost no time in giving first aid to those in distress and in starting the work of reconstruction.[42]

The panic of 1907 in the United States was preceded by liquidation in Cuba and the depression in the island continued almost to the end of the second intervention. In 1906 the tobacco and vegetable crops were greatly reduced by a prolonged drouth.[43] The excess value of sugar and allied industries was over five million dollars less in 1906 than in 1905.[44] The August Revolution had added to the economic plight of

---

[41] *Ibid.*, p. 399.
[42] *La Lucha*, Havana, October 20, 1906.
[43] Magoon, *Report*, I, 36.
[44] Olmsted and Gannett, *op. cit.*, p. 71.

the island by destroying crops and causing foreign and domestic creditors "to seek to collect their accounts." [45] The October cyclone added to a dismal picture with its destruction of life and property. In view of such misfortunes it was generally thought that the credit of the island had been destroyed and that revenues would decline. It was in the face of these conditions that Magoon took charge in Cuba to restore prosperity and to keep things quiet.

In November, 1906, the question of annexation again came to the front. A movement was started in Cuba to send a petition to Washington asking that the island be declared a protectorate of the United States. Cubans charged that secret agents were busy fomenting trouble and that New York capitalists wanted annexation.[46] One Cuban magazine stated that foreigners in Cuba desired annexation because they feared their interests would not be well protected after the United States officials left.[47] The annexationists were greatly encouraged when Senator J. T. Morgan of Alabama renewed his fight to have the Isle of Pines declared United States territory, and when Senator Cullom, chairman of the Senate Foreign Relations Committee, declared for annexation.[48] Roosevelt settled the question in favor of Cuban independence, and in his message to Congress December 3, 1906, warned the Cubans "to preserve order among themselves" and declared that the United States wished nothing of Cuba except that the island should "prosper morally and materially." [49]

On October 24, 1906, all weapons which had been turned in by the insurgents were towed out of Havana harbor and thrown into the Gulf of Mexico off Morro Castle.[50] The guns

---

[45] Magoon, *Report*, I, 54.
[46] *Havana Post*, November 23, 1906.
[47] *Cuba y América*, p. 228, November 24, 1906.
[48] *Havana Post*, December 1 and 4, 1906.
[49] Roosevelt, *op. cit.*, p. 390.
[50] *La Discusión*, Havana, October 25, 1906.

were practically worthless and the provisional government hoped the manner of destroying them would serve as a warning to future rebels. That the warning was not accepted by all is shown by the fact that troops had to be sent the following month to restore order in Palmira in Santa Clara Province.[51]

Aside from a little trouble in Santa Clara, the Liberal stronghold, and some petty stealing here and there, law and order, generally speaking, were good. This was remarkable in view of the extreme poverty of many of the people and the fact that the country had just passed through a period of revolt and anarchy. Much credit was due the rural guard which was advised by officers of the United States Army.

When the provisional government was established the rural guard was without force and prestige because it had engaged in political activity in behalf of the Moderates. The provisional governor ordered an investigation of the charges and they were found to be true. "Justice to the Rural Guard, however, requires that the statement be made that this service was contrary to the desire of a large majority of the officers and enlisted men." [52] Major Herbert J. Slocum, who had helped organize the rural guard at the close of the Spanish-American War, was sent to Cuba for service with the provisional government. He was detailed as adviser to Major-General Alejandro Rodríguez who was then commanding the armed forces of Cuba. These officials, with the assistance of Major Henry A. Barber, and Captains Powell Clayton, Jr., George C. Barnhardt, Andrew J. Dougherty, and Edmund Wittenmyer, all of the United States Army, set about reorganizing the rural guard.[53] All political activity was prohibited and promotion was no longer based on influence, but

[51] *Havana Post*, November 26, 1906.
[52] Magoon, *Report*, I, 18.
[53] *Ibid.*, p. 19.

on merit. Within a short time the rural guard had regained the confidence and good will of the public.

On November 27, 1906, Magoon named a claims commission to investigate and report on the many claims for damages against the government on account of the August Revolution. Francis J. Kernan of the United States Army was named chairman, but soon retired and was replaced by Captain George W. Read of the United States Army. The commission considered 6,557 claims for horses and mules taken by the rebels. The total amount asked was $653,027.20 and the commission recommended that the government pay $296,508.84.[54] While this was less than half the sum claimed, the *Havana Post* stated that the government was having to pay a high price for stolen horses.[55] Some 5,500 miscellaneous claims presented amounted to $1,035,079.56 and the commission allowed $441,920.55. Many of these claims were filed by nationals of the United States, Mexico, Spain, Germany, Great Britain, Italy, Arabia, Turkey, France, China, and Colombia. The amount claimed by aliens was $436,413.98, and the commission approved $179,330.55. All told some 15,027 claims were made, totaling approximately $3,803,385.55. These were all investigated and settled for $1,389,827.39.[56] The commission, with the assistants who were appointed to make local investigations, handled an enormous amount of work and did it in a thorough and satisfactory manner.

Taft, having found that the congressional elections of 1905 were illegal because of fraud, issued a decree on October 12, 1906, providing that congress should remain in recess during the continuance of the provisional government.[57] This left the legislative as well as the executive power in the hands of

---

[54] *Ibid.*, p. 83.

[55] *Havana Post*, December 21, 1906; Magoon, *Report*, I, 83-84.

[56] *Ibid.*, II, 119.

[57] *Decrees, 1906*, no. 11.

the provisional governor. On November 29, 1906, Magoon issued a call for the members of congress to assemble in Havana on the first of December. It was generally understood that the provisional governor would declare the elections of 1905 void and accordingly the Moderates announced that they would resign if Magoon would set a date for the holding of new elections.[58] The suggestion of the Moderates was ignored and on December 3, 1906, Magoon, after receiving instructions from Roosevelt, through Taft, decreed that the terms of all representatives elected on December 1, 1905, and all senators elected March 19, 1906, would be considered terminated from and after October 12, 1906. The decree provided that those whose offices were vacated should receive their pay through the twelfth of October, 1906. The senators elected in 1902 and the representatives elected in 1904 were permitted to draw full salaries until their terms expired. The decree also stated that elections required to give effect to Taft's proclamation instituting provisional government would be held when tranquillity and public confidence were fully restored.[59] This decree was criticized by those whose pay was stopped and by others who accused Magoon of using force and power instead of justice and reason.[60] Magoon only carried out the work started by Taft and as already indicated the decision in this case was made by Theodore Roosevelt.

The Army of Pacification remained in Cuba during the second intervention. About six thousand men, commanded at first by General J. Franklin Bell and later by General Thomas H. Barry, were stationed at some twenty-seven posts throughout the island. The United States troops were kept in the background as much as possible. Not once did they march

---

[58] *La Discusión*, Havana, December 1, 1906.

[59] *Decrees, 1906*, no. 206.

[60] Martínez Ortiz, *Cuba*, II, 406; *Havana Post*, December 4, 1906; *The Cuban Interpreter*, I, 50, November 12, 1907.

through the capital city of Havana. They did not perform any military operations, but gave confidence to the civil government and assisted in the work of restoring order. After the troops were located at their stations they were engaged in revising the map of Cuba and in making topographical surveys of the various provinces. Information was also secured concerning railroad bridges which would be vulnerable points in the event of trouble and every such bridge and culvert in Cuba of more than a twenty-foot span was photographed and measured.[61] The men detailed to that work "wore civilian clothes and did not carry weapons of any kind." They spoke only broken Spanish and spent five months traveling some eighteen hundred miles over the entire island without "one instance of trouble or friction with the Cubans." [62] The work of the army served to acquaint the officers and men with all parts of Cuba and its people and as a rule they were received everywhere as friends. The troops were well behaved, but to avoid any possible conflict with Cuban authorities a decree was issued which provided that soldiers, sailors, or marines accused of breaking Cuban laws should be tried in special provisional courts and not in Cuban courts.[63]

The Cuban government paid the expense of constructing and maintaining quarters for the United States troops and also furnished quarters for officers who were detached for special service under the provisional governor.[64] Most of the new quarters were built by the United States as the Cuban Department of Public Works was not organized to carry on large scale rapid construction at that time. Following the cyclone in October, 1906, several buildings and practically all

---

[61] Magoon, *Report*, I, 86-87.
[62] Col. Harold C. Fiske, United States Army, retired, to the author, February 26, 1934. Col. Fiske served with the Engineer Corps in Cuba during the second intervention.
[63] *Decrees, 1906*, no. 16.
[64] Taft and Bacon, *Report*, pp. 489-90.

the roofs had to be replaced at Camp Columbia. By special decree all military supplies from the United States were admitted into Cuba free of duty.[65]

In the work of sanitation the Medical Corps of the United States Army rendered valuable service. One of the first decrees issued by Magoon dealt with the necessity of bringing yellow fever under control and preventing its propagation. The Cuban congress under Estrada Palma had been reluctant to vote money to continue and expand the excellent sanitation projects started by the United States military government. During the August Revolution sanitation service was stopped in many towns and early in October yellow fever appeared in the provinces of Santa Clara and Havana. The provisional government appropriated large sums for medical inspectors, nurses, detention camps, screened isolation rooms, and oiling and fumigating brigades.[66] The army, the police, and the rural guards were called on to fight in the war for health. To protect United States soldiers who were not immune to yellow fever, army medical officers were ordered to serve on municipal boards of health in each garrisoned town.[67] The prompt and thorough measures taken by the government were effective. All fever cases were brought under control and it was not necessary to quarantine Cuban ports.

The Cuban people would not make much individual effort to secure sanitary conditions. They expected the government to do all necessary sanitation work and enforce health regulations. Finding that local sanitation officers, appointed by and subject to the municipal authorities, were inefficient, the provisional governor issued a decree nationalizing the sanitation service of Cuba. This decree abolished all local boards and established a National Board of Sanitation which appointed

---

[65] *Decrees, 1906,* no. 13.
[66] *Ibid.,* no. 28; *Havana Post,* October 2, 1906.
[67] *Ibid.,* no. 30.

officers for each municipality. The municipalities were required to pay one-tenth of their revenues to the national government to defray the cost of the sanitation services. Expenditures in excess of the amounts contributed by the municipalities were paid by the central government.[68] The plan of making sanitation a national matter worked well, and in general the health of the people of Cuba was good during the period of the second intervention.

One of the most important acts of Magoon while in Cuba was the appointment of the Advisory Law Commission on December 24, 1906. This commission grew out of the plan approved by the United States peace commissioners which called for the enactment of the following laws: first, a municipal law embodying the requirements of the constitution; second, an electoral law containing sufficient provisions to secure representation by the minority and providing for the conduct of registrations and elections under a nonpartisan bureau having charge of police during the registration and election periods; third, a law providing for the reorganization and increased independence of the judiciary; and fourth, a civil service law.[69] The advisory commission performed its task so well that the legislative program was later extended to cover other matters all of which will be treated later in a separate chapter.

Another group which rendered excellent service under the provisional administration was the Advisory Commission of Agriculturists. At the time of the second intervention there was in Cuba an association of sugar planters known as the Agricultural League. That body requested the provisional government to select members from the league to serve on a commission which would after careful study make recommendations to the government concerning measures affecting

---

[68] Magoon, *Report*, I, 46-47.
[69] *Ibid.*, p. 21; *Decrees, 1906*, no. 284.

their industry. The request was granted and the membership was enlarged to include representatives of the tobacco industry. The following were named: Rafael F. de Castro, president; Gabriel C. Casuso, Manuel Froilán Cuervo, Leopoldo Sola, Eduardo Dolz y Arango, Claudio G. de Mendoza, Luis S. Galbán, José María Espinosa, Luis Marx, Lorenzo D. Beci, Juan María Cabada, Roberto B. Hawley, Miguel Machado, and Gabriel Camps. This commission made practical suggestions to the government concerning the two principal agricultural crops of the island during periods of economic unrest. It is worthy of note that this body served without pay even after "being informed that the Government felt that they were entitled to compensation." [70]

When Estrada Palma turned the national treasury over to the United States Peace Commission it contained $13,625,-539.65.[71] Part of this sum was in bonds which were carried as assets by the government. Some critics of the provisional government have accused Magoon of wasting the ten to twenty-five millions that Estrada Palma is supposed to have saved. They have also charged that he increased government expenses and left Cuba with a huge deficit.[72] The facts and figures indicate that the provisional administration in the fall of 1906 was faced with a deficit of approximately $4,000,000 and that Estrada Palma left no real surplus. On October 26, 1906, Major E. F. Ladd, supervisor of the treasury, submitted the following figures on "the condition of the Cuban treasury relative to its ability to meet the current and extraordinary expenses of the Republic for the current year and at the same time carry on the numerous projects imposed by the regular budget and special appropriation acts." The balance required to meet budgets from October 1, 1906, to July 1, 1907, was $17,448,424.75. Other expenses which had to be

---

[70] Magoon, *Report*, I, 60; *The Cuban Interpreter*, October 10, 1907, p. 23.

[71] Taft and Bacon, *Report*, p. 463.

[72] Enrique Barbarrosa, *El proceso de la república*, pp. 77-78; Trelles, *op. cit.*, p. 9; Carleton Beals, *The Crime of Cuba*, p. 209.

paid—for example, sums due for war expenses, increase in rural guard, military occupation, claims incident to the revolution, and special acts outstanding—amounted in round numbers to $13,500,000. To offset liabilities totaling approximately $31,000,000 the government had available in the treasury approximately $11,000,000 and an estimated revenue for the remaining nine months of $16,000,000. The total cash and expected assets of $27,000,000 when taken from the total liabilities of $31,000,000 account for the $4,000,000 deficit which faced Magoon at the beginning of his administration.[73]

Fortunately, the estimates on expected revenue proved to be wrong, for in spite of the drouth and the cyclone, agricultural products were adequate and brought top prices. The customs receipts were higher than those of any preceding year. The fact that the country had just passed through a period of disorder did not prevent an increase in foreign and domestic trade. The receipts of the treasury from sources other than the customs showed an increase and gains were also reported by the Post Office Department.[74] Because of this sudden turn for the better the government collected revenue amounting to $28,821,963.64 instead of the estimated $16,000,000 for the nine months following October 1, 1906. The disbursements for the same period amounted to $25,393,840.03. Cash and bonds in the treasury totaled $13,625,539.65 instead of the $11,000,000 of nine months before. Thus the government, to the surprise of everyone, instead of having the expected deficit of $4,000,000 on July 1, 1907, was able to show a treasury balance of $17,053,663.26.[75]

---

[73] Magoon, *Report*, II, 155-58; Taft and Bacon, *Report*, pp. 534-40; *New York Herald*, October 28, 1906. The figures given do not account for the expenditure of over $2,500,000 for ordinary and emergency items between September 28 and October 26, 1906.

[74] Magoon, *Report*, I, 36-38.

[75] Magoon, *Report*, II, 173. Cf. *infra*, pp. 200 *et seq.*, for condition of the treasury at the end of the intervention.

Magoon authorized money spent when and where it was needed. He did not follow the example of Estrada Palma and keep a surplus in the treasury as a temptation for Cuban politicians.[76] In addition to meeting current government expenses, revenues were used to pay war claims and to fight yellow fever. Large sums were also required to pay for the public works program which Magoon launched to provide much needed public buildings and improvements and to relieve the serious unemployment situation.

Following the August Revolution large numbers of militiamen and insurgents were without employment and their ranks were increased by the agricultural unemployed. During the sugar cane cutting, hauling, and grinding season, which lasts from December until May, large numbers of men are employed. This dry season from December to May is also the period for the growth and harvest of vegetables, fruit, and tobacco. During the rainy season, which lasts from May to December, there is little agricultural employment and thousands of laborers are idle. Unable to save enough from their wages to support themselves and their families they frequently become charges on the country and ready followers of politicians and revolutionary leaders. It was to solve this important economic problem and to secure needed public buildings and improvements that Magoon instituted the broad program of public works which was continued throughout the second intervention.[77] This program, which will be treated more in detail later in this work, was under the supervision of the Department of Public Works. It included the repair and construction of highways, roads, and bridges; the improvement and building of harbors, lighthouses, buoys, and bea-

---

[76] Barbarrosa, *op. cit.*, p. 65, described the August Revolution as "the conquest of the twenty millions of the treasury."

[77] A striking comparison can be drawn between the Magoon program of public works in Cuba and the New Deal P. W. A. and C. W. A. projects in the United States.

cons; and the construction and repair of sanitary works, water systems, and state buildings. The total expenditures on such projects from October 1, 1906, to September 30, 1908, amounted to $23,965,280.67.[78]

In addition to dealing with the problems of the unemployed, Magoon was faced throughout his administration with several strikes of serious proportions. The first was started by the cigar makers in Havana and lasted from February to July, 1907. The employees of about half the cigar factories in Havana demanded their wages in United States money "at the same schedule theretofore paid in Spanish gold." [79] This was equal to a ten per cent raise in wages. To break the strike the owners of all cigar factories declared a lockout. The union workers secured aid from cities in Canada, from Key West, and New York City. They also received aid and sympathy from the general public. Magoon was friendly to labor and urged the employers to pay the workers wages in United States currency. Eventually all the factory owners granted the full demands of the strikers. Magoon was credited with having ended this strike and on July 21, 1907, some 30,000 workers held a fiesta and parade in honor of the provisional governor.[80]

The success of the cigar makers induced other workers to strike. Masons and plasterers demanded their wages in United States money and an eight-hour day and forced the manufacturers of cement, brick, and tile to close their factories.[81] Perhaps the most serious strikes were those of the engineers, firemen, and shopmen of the United Railway Company and of the Western Railway; of less importance was the strike of the shopmen of the Havana Central. The

---

[78] Magoon, *Reports*, II, Appendix A, p. xxx.
[79] Magoon, *Report*, I, 63.
[80] *Havana Post*, June 28 and July 22, 1907; Jenks, *op. cit.*, p. 99.
[81] Magoon, *Report*, I, 64.

strikers wanted their pay in United States currency and demanded a working day of eight hours.[82] These strikes resulted in the partial suspension of railway service throughout the island and in great inconvenience to the general public. The strikes of the railway employees lasted several months and the situation eventually forced a compromise settlement.[83]

In addition to the above strikes there were lesser strikes by the stevedores, omnibus drivers, box makers, plumbers, broom makers, and carpenters. The strikes of the masons, plasterers, plumbers, and carpenters took place in the dry season when most building work was done and thus tied up construction in Havana for months. These strikes injured trade and commerce and increased the unemployment problems of the provisional government. In most cases a compromise was reached, under the terms of which some of the workers' demands were granted and others were withdrawn.[84]

The strikes of the masons, railroad men, and stevedores were attended with violence and litigation. Many individual acts of violence were committed and attributed by the employers to the strikers. In general the labor unions and workmen's associations were active in preserving order. On one occasion a Cuban judge ordered all persons at labor headquarters arrested and 213 men, including the president of the Federation of Labor, were taken into custody. When Governor Magoon heard of this action he was incensed at the stupid abuse of discretion on the part of the judge. He could hardly afford to interfere with the judiciary, but he had the Department of Public Prosecution hasten the examination of the prisoners. All except ten were released under bond pending a hearing before the courts. During this period the strikers alleged that strike breakers were being imported from the

---

[82] *La Discusión*, Havana, September 26, 1907.
[83] Magoon, *Report*, II, 12.
[84] *Loc. cit.*

United States. However, as necessary proof was lacking, the chief of the immigration service was unable to bar immigrants on the ground they were under contract to work upon their arrival in Cuba.[85]

The provisional governor refused all requests to intervene in the strikes and force the men to return to work. The position taken by the government was well stated in a letter which Magoon sent to the cigar manufacturers:

The strikers decline to work unless paid the prices fixed by them for their labor. This is a right which every freeman possesses. They offer no obstacles to the manufacturers employing others; and they have not resorted to violence or other unlawful means of coercing the manufacturers into compliance with their requirements.

Their refusal to work may be ill advised, or based upon imperfect understanding, or misinformation, but so long as they conduct themselves in orderly manner as peaceable law abiding citizens, I cannot interfere officially, for the occasion for the exercise of official powers is not presented.[86]

Considering the numbers and industries involved and the grievances and passions of some of the workers, it may be said that the provisional government handled the strike situation in a fair and creditable manner.

Magoon often rewarded honest and efficient service with promotion, but he was quick to dismiss inefficient and dishonest employees. Some of those discharged for betterment of the service and for defalcations were J. Agustin Agramonte, collector of the customs of Neuvitas, Angel José Acosta, municipal judge of Cartagena,[87] Luis Yero, captain of the port of Havana,[88] G. Escoto, the appointment clerk of the Depart-

---

[85] *Loc. cit.*; Magoon, *Report*, I, 67-68.
[86] Magoon, *Report*, I, 66.
[87] *Decrees, 1906*, no. 214; *Decrees, 1907*, no. 20.
[88] *Havana Post*, March 21 and March 28, 1907.

ment of Public Instruction, Ricardo Rodríguez, postal clerk in charge of the division of stamps and supplies, and Miguel de la Torre, treasurer of the Fiscal Zone of Havana, who made away with $195,000 after thirty-six years of government service.[89]

Magoon made several political appointments in line with the policy of "keeping Cuba quiet," but he also economized by dismissing unnecessary employees and by consolidating and reorganizing various offices and departments. To the disgust of all politicians a real retrenchment policy was started with the year 1907. The Departments of Posts and Telegraphs were consolidated and twenty postal clerks were cut from the payroll at a saving of $20,000 a year to the government. It was estimated that the decree dismissing various first and second class revenue inspectors would save Cuba some $25,000 per year.[90] Expenses at the palace were also reduced by more than half under the efficient management of Captain J. A. Ryan.[91] Economy measures enforced by Governor Magoon accounted for part of the surplus in the treasury on July 1, 1907.

In addition to his other powers Magoon had authority to modify judgments and issue pardons. When the provisional government was instituted it was thought that many were in prison for political reasons and therefore pardons were liberally granted.[92] Because of severe penalties in the Spanish codes Cubans had come to consider pardons as acts of justice rather than grants of grace. Estimates of the pardons granted by Magoon differ, and little or no distinction has been made between full and partial pardons. According to his report to

---

[89] Magoon, *Report*, II, 117; *Havana Post*, October 20, 1908.

[90] *Havana Post*, December 28, 1906; *Decrees, 1907*, no. 24.

[91] Figures submitted by General J. A. Ryan, United States Army, retired. Ryan was aid to Governor Magoon and manager of the palace during the second intervention.

[92] Jenks, *op. cit.*, p. 97.

the Secretary of War, Magoon granted 1,110 pardons, commutations, and remissions up until September 30, 1908, and denied 4,073 requests for pardons during the same period.[93] Fernando Ortiz states that Estrada Palma granted an average of six pardons per month, Magoon 46, Gómez 29, and Menocal and Zayas 33 per month each.[94] Magoon, in discussing amnesty laws and special pardons, pointed out that an annual average of 2,092 persons received benefits from pardons and amnesty laws under the military government; that the average number benefiting from amnesty laws and pardons during the first two years under Estrada Palma was 648 per year; and that the average number benefiting from amnesty laws and pardons under the provisional government was 555 per year.[95]

It is a known fact that Magoon granted many individual pardons for which he has been roundly criticized. It has been intimated that pardons were bought and sold, but no proof has been presented to show that Magoon or any member of the provisional administration were parties to such corruption. It is known that José Miguel Gómez, Zayas, Asbert, and numerous other leading Cubans interceded with Magoon for their clients and friends. They may even have received fees for their services as attorneys and agents, but there is nothing to show that Magoon received any of the fees paid or that he was unduly influenced by the standing and reputation of the person recommending the pardon.

Practically all, if not all, of the pardons were granted on the recommendation of the acting head of the Department of Justice. This office, during most of the Magoon administration, was held by Manuel Landa who was advised by Colonel

[93] Magoon, *Report*, II, 87.
[94] Fernando Ortiz, "La decadencia cubana," *Revista bimestre cubana*, XIX (Enero-Febrero, 1924), 17-44.
[95] Magoon, *Report*, II, 89-94.

E. H. Crowder of the United States Army. No suggestion has been made and no evidence adduced to show that these gentlemen made false or unworthy recommendations or that they were bribed for their work.

It is not generally known or stated that the Cuban law required the executive to review sentences of conviction in criminal cases. Unlike the English and United States legal systems where the exercise of the pardoning power is discretionary, the Cuban system made review of sentences of conviction by the pardoning power compulsory when a pardon was requested. Because of this system more convictions were secured in lower courts and harsher penalties were meted out than would be the case in England or the United States.[96] This practice accounts in part for the large number of pardons granted by Magoon. Then, too, the United States probably pursued too gentle a policy in Cuba by way of being good and kind to the Cubans, when a firm and unyielding policy would have secured more respect. Governor Magoon signed no death warrants while in Cuba and on one occasion after commuting a death sentence to that of life imprisonment is reported to have said that he was opposed to signing death warrants and that he would leave that task for his successors.[97]

The executive officials under the provisional government handled a vast amount of work. In reality they had to serve two masters, Cuba and the United States. All government reports and decrees were required to be published in both English and Spanish. Taft allowed the chief clerks of the various departments to serve as cabinet officers. To avoid trouble with the Cuban politicians, Magoon followed this policy and designated the chief clerks as acting secretaries. Each acting secretary was advised by an officer of the United

[96] *Ibid.*, p. 88.
[97] *Decrees, 1907,* no. 31.

States Army. This plan was used during all of the second intervention and proved very satisfactory. With but few changes, the acting secretaries during the second intervention were as follows: Justo García Vélez, Department of State; Manuel Landa, Department of Justice; Manuel Sobrado, Department of Government; Gabriel García Echarte, Department of Treasury; Lincoln de Zayas, Department of Public Instruction; Diego Lombillo Clark, Department of Public Works; and Francisco I Vildósola, Department of Agriculture, Industry, and Commerce. The United States officers who served as advisers were: Colonel E. H. Crowder, Department of State and Justice; Lieutenant-Colonel E. St. J. Greble, Department of Government; Lieutenant Colonel W. M. Black, Department of Public Works; Major J. R. Kean, Department of Sanitation; Major H. J. Slocum, Commanding General of Armed Forces; and Major J. D. Terrill, Department of Treasury.[98]

The Cuban constitution, based on that of the United States, provided for separate executive, legislative, and judicial departments. During the provisional administration all departments were brought under the control of the provisional governor. However, the judicial department was virtually independent and all courts and judgeships which had existed under Estrada Palma were continued by the provisional government. The judges, in the main, were men of character and ability and were generally held in high esteem by the people. Cuban laws were very complicated and were "not adapted to the form of government or the conditions of society and business" existing in Cuba.[99] Those laws were soon to be greatly revised and improved by the Advisory Law Commission.

It has been stated that the United States preserved the

---

[98] Magoon, *Report*, I, 92-93.
[99] *Ibid.*, p. 69.

fiction of Cuban sovereignty.[100] Additional evidence of this point is furnished by the fact that Magoon as head of the Cuban government signed an extradition treaty entered into between Cuba and Santo Domingo.[101] Also, Cuba was represented in the family of nations at the Second International Peace Conference which met at The Hague on June 15, 1907. The delegates named by the provisional governor were Doctor Antonio Sánchez de Bustamante, Doctor Gonzalo de Quesada, and Licentiate Manuel Sanguily.[102] Governor Magoon also ratified for Cuba the Sanitary Convention of the American Republics, the principal convention and the final protocol of the Universal Postal Union, the convention for the establishment of an International Institute of Agriculture in Rome, and approved the adhesion of Cuba to the Geneva Convention of 1864 to improve the condition of soldiers wounded on the field.[103]

When Taft took charge in Cuba it was thought that the intervention would end in a short time, but by the spring of 1907 it was seen that a census would have to be taken before elections could be held. More time was required for the Advisory Law Commission to prepare the necessary laws than had been anticipated, and many public works had been started which the provisional government desired to complete. It appeared that the United States, once in Cuba, had resolved to do a thorough job, and as conditions in 1907 hardly warranted withdrawal, Magoon and his assistants prepared to remain in Cuba a while longer.

---

[100] Cf. *supra*, p. 58.
[101] *Official Gazette*, Havana, January 16, 1907.
[102] *Decrees, 1907*, no. 529.
[103] Magoon, *Report*, I, 150.

V

Public Works, Health, and Sanitation

THE PROVISIONAL GOVERNMENT did not limit its activity to the writing of laws and the holding of elections, but inaugurated a general program of reform and improvement for Cuba. Transportation, communication, public works, health, sanitation, and other like matters affecting the welfare of the people received attention with notable results.

When Magoon took charge there were less than five hundred miles of macadamized roads in the entire island. The lack of improved roads and bridges retarded agricultural development and made it difficult to get to market such products as sugar, tobacco, timber, fruits, vegetables, and ores. The small landowners suffered most, since many of the great sugar estates had private railroads connecting them with main line railroads or with seaports.[1] In some sections of the island, notably in Oriente, whole districts were uncultivated and nearly depopulated because of the difficulties of transporting the products of the soil to markets at a cost which was commercially profitable and of obtaining the necessities of life which the soil failed to provide. Many supposed roads were

---

[1] Magoon, *Report*, I, 48.

merely right-of-ways which could be used only during the dry season, and even then with difficulty. Bridges were often lacking or unfit for heavy traffic because of long usage and few repairs.[2]

Poor roads caused the Cubans to make use of the *carreta*, a clumsy cart with two large wheels set on the axle in such a manner as to permit a side play of several inches. These carts were generally pulled by teams of oxen, and often as many as ten were required to do the work of a good team of mules. Days were taken for trips that should have been completed in a few hours.[3] In hauling cane or hardwood logs the *carretas* often carried loads of from four to six tons. Since these carts were destructive of the roads, the provisional governor encouraged the use of four-wheel vehicles with wide-tired wheels by decreeing a law which limited the load to be carried over highways in *carretas*.[4]

During some 386 years of Spanish rule, 256 kilometers of roads were built in Cuba; the United States military government constructed 98 kilometers in three years; and Estrada Palma, fully realizing the need of better transportation, built 382 kilometers of highways in a period of four years.[5] Magoon, to speed up transportation and communication, aid agriculture and commerce, and relieve the unemployment situation, supervised the construction of 570 kilometers of roads in two years.[6] In fact much of the provisional governor's

---

[2] Ramiro Guerra y Sánchez, *Un cuarto de siglo de evolución cubana*, pp. 67 *et seq.*

[3] William A. DuPuy, "Road Building by the United States in Cuba," *Scientific American*, C-CI (February 13, 1909), 136.

[4] *Decrees, 1909*, no. 142.

[5] Trelles, *op. cit.*, p. 18. This work, by a distinguished Cuban scholar, is of great importance. Its thirty pages contain a wealth of data on such topics as roads, schools, criminality, and national expenditures. The figures given by Trelles are cited with approval by Ortiz, "La decadencia cubana," *Revista bimestre cubana*, XIX (Enero-Febrero, 1924), 40-41.

[6] Magoon, *Report*, II, 330. Trelles, *op. cit.*, p. 18, credits Magoon with 608 kilometers for a two-year period. His total was probably intended to cover the

time was spent in receiving delegates and petitions from various towns requesting that this or that road be extended to or through their particular locality.

The extensive road-building program of the provisional government, which included the completion of roads planned by the Estrada Palma government but abandoned because of the August Revolution, were carried out by the Department of Public Works which had a central office in Havana and branch offices in the various provinces. The Acting Secretary, D. Lombillo Clark, was advised by Colonel W. M. Black of the Engineer Corps of the United States Army.[7] The administration found that the technical force of 251 was inadequate to handle the various projects launched, and decided that additional men would have to be employed. Accordingly, engineers of the United States Army were ordered to various parts of the island to make surveys and other engineers were imported from the United States.[8] By September 30, 1908, the department had a technical force of 526 with more than 900 non-technical assistants. The personnel of the department was never more than 1,436 as several works were completed and no new works were started after July, 1908. The department was so organized that its personnel could be increased or diminished as the work required.[9]

On April 19, 1907, Governor Magoon added to the projects already under way by approving a carefully planned

---

entire period of the second intervention, or twenty-eight months. The figures in the Magoon Report cover the period to September 30, 1908. They do not include the 395 kilometers of roads which were then under construction and on which sixty per cent of the work had been completed. The completion of 38 of those kilometers during the remainder of Magoon's term would account for the difference in the two figures. The official reports do not give total kilometers for the twenty-eight months.

[7] Magoon, *Report*, I, 361 *et seq.*

[8] General Mason M. Patrick to the author, March 13, 1934. General Patrick served with the Engineer Corps in Cuba during the second intervention.

[9] Magoon, *Report*, II, 329.

road program which called for the construction and improvement of 2,304 kilometers of roads. The cost to be spent over a three-year period was estimated to be $13,000,000. In fact, the provisional government up to September 30, 1908, spent $13,361,406.70 for the construction of 570 kilometers and the repair of 200 kilometers of roads. Thus with less than half the proposed work completed, the provisional government, in a two-year period, had exceeded the total cost estimate for the three-year period by $361,406.70. However, hundreds of unemployed were given work and road mileage was increased 125 per cent over that existing when Magoon took charge, or 158 per cent if those roads left to be completed during the Gómez administration are counted.[10]

Most of the construction work was done under contract at unit prices but exceptions were made when bids were unreasonable or when time did not permit the delay necessary for public bidding.[11] Several contracts were awarded to United States firms and it has been charged that these firms were unduly favored, that they constructed poor roads, and that some of the contracts were tainted with fraud. These charges, as well as other criticisms of the provisional administration will be discussed in detail in another chapter of this work.[12]

The road program was retarded because most of the contracts required the use of improved road-making machinery. Most of this machinery had to be imported from the United States and when it arrived in Cuba, it was found difficult to move it and the necessary supplies to the site of the work. Delays were also occasioned by the rainy seasons. Notwithstanding these obstacles, satisfactory progress was made and

---

[10] *Ibid.*, Appendix A, p. xxx; *ibid.*, p. 330; *La Discusión*, Havana, June 7, 1907.
[11] Magoon, *Report*, I, 363.
[12] Cf. *infra*, pp. 209-12.

at costs which in some cases were 30 per cent below former prevailing prices.[13]

The beds of the new roads were thirty-four feet wide, and the pavement was sixteen feet in width. The culverts were made of concrete and the bridges of steel. The pavement was placed on ten inches of limestone rock and packed by heavy imported steam rollers. Many swamps were drained and right-of-ways ditched. The new roads were free from sharp turns, and no grade was more than 6 per cent. After the highways were completed, "flying gangs" were stationed over the island at fifteen-mile intervals to keep them in good repair.[14]

Magoon considered the building of roads and the consequent improvement of transportation and communication his greatest achievement in Cuba.[15] Only those who can visualize the tremendous social and economic benefits to be derived through improved means of transportation and communication by a people almost isolated can fully appreciate the significance of the road program. One road built in Matanzas reduced the cost of getting sugar to port from ninety to fifty cents per bag. "The road from Pinar del Rio to Viñales and Esperanza reduced the price of passenger transportation from $15.00 to $1.50 and the time of trip from three days to less than three hours." [16] Such savings in time and money were typical of those throughout the island. It is only natural, therefore, that Magoon's service to Cuba in the field of transportation and communication should be compared with Wood's health and sanitation work.

One writer in discussing Cuban roads states that the great-

[13] For comparative tables showing reductions on various projects see Magoon, *Report,* I, 370-72; *ibid.,* II, 335.

[14] DuPuy, "Road Building by the United States in Cuba," *Scientific American,* C-CI (February 13, 1909), 136; Irene A. Wright, "The Cart Roads of Mister Magoon," *The World To-Day,* XVI (June, 1909), 641.

[15] Dr. Charles E. Magoun to the author, February 20, 1934.

[16] Magoon, *Report,* II, 35.

est accomplishment of Magoon, "representing the United States," was "the opening up of the island from end to end, and in dozens of places from coast to coast, laterally, with excellent macadamized roads built on the most approved modern principles." [17] An American journalist residing in Cuba during the second intervention states that "the building of these roads has not only been of vast commercial benefit to the island, but it has also disposed of a large treasury balance which might have been an incentive to revolution." [18] The construction of these roads made revolution in the remote districts almost impossible. While the highways were being constructed in the province of Pinar del Río, rebels and "picnickers" actually came out of the "weird limestone vales" to work on the roads for cash wages.[19]

Improvements in transportation and communication did not stop with road building. Harbors and rivers were widened and deepened as rapidly as dredging equipment and government revenues would permit. Several new lighthouses were constructed, and new beacons and buoys were placed and others were painted and repaired. To facilitate harbor improvements the government purchased a large dipper dredge and four dumping scows. These purchases increased its dredging capacity five times over that of 1906. However, there was more work than the government could do and many projects were completed under contracts by private companies.[20]

A dredging plant and two scows were sent to the Isle of Pines where the bars of the Nueva Gerona and Jucaro rivers were cut by channels nine feet deep, one hundred feet wide, and some fifteen hundred to two thousand feet long. Canals

---

[17] DuPuy, "Road Building by the United States in Cuba," *Scientific American*, C-CI (February 13, 1909), 136.

[18] Wright, "The Cart Roads of Mister Magoon," *The World To-Day*, XVI (June, 1909), 641.

[19] *Ibid.*, p. 644.

[20] Magoon, *Report*, I, 374-81.

were dug along the coast between Cárdenas and Nuevitas to open up an important sugar cane area. Channels were dredged in the Matanzas harbor, and a bar across the San Juan River at that port was cut twelve feet deep, two hundred feet wide, and two thousand feet long. The government wharf at Casilda was repaired and a new customhouse and pier were constructed at Santiago de Cuba. The improvements were made for the small coastwise ships as well as for the large vessels carrying foreign commerce. One of the last appropriations made by Magoon during his term as provisional governor was an order on January 11, 1909, that $100,000 be used to dredge the harbor in the bay of Isabel de Sagua in the sugar area.[21]

On July 15, 1907, the provisional governor appointed a board consisting of Colonel W. M. Black, and Major Mason M. Patrick, Corps of Engineers, United States Army, and José R. Villalón, Professor of Mathematics at the University of Havana, to examine the harbor of Havana and make recommendations for its improvement. The board recommended the dredging of the harbor and the construction of sea walls, piers, and sheds. These improvements were made from the Punta to the south end of Almeda de Paula. As soon as the work was completed, lighters used in transporting goods from ships anchored in the harbor to the government wharves ceased to be in demand and the previous overcrowded conditions were for the time ended.[22]

Most of the harbor improvements were necessitated by ravages of time which had rendered the wharves and piers at various ports unfit for use. Much of the dredging was required because of the increased size of ships. "In 1899 the average tonnage of vessels engaged in domestic trade was 157, and the average for the foreign trade was 1,374; in 1906 the

---

[21] *Ibid.*, II, 345-47; *Decrees, 1909*, no. 22.
[22] *Havana Post*, July 16, 1909; Magoon, *Report*, II, 348.

corresponding averages were 283 and 2,179." [23] Considering all work done, the $1,487,314.52 spent over a period of two years for better harbors, lighthouses, buoys, and beacons does not seem excessive; and it denotes more than a passive interest on the part of the provisional government for Cuba's maritime transportation and commerce.[24]

In 1908 there were 2,330 miles of railroad lines in Cuba. These were owned chiefly by English and United States companies, and they connected most of the important cities and ports of the island. These railroads were the principal means of transportation and communication in some parts of Cuba before the system of public roads started under Governor Magoon was finished. The prolonged strike in 1907 of the engineers, firemen, and shopmen of the United Railway Company and the Western Railway, and the strike of the shopmen of the Havana Central reduced railroad earnings and paralyzed transportation throughout the island. Finally, the warring factions reached a compromise and the prosperity of the railroads improved. The average earnings of the various railroads were greater in 1908 than in 1906 or 1907.[25]

On July 30, 1908, the provisional governor signed a decree providing for extensions of the lines of the Havana Electric Railway Company. The extensions were recommended by D. Lombillo Clark, Acting Secretary of the Department of Public Works, and approved by Luke E. Wright, Secretary of War of the United States.[26] Upon the recommendation of Colonel E. H. Crowder, the franchise for the extensions was awarded to Frank Steinhart. Contrary to current gossip, that

---

[23] Olmsted and Gannett, *op. cit.*, p. 55.

[24] Magoon, *Report*, II, Appendix A, p. xxx.

[25] Olmsted and Gannett, *op. cit.*, p. 119; *The Cuba Review*, VIII (January, 1909), 19. Cuba was the second country in America to operate a steam railroad, the first road being opened to traffic in 1837. Railroads were not operated in Spain until 1848. Gonzalo de Quesada, *Cuba*, p. 243.

[26] *Decrees, 1908*, no. 816.

was the only franchise granted to Steinhart by Magoon and it was a matter of record, open and above board.[27] The extensions of the street railway system following the granting of that franchise were of great service to the thousands of inhabitants of Havana and its suburbs.

During the first intervention the postal and telegraph services of Cuba were completely reorganized. Cuban stamps were issued, money order and parcel post systems were created, and a dead letter office was established. Telegraph lines were restored and new ones were built. When Estrada Palma took charge the island had a well organized post office system and 3,499 miles of telegraph lines.[28] The postal and telegraph systems were expanded by the Estrada Palma administration, but both were damaged by the August Revolution.

When Magoon arrived in Cuba there were thousands of undelivered letters and registered articles. Telegraph lines were in a bad state of repair and many had been destroyed by the troops during the August Revolution and by tropical storms. On October 28, 1906, the provisional governor named Colonel Carlos Hernández Director-General of Posts and Telegraphs. This officer reorganized the department and reduced the force, thereby saving the government over $20,000 a year. Some forty-nine post offices were added and thirty-two new telegraph offices opened. Faster and better mail service was given. Government telegraph lines were increased from 2,754 miles to 6,168 miles and so improved that service was seldom interrupted, even during the rainy season, for more than two hours.[29] On May 31, 1907, Cuba, by order of the provisional governor, became a member of the Universal

---

[27] Chapman, *op. cit.*, p. 267. Interviews with Frank Steinhart and General J. A. Ryan.

[28] Quesada, *op. cit.*, p. 253.

[29] Olmsted and Gannett, *op. cit.*, pp. 74-76; Magoon, *Report*, I, 263; *ibid.*, II, 123.

Postal Union. Throughout the period of the second intervention the Department of Posts and Telegraphs rendered efficient service. The total expenses of the department during the Magoon administration amounted to approximately three million dollars.[30]

During the second intervention six wireless telegraph stations which had been contracted for by the Estrada Palma government were built. Also, the United Fruit Company was granted permission to establish a wireless station at Cape San Antonio.[31] With these wireless stations and several cable connections, Cuba was well supplied with rapid communication services to the outside world.

On September 29, 1906, government telephone lines extended some 284 miles. The October cyclone of that year destroyed 120 miles of lines, but by November, 1908, these had been replaced and the total mileage increased to 322 miles.[32] In addition to the government telephone system several private lines were operated by virtue of Spanish concession. Spanish laws continued to regulate the telephone service during the second intervention. This system of public and private telephone lines operating under various permits and obsolete laws caused the provisional government no end of trouble. The Cuban American Company had a twenty-year franchise for the city of Havana which would expire in June, 1910. The owners tried in vain to secure a renewal of the franchise from the Estrada Palma government; but they did secure a concession for Marianao in 1905. This concession gave the company the right to build and operate telephone lines within a circle having a radius of ten kilometers from the central station in Marianao. The franchise failed to locate the position of the central station in Marianao and since that city

[30] *Decrees, 1907,* no. 618; Magoon, *Report,* II, 275.
[31] Magoon, *Report,* I, 263.
[32] *Ibid.,* II, 123; Guerra y Sánchez, *op. cit.,* p. 67.

joined Havana it was possible for lines to embrace practically all the business district and a large part of the residential section of Havana. This concession was transferred to the Havana Telephone Company, which constructed a line from its station in Marianao into Havana. Public complaints ensued and the Havana Telephone Company was finally enjoined from doing business in Havana. There the matter stood when the provisional government was established.[33]

The Havana Telephone Company had floated bonds in England and spent considerable sums of money. It was insistent for some favorable action and requested Magoon either to extend the old franchise or to amend the Marianao franchise to make it include Havana. It was also proposed that Magoon issue a decree which would permit any person or corporation to establish a telephone system anywhere in Cuba. All of these requests were denied by the provisional governor who held that the valuable Havana franchise should await the action of the new Cuban government. There was strong sentiment for government ownership of telephone lines and Magoon did not wish to prevent this outcome, should the Cubans desire it, when the old Spanish franchise expired in 1910.[34]

Thwarted by Magoon, the telephone company sent its agents to Washington to secure the support of the War Department and the President. They asserted that there was a strong public demand for telephone legislation of a type which would have been most favorable to the company. The company wanted Magoon to act in their favor or they wanted Roosevelt to remove him and send down a governor who would. Magoon not only sent a full report on the subject to Washington, but was called to Washington to discuss this and other matters with the President and the Secretary of War.

[33] Magoon, *Report*, II, 96-97.
[34] *Ibid.*, pp. 97-98.

To the great dissatisfaction of the company Roosevelt supported Governor Magoon.[35]

Later the provisional governor submitted the question of telephone legislation to the Advisory Law Commission. That body was unable to agree, but a majority of the commission submitted a draft of a telephone law which was based upon one that had been vetoed by Estrada Palma. This law was published for public criticism, and copies were sent to municipal councils throughout the island with the request that they study the law and report their approval or disapproval of it. Out of eighty-two reports received, ten favored the immediate enactment of the law, while seventy-two opposed any action on the part of the provisional governor and suggested that the matter await the action of the new Cuban congress. Accordingly, the telephone law was not enacted, but Magoon submitted it together with all records to the Cuban congress on January 28, 1909.[36]

The provisional government in addition to its general supervision over and construction of highways, waterways, and other means of transportation and communication also supervised through the Department of Public Works the construction and repair of state buildings, sanitation works, and water supply and drainage systems. This department made surveys, repaired and paved city streets, and in general did all kinds of national and local work. Many of the projects undertaken were of the sort that the municipalities should have executed had their finances permitted.

Until September 30, 1908, one hundred and fifty-six state buildings were constructed, improved, or repaired at a cost of

[35] *Ibid.;* interviews with Robert J. Flick and General J. A. Ryan.

[36] Charles E. Magoon, *Supplemental Report of Provisional Governor, for the Period from December 1, 1908 to January 28, 1909*, p. 30. Hereafter cited as Magoon, *Report,* III. On April 27, 1909, the Cuban-American Company surrendered its franchise which would have expired in June, 1910, and secured from President Gómez an eighteen-year franchise for $24,000 per year for the first two years and $15,000 per year thereafter. *The Cuba Review,* May, 1909, p. 7.

$2,033,724.81. Courthouses throughout the island were over-hauled, customhouses were practically rebuilt in Matanzas, Cienfuegos, and Baracoa, and a new one was constructed in Santiago de Cuba. Other government buildings constructed and repaired were schools, asylums, hospitals, jails, slaughter houses, post offices, and military barracks.[37] Some of this work was done by the government with hired labor, but most of it was completed under contract. Here again charges of graft and fraud were made, but aside from some sewer and water supply contracts there was no evidence to support the charges.

The money to pay for the public improvements made by the provisional government was derived from current revenues. The apparent surplus left by Estrada Palma went to discharge the debts of the revolution, to extirpate yellow fever, and to hold fair elections. Up to November 1, 1908, all work done by the provisional government and all obligations incurred prior to that date were paid.[38] However, the drouth and panic of 1907 forced the government to reduce its public works program, and the withdrawal of the provisional administration in January, 1909, the continued enforced liquidation of private indebtedness, and the reduction of credit left the island with several works only partially completed and not paid for. In this particular Magoon passed obligations to his successor, Gómez, similar to those left him by Estrada Palma.

The end sought by the program of public improvements was achieved. Cuba received permanent benefits essential to the welfare of its people and the development of the country, and "Magoon kept Cuba quiet." Laboring classes secured employment and wages during a period in which they would

---

[37] Magoon, *Report*, II, 131. For list of construction work and repairs with prices paid, see Magoon, *Report*, II, Appendix A, Department of Public Works, pp. 1 *et seq.*

[38] Magoon, *Report*, II, 33.

otherwise have been destitute; trade and commerce were tided over a period of business depression, and large sums of money were put into circulation throughout the island at a time when money was scarce in all parts of the world.

Mention has already been made of the health and sanitation work of the provisional government. On August 26, 1907, Magoon issued a decree creating a National Sanitary Department. This department began its work early in September with the following members: Dr. Carlos J. Finlay, chief of the National Board of Sanitation; Dr. Juan Guiteras, president of the Board of Infectious Diseases; Dr. Enrique Núñez, president of the Commission of Special Hygiene; Dr. J. A. López del Valle, chief of sanitation of Havana; Dr. Emilio del Junco, legal adviser; Mr. Rogelio Espinosa, engineer; and Dr. Enrique B. Barnet, executive officer of the department. On November 22, the Maritime Quarantine Service was transferred from the Treasury Department to the National Sanitary Department. The chief of the quarantine service, Dr. Hugo Roberts, accordingly became an ex-officio member of the National Sanitary Department. Yellow fever and infectious diseases received the special attention of the Sanitary Department. To diffuse information among the public concerning various diseases and the manner of preventing their spread, the government printed and distributed thousands of pamphlets.[39]

At the close of the first intervention Cuban sanitation suffered a serious loss when the United States officers engaged in that work were withdrawn. The Cuban congresses under Estrada Palma failed to appropriate sufficient sums to continue the work already under way. With a large non-immune population and with travelers coming in from various foreign ports it was not surprising that the scourge of yellow fever broke out again during the last year of the Estrada Palma

---

[39] *Decrees, 1907,* nos. 894 and 1127; Magoon, *Report,* II, 450.

government. The Magoon administration had to fight this fever from the first. During the first intervention the native Cuban population was immune and yellow fever rarely prevailed in the interior but took its toll in the seaports among the non-immune immigrants who soon either received immunity or died. A thorough clean-up campaign of the chief cities of the island had ended yellow fever in Cuba by 1902. After that date many immigrants entered Cuba. Spaniards entering averaged 30,000 a year and many Americans also took up residence there. These non-immunes went into rural areas and consequently the fever spread rapidly and its detection and isolation by government authorities became increasingly difficult. Rural municipalities paid little attention to attacks of fever, especially where the case was mild and of short duration. In some cases only death caused the presence of fever to be reported to the Department of Sanitation. It was in this manner that the disease appeared and spread during the second intervention.[40]

The fight against this scourage was just as thorough and covered a wider area than that conducted by United States officials during the first intervention. From October 1, 1906, to November 1, 1908, some 174 cases of yellow fever from all parts of the island were reported; forty-seven of these proved fatal.[41] Under the leadership of Dr. Carlos J. Finlay, Major J. R. Kean, Captain H. D. Tomason, and others, yellow fever was brought under control, and by September, 1908, not a known case existed. By 1909 the death rate in Cuba from all causes had dropped to twelve per one thousand population, one of the lowest death rates in the world.[42]

The presence of many tourists and government officials in Cuba and some 6,000 United States soldiers scattered

---

[40] Magoon, *Report*, I, 457; Quesada, *op. cit.*, p. 259.
[41] Magoon, *Report*, I, 469; *ibid.*, II, 442.
[42] *Ibid.*, I, 460; Trelles, *op. cit.*, p. 17.

throughout the island caused the provisional government and the Cubans to be all the more careful in matters of public health and sanitation. The threat by the United States of a quarantine for the city of Havana was sufficient to make health a national concern. In fact on April 6, 1908, the United States "on suspicion" imposed a quarantine on the entire territory of Cuba, including the Isle of Pines, with the exception of the cities of Havana and Marianao. This action was violently opposed by Major J. R. Kean, adviser to the Sanitary Department, as being in violation of the Sanitary Convention signed in Washington, October 14, 1905.[43] However, as yellow fever disappeared from the island and general sanitary conditions improved, this quarantine was removed. During its first two years, the provisional government spent $1,130,000 in the fight against yellow fever alone, and an additional sum of $2,200,000 or more than one-tenth of the national income for sanitation projects.[44]

Tuberculosis has long been a plague in Cuba. A national sanatorium for the control and treatment of this disease had been planned during the first intervention. These plans were executed under Magoon. The national sanatorium, La Esperanza, was erected and equipped in conformity with the best ideas of medical science. A dispensary service was conducted in Havana, and for the care of those who lived out of the Havana area, provision was made for treatment at the local hospitals, some of which had special tuberculosis wards. This disease was especially active among the poor and ignorant. To meet this condition the health and sanitation agencies of the provisional government carried on an intensive educational campaign for the prevention and care of the disease.[45]

---

[43] Magoon, *Report*, II, 437-38. Just previous to this quarantine the Health Commissioner of New York on a visit to Cuba had described the island as "spotless." *Havana Post*, April 2, 1908.

[44] *Ibid.*, 143.

[45] *Ibid.*, 445.

Magoon did not consider health and sanitation a purely local matter. In behalf of Cuba he accepted an invitation to the Third International Sanitary Congress of the American Republics which was held in Mexico City. Dr. Hugo Roberts and Dr. Juan Guiteras were named as delegates and during December, 1907, attended the Congress.[46] Cuba was also represented at the International Tuberculosis Congress which was held in Washington, D. C., from September 21 to October 12, 1908. The provisional governor named Doctors J. R. Kean, Juan Guiteras, Fernando Rensoli, Joaquín Jacobsen, and Mario G. Lobredo to attend the Congress as delegates. Dr. José M. Peña served as secretary to the delegation.[47]

In its health program the provisional government was not unmindful of the hospitals, asylums, penal, and charitable institutions of Cuba. These institutions were under the Department of Government of which Manuel Sobrado was the acting secretary. He was assisted by Captain James L. Bevans, Medical Corps, United States Army, and advised by Colonel E. St. J. Greble. Hospitals were classified and their administrations and equipment improved. Hospitals, penal institutions, correctional schools, and asylums were inspected, repaired, and proper sanitary equipment was installed. Perhaps the outstanding work in this field was at the National Hospital for the Insane at Mazorra. Conditions there at the time of the second intervention were unspeakable, and Estrada Palma had called Mazorra a national shame and an insult to Cuba.[48] The Cuban congress on July 18, 1906, had appropriated $150,000 for repairs. The provisional government spent most of this for equipment, and additional sums for repairs. Beds,

---

[46] *Decrees, 1907,* no. 857.
[47] *Ibid.,* no. 802.
[48] James L. Bevans and L. Alvarez Cerice, *Report of the Hospitals and the National Insane Asylum of the Republic of Cuba, 1909,* p. 60. For Estrada Palma's recommendations to congress concerning this and other state institutions see *Mensajes presidenciales,* p. 166.

furniture, sanitary fixtures, mosquito bars, electrical equipment, and trees were purchased. Roofs were repaired, barracks built, fences erected, sidewalks restored, porches added, and barracks and other buildings were painted. With these improvements, the establishment of a dairy, and the purchase of pigs and chickens, the unfortunates at Mazorra received the best of care and treatment under the Magoon administration.[49]

On October 7, 1907, the provisional governor appropriated $22,271.08 for the construction and equipment of a nurses' home as an addition to Mercedes Hospital in Havana.[50] Hospitals at Matanzas, Cárdenas, Colón, Pinar del Río, Guanajay, Santa Clara, Cienfuegos, Camagüey, Santiago de Cuba, Guantánamo, Baracoa, and at other places throughout the island were supplied with new equipment and repaired by the government. Improvements were also made at homes which housed the aged, foundlings, and orphans. From October 1, 1906, to September 15, 1908, the expenses of the Department of Charities were $2,381,851.07.[51]

During the second intervention the penitentiary and jails throughout the island were inspected and repaired. As a rule they were poorly equipped and without sanitary installations.[52] The Department of Public Works built several new jails and others throughout the island were modernized. An effort was made to secure better methods in penal institutions and to employ more efficient and honest keepers. To this end General Carlos García Vélez, Inspector General of jails, the penitentiary, and charitable institutions, was authorized to attend the meeting of the executive committee of the Associa-

---

[49] *Decrees, 1906,* no. 84; Bevans and Cerice, *op. cit.,* p. 85.

[50] Magoon, *Report,* I, 252.

[51] *Ibid.,* II, 275.

[52] *Ibid.,* I, 259. For data concerning the age, race, number, sex, education, etc., of the prisoners, patients, insane, aged, orphans, and foundlings in Cuba in 1907 see Olmsted and Gannett, *op. cit.,* pp. 115-19.

tion of Governing Boards of the American Prison Association which met on August 18, 1908, at the reformatory in Mansfield, Ohio.[53] The provisional administration from October 1, 1906, to September 15, 1908, spent $1,369,675.67 to cover the expenses of the penitentiary and prisons in Cuba.[54]

Other improvements made by the provisional administration in Cuba as a part of the public health and sanitation program were the construction, extension, and repair of sewerage, drainage, and water supply systems. The water lines of Havana were extended to the neighboring towns of Marianao, Camp Columbia, and Guanabacoa. Waste in the water system of Havana was reduced and the pressure increased. The water supply systems of Mariel, Consolación del Sur, San Nicolás, Unión de Reyes, Trinidad, Camagüey, Santiago de Cuba, and other places were repaired and extended. The town of Sagua la Grande was protected against floods by the construction of a dyke. Drainage works were built near Colón, Güira de Macuriges, and Vieja Bermeja. In two years the Magoon administration spent $1,464,041.95 for water systems and drainage.[55]

During the first intervention in Cuba a plan was devised for the sanitation of Havana. This called for the sewering and paving of the city. The military government on January 10, 1902, entered into a contract with the lowest bidders, Messrs. McGivney and Rokeby for this work. These men deposited $500,000 as security for their due performance of the contract.[56] The military government ended on May 20, 1902, and although General Wood called the contract to the attention of the Cuban officials, nothing was done about it. The

---

[53] *Decrees, 1908*, no. 801.

[54] Magoon, *Report*, II, 275.

[55] *Ibid.*, I, 106; *ibid.*, II, 131.

[56] *Ibid.*, II, 132; R. Floyd Clarke, "The Havana Paving and Sewering Contract" (a confidential brief by the counsel for the contractors), p. 5. *Crowder Papers*.

contract became the subject of diplomatic correspondence between Cuba and the United States, and Estrada Palma called it to the attention of the Cuban congress in 1905 and again in 1906, but no action was secured.[57]

The contractors appealed to Magoon for relief, and he took the matter up with the officials of Havana and with Secretary of War Taft and Secretary of State Root. The matter was thoroughly investigated and President Roosevelt was consulted. On the recommendations of Taft and Root, Roosevelt through Taft on March 5, 1908, ordered Magoon to issue a decree sanctioning the execution of a supplemental contract.[58] Under this agreement the government was to pay two-thirds and the city one-third of the total cost. The payments were assured by a pledge of 10 per cent of the customs receipts of the Port of Havana. That paving and sewerage project, involving between eleven and twelve million dollars, after having been approved by the President of the United States and the city council of Havana, was authorized by Magoon on June 22, 1908.[59]

The provisional government advanced Vedado, Havana's most beautiful suburb, $360,834.17 with which to purchase its water system from a concessionnaire. This sum represented two-thirds of the purchase price and the municipality agreed to repay the money advanced in ten equal annual installments. This purchase carried out a recommendation previously made by Estrada Palma and put an end to expensive litigation which had been in progress for several years.[60]

When the provisional government took charge in Cuba the city of Cienfuegos secured its water from a private system which could only furnish water to about one-third of the

[57] *Mensajes presidenciales,* pp. 133 and 170.
[58] Clarke, *op. cit.,* pp. 117-21; Magoon, *Report,* II, 133.
[59] *Decrees, 1908,* no. 681.
[60] Magoon, *Report,* II, 135.

population. The city had no sewer system and public health demanded a modern sanitation system. In 1905 the people voted a loan of $3,080,000 at 5 per cent and payable in fifty-five years for the establishment of modern sewer and water systems. Some claimed that the vote was tainted with fraud, but no charges were filed. A contract for the work was approved and entered into between the city and Hugh J. Reilly on June 17, 1906. The bonds for the loan had been printed, but not issued when Reilly began work with the permission of the mayor on November 13, 1906.[61]

During the elections of 1905 the Estrada Palma government had illegally interfered with the municipal council in Cienfuegos. Accordingly, after the Liberals were restored to the council, they refused to make the first payment and annulled the loan and improvement contracts. Reilly suspended work and appealed through regular channels. The governor of the province sustained Reilly's appeal and the municipal council then took the matter to the provisional governor. Colonel Enoch Crowder, adviser to the Department of State and Justice, made a thorough investigation of the case, and reported certain irregularities and recommended that the contracts be modified and new bids received. It was also suggested that the government take over the bonds and assume part of the expense. These suggestions were not acted upon and Magoon, on December 31, 1907, settled the matter by a decree in which he sustained the Cienfuegos council.[62] The Havana Bond and Loan Company, considering its loan contract illegally breached, appealed to the Supreme Court against the decree on the ground of unconstitutionality, but the court upheld Magoon's decision.[63]

The annulment of the Havana Bond and Loan Company's

---

[61] *Ibid.*, pp. 135-36.
[62] *Decrees, 1907*, no. 1317; *La Lucha*, Havana, December 31, 1907.
[63] Magoon, *Report*, II, 137; *Havana Post*, October 24, 1908.

contract did not injure third parties, but the cancelling of the Reilly contract worked a great hardship upon sub-contractors who had in good faith done much work and invested large sums of money. To settle this matter, Magoon suggested that the government take over the work and pay Reilly and his sub-contractors whatever sum an impartial commissioner would say was equitable.[64] Taft, Secretary of War, and Magoon's superior, decided that it would be more equitable and expeditious to modify the Reilly contract so as to make it legal rather than to invite bids for a new contract. This left Reilly and his sub-contractors with nothing but claims for damages. Taft further recommended to the President of the United States that a new contract be made between the provisional government and Reilly similar to the one between the municipality and Reilly, and that the government take charge of and pay for two-thirds of the work. Roosevelt approved Taft's plan and after the City of Cienfuegos agreed to assume three-fifths of the cost of the work the provisional governor was ordered to issue the necessary decree.[65] Accordingly, Magoon was forced to issue a decree on August 11, 1908, thereby revoking his decree of December 31, 1907.[66]

There was much hostility to the new contract, and demonstrations were held in Cienfuegos. The contract was the chief issue in the city election of August 1, 1908, and the candidates opposing the contract were successful.[67] When Reilly started to resume work he had difficulty in securing a permit to tear up the streets. On September 17, 1908, the municipal council passed a resolution withdrawing its consent to pay three-fifths of the cost of the works. Magoon by decree had to declare this act illegal before the works really got under way.[68]

[64] Magoon, *Report*, II, 137.

[65] *Ibid.*, p. 138; *Havana Post*, June 6, 1908.

[66] *Decrees, 1908*, no. 813; *New York World*, October 19, 1908.

[67] *La Lucha*, Havana, October 26, 1908; Magoon, *Report*, II, 138.

[68] *Decrees, 1908*, no. 973.

The Cienfuegos loan and water supply and sewerage contracts have been the source of much criticism against the Magoon administration.[69] The people of Cienfuegos felt outraged but since they understood the situation they did not blame Magoon.[70] The whole matter was unfortunate, and the blame, if blame there must be, lies with the government's interference with the municipalities in the elections of 1905 and with Taft in overriding the decision of Magoon which approved the act of the city council and which was in turn approved by the Supreme Court of Cuba. Magoon's disagreement with the Secretary of War in this matter was one of the factors which caused him to lose Taft's support after his services in Cuba were ended.[71]

At the same time that the provisional government was carrying out its public works, health, and sanitation programs, it was attending to routine matters of government and considering and working on other problems of vital importance. Its treatment of agriculture, commerce, mining, education, and other national matters must now be considered.

---

[69] Cf. *infra*, pp. 202-3. To finish the water and sewer works in Cienfuegos and the paving and sewer projects in Havana, Taft ordered Magoon to authorize a loan for $16,500,000. *Havana Post*, January 26, 1909; *Decrees, 1909*, no. 114. Thus Magoon was not only accused of wasting the thirteen millions Estrada Palma had saved, but of leaving the nation with a debt of sixteen and one-half million dollars.

[70] *Havana Post*, December 13, 1908; *La Lucha*, Havana, January 4, 1909.

[71] Interviews with General J. A. Ryan and Robert J. Flick. Flick, a reliable witness who was in Cuba when Taft visited Magoon there, states that he heard Taft promise "Charlie" (Magoon) that he would appoint him Secretary of War in his cabinet should he be elected President of the United States. Taft was elected, but Magoon did not become Secretary of War.

VI

Improvements and Problems Under Magoon

THE PROSPERITY OF CUBA depends chiefly on its agriculture. Fortunately the island has an abundance of arable land and is blessed with a climate which permits the growing of a wide variety of crops. The soil is unusually rich and many a Cuban with nothing but a crooked limb for a plow, a team of oxen, and a *machete* has been able to earn a comfortable living for himself and family. The average temperature of the island is 77 degrees Fahrenheit. On the warmest July day the temperature rarely goes above 95 degrees. Rainfall varies more than temperature in different parts of Cuba, being least upon the coast and greatest in the interior. The so-called wet season during which 72 per cent of the annual rainfall is received extends from May to October. The average annual rainfall on the northern coast of Cuba is 50 inches, on the southern coast 45 inches, and in the interior 60 inches.[1]

The central provinces of Cuba, Havana, Matanzas, Santa Clara, and Camagüey, consist mainly of rolling plains with shallow stream valleys, and they furnish the principal sugar

---

[1] Olmsted and Gannett, *op. cit.*, pp. 45-51; Gonzalo de Quesada, *op. cit.*, p. 11.

and tobacco areas. The western province, Pinar del Río, is broken by ranges of hills which in many places exceed 2,000 feet, and in the eastern province of Oriente the surface is broken by sharp mountain ranges which have an altitude of more than 5,000 feet. The agricultural products of these two provinces, tobacco, coffee, and cocoanuts, are of high quality, but the areas are best known for their timber and minerals.[2]

The soils of Cuba suitable for agriculture have been divided into four groups: the red cane lands, the black cane and grass lands, the sandy tobacco lands, and the prairies. The first three types of soil give rise to the principal Cuban crops, sugar cane and tobacco. In addition to these principal crops, cocoanuts, coffee, cacao, citrus fruits, pineapples, textile plants, wheat, rice, corn, vegetables, and medicinal plants are grown.[3] The prairies furnish excellent pastures for stock raising and that industry has always ranked high in Cuba. The most important animal products of the island are cattle, horses, swine, poultry, bees, and fish. Sheep and goats are raised in smaller numbers. Herbivorous animals multiply rapidly and thrive in Cuba. Fish, turtles, and sponges abound in surrounding waters and add to the natural wealth of the country.[4] In 1907 the public forest lands contained 1,226,454 acres. Although there had been widespread vandalism, sufficient trees remained to meet the timber requirements of domestic and foreign markets.[5]

Citizens of the United States who knew of the wealth and possibilities of Cuba were dismayed at the sorry plight agriculture presented in the fall of 1906. A prolonged drouth

---

[2] Gonzalo de Quesada, *op. cit.*, p. 7.

[3] F. S. Earle, "Agricultural Cuba," *The World To-Day*, XI (November, 1906), 1177; Gonzalo de Quesada, *op. cit.*, pp. 73 *et seq.* Cubans are great coffee drinkers and their country produces excellent coffee, yet during the second intervention practically all the coffee used was imported from other nations. *Harpers' Weekly*, LII (October, 1908), 31.

[4] Olmsted and Gannett, *op. cit.*, pp. 14-16.

[5] *Ibid.*, p. 24.

threatened the cane, tobacco, fruit, and vegetable crops. During the August Revolution crops had been neglected, cane fields burned, and cattle and horses seized by the rebels wherever they were found. Farmers were isolated by broken bridges and impassable roads, markets were paralyzed, and farm credit was destroyed. The great cyclone and storm of October seemed to climax the picture of desolation and ruin.

The provisional government took charge in an attempt to make agriculture prosperous. Fortunately the drouth did not injure the cane crop as had been expected and the yield for 1906–1907 exceeded that of the previous year by 214,573 tons. This increase was due in part to timely rains and to increased acreage. The tobacco crop for the same period was short, but because of its superior quality brought the highest price ever known in Cuba.[6] Following the successful season of 1906–1907 more acreage was added for cane and tobacco, and fruit trees and coffee groves were planted. Winter vegetables were grown to supply the demand of the United States. Unfortunately, irregular rains during the 1907–1908 season hindered plantings and replantings of some crops, damaged many of the cane fields, and caused various crop diseases to appear. These factors, together with the Panic of 1907, were injurious to agriculture and farm prices. The economic crisis also affected the cattle industry and caused serious losses to owners who were forced to sell at low prices.[7] However, by the end of 1908 agricultural conditions were better and trade had increased, especially with the United States.[8] Agriculture was benefited by the harbor improvements, the increased railroad mileage, and the new roads built during the Magoon administration.

---

[6] *Ibid.*, p. 69; Magoon, *Report*, I, 36. See also David A. Lockmiller, "Agriculture in Cuba During the Second United States Intervention, 1906–1909," *Agricultural History*, XI (July, 1937), 181-88.

[7] Magoon, *Report*, II, 408-09; Chapman, *op. cit.*, p. 241.

[8] *Monthly Consular and Trade Reports*, October, 1908, p. 76.

Agriculture received attention from the Department of Agriculture, Industry, and Commerce as well as from the Advisory Commission of Agriculturists previously mentioned.[9] The Acting Secretary of the Department of Agriculture, Industry, and Commerce was Francisco I. Vildósola, who with his small force of 134 employees rendered efficient service. They looked after the weather stations, fisheries, forests, mines, vaccines, and brands for cattle, experiment stations, colonization and immigration, and agricultural statistics; and they published and distributed agricultural circulars and a monthly bulletin.[10] The expenditures of this department from September 29, 1906, to June 30, 1908, amounted to the small sum of $490,315.27.[11]

Mining has been an important industry in Cuba since 1830 when companies were formed to exploit the copper mines of Oriente. In that province and to a lesser extent in Santa Clara, Camagüey, and Pinar del Río, deposits of iron, copper, gold, manganese, zinc, coal, and asphalt existed in marketable quantities.[12] Much of the abundant iron ore was secured through surface mining. By that method the side of a hill was cut and terraced, tracks were run off the terraced ledges, and foot by foot the hill of almost solid ore was removed. This process avoided underground work with its cave-ins and explosions. The surface work was not only safer for the employees, but more healthful, and it was also economical because no expensive equipment was required. Most of the work at the mines was done by Gallegos from Spain since the Cubans disliked pick and shovel work.[13]

---

[9] Cf. *supra*, p. 87.

[10] Magoon, *Report*, I, 403-29.

[11] *Ibid.*, II, 172. This sum covered the activities of the bureaus of industry and commerce as well as agriculture.

[12] *Monthly Consular and Trade Reports*, March, 1907, p. 58; Gonzalo de Quesada, *op. cit.*, pp. 113 *et seq.*

[13] L. B. Ward, "The Economical Surface Mining Operations of Cuba," *Scientific American*, XCVII (July 6, 1907), 11.

During the second intervention considerable iron, copper, and gold was mined. The Juragua Iron Company shipped from 300,000 to 350,000 tons of ore annually. The annual shipment of the Spanish-American Iron Company, which operated ten mines during that period, was between 400,000 and 500,000 tons. Most of the ore was sent to the United States, where it was made into steel by the Bethlehem and Maryland steel companies. Orders for iron ore also came from England, Germany, Belgium, and Nova Scotia.[14] During 1907 copper was exported to the value of $624,103, and from May, 1907, to May, 1908, the Holguín-Santiago Mine Company produced gold worth $84,304.55.[15]

All forms of industry and commerce were stimulated by the Magoon program of public works. To further remedy the economic ills of Cuba, which resulted from the August Revolution, the Panic of 1907, and unfavorable weather conditions, the provisional governor issued a decree on November 11, 1907, which authorized the government to loan $5,000,-000 to Cuban banks. Banks securing loans from the government were required to deposit with the national treasury approved collateral for the repayment of the loans, and to pay 6 per cent interest on all loans after July 15, 1908. The decree provided that the money borrowed should be used to meet the various needs of the farmers and planters of Cuba, and the government reserved the right to recall a loan should the money be used for undesignated purposes.[16] At this time the government was well able to spare the money. The decree not only provided credit for agriculture during the depression

---

14 Magoon, *Report*, II, 43-44; Ward, "The Economical Surface Mining Operations of Cuba," *Scientific American*, CXVII (July 6, 1907), 11.

15 Magoon, *Report*, II, 42-45.

16 *Decrees, 1907*, no. 1,085. At first the government wanted to loan this money at 2 per cent interest. *Havana Post*, April 18, 1907. The banks did not care to help the country on those terms, so better conditions were later offered and accepted.

but it did much to win confidence in the government and was approved throughout Cuba.[17]

To improve local conditions in Cuba, Magoon extended government aid to municipalities. Old Spanish tax laws which were still in force did not allow the municipalities sufficient funds to provide those improvements considered essential to modern life. Accordingly the Spanish government, the Wood administration, and the Estrada Palma government made grants to the municipalities from national funds as they deemed proper. Magoon continued this policy, but whenever possible the municipalities were "required to participate in the cost by appropriation of municipal funds or private subscription, and also to make provision for the maintenance of the improvement at the expense of the municipality." [18]

To consider applications for aid and to prevent unwise expenditures the provisional governor appointed a Board of Municipal Aid. Colonel W. M. Black was named president and Colonel E. St. J. Greble and Major J. R. Kean were appointed to assist him. Up until November, 1908, this board had passed on 143 petitions for state aid, and on its recommendation the provisional governor appropriated $405,211.33 for municipal works.[19] Under this plan water systems were extended and repaired, streets and sidewalks built, slaughter houses constructed, market houses provided, and cemeteries enlarged. The Board of Municipal Aid denied many requests and referred those made by private citizens to the authorities of their respective municipalities. In denying petitions this body pointed out ways and means whereby towns could raise funds and make their own improvements. Under the supervi-

---

[17] Magoon, *Report*, I, 63; *Monthly Consular and Trade Reports*, February, 1908, p. 35. The *Havana Post*, November 7, 1907, had advocated government aid; and *La Lucha*, Havana, November 12, 1907, hailed the loan as a great boon to agriculture.

[18] Magoon, *Report*, I, 52.

[19] *Decrees, 1907*, no. 62; Magoon, *Report*, II, 146.

sion of the board much advice and little money brought about many civic improvements.[20]

Generally speaking, Cuban commerce prospered during the Magoon administration. In proportion to its population, Cuba's foreign commerce had always been large, and after the first intervention, foreign commerce increased and exports more than doubled. "In 1907 imports were valued at approximately $47.00 and exports at $56.00 per capita of the population." [21] During that year imports were received to the value of $97,334,195 and exports totaled $114,812,846. Approximately 50 per cent of Cuba's imported goods came from the United States and about 90 per cent of the exported articles were sent to that country. From September 29, 1906, to June 30, 1907, customs collections amounted to $18,881,-414.12 and from July 30, 1907, to the same date in 1908 customs receipts totaled $24,794,966.07. During 1907, a total of 4,294 ships from foreign ports arrived in Cuba with a total gross tonnage of 9,852,115. The outgoing ships destined for foreign ports during the same year numbered 4,266 with a gross tonnage of 9,818,261.[22] While the majority of these ships came from and went to the United States, a large number carried on trade with England, Germany, France, Spain, countries of South and Central America, and various islands in the Caribbean.

The chief imported articles during this period were foodstuffs, iron and steel, textiles, woods and their manufactures, chemical products, oils and fats, paper and its manufactures, stoneware, earthenware and pottery, gold, silver, platinum, animals and their by-products, machinery, and implements. Many food products such as corn, rice, meats, fats, and the like were imported in large quantities, chiefly from the United

[20] Jenks, *op. cit.*, p. 99.
[21] Olmsted and Gannett, *op. cit.*, p. 80.
[22] *Ibid.*, pp. 80-84 and 100-101; Magoon, *Report*, II, 173-74.

States, although they could easily and profitably have been produced in Cuba. The principal exports were sugar and its by-products, tobacco, fruits, minerals, forest products, sponges, and animals and their by-products.[23]

Climatic conditions work great hardships in Cuba, especially on agriculture and labor. During the dry season from November to April, tobacco is planted and harvested, sugar cane is cut and most of the sugar marketed, fruit products ripen and are marketed, and vegetables are grown, especially for United States markets. Cubans, during the second intervention as at present, were busy during the dry months; and to meet the heavy demands for laborers, planters were accustomed to secure workers from the West Indies, the Canary Islands, Spain, Italy and other countries.[24] Most of the transients returned home at the close of the season and took with them all the money they had saved while in Cuba. Those who left drained Cuba's specie, and those who remained increased the ranks of the unemployed during the rainy season.[25] During the wet months most of the field hands were discharged and thousands were out of work. This annual unemployment problem was aggravated during the Magoon administration by the August Revolution, unfavorable climatic conditions, and poor market conditions abroad. Magoon helped the situation by his extensive public works program. He also advocated a greater diversification of crops, encouraged saving accounts, and boosted mining, manufacturing, and other year-round industries whenever possible. However, there was and is no permanent solution to this phase of Cuban life as long as sugar production ranks first among the industries and rainy and dry seasons continue.

---

[23] Olmsted and Gannett, *op. cit.*, pp. 85-88; Gonzalo de Quesada, *op. cit.*, pp. 88-89.

[24] *Monthly Consular and Trade Reports,* March, 1907, p. 18.

[25] Magoon, *Report*, II, 13.

Other economic matters receiving the attention of the provisional administration were the high cost of living, the small margin of profit in the production of sugar, the high rate of interest for money, the low wages paid for common labor, customhouse regulations, banking laws, and currency reform.[26] Neither Magoon nor any one else had been able to do much about the high cost of living or the small margin of profit in the sugar industry. Government loans to the banks and cities and the public works program served to expand credit and lessen interest rates. The public works program and some successful strikes during the second intervention helped the wages of the laborers. Magoon recommended banking laws and a national currency based on the United States dollar. However, Cuba did not establish a national currency until 1915 and coins of other nations, chiefly the United States and Spain, continued to be used.

In the matter of tariffs and customhouse regulations Magoon was more successful. Early in his administration he received complaints against tariff charges and customhouse practices and regulations.

Practically all of them could be grouped as complaints against (1) erroneous classification of imports under existing regulations; (2) changes in classification of goods after entry and payment of the amount of duties demanded; (3) improper interpretation and application of the regulations governing coastwise trade and navigation; and (4) arbitrary levy of fines and penalties.[27]

All of these complaints were investigated and finally settled to the satisfaction of the complainants and treasury officials. The provisional governor issued numerous decrees relative to tariff charges, inspection of ships, duties, goods not on the

---

[26] *Ibid.*, I, 45; *Monthly Consular and Trade Reports*, October, 1907, p. 77.
[27] Magoon, *Report*, I, 42.

manifests, merchandise landed through error, tonnage dues, fees, and various port regulations.[28]

Another problem requiring the attention of the provisional administration was the matter of a census. The last census of the island had been made under the United States military government in 1899. Since that date many immigrants had arrived in Cuba, the native population had increased, and people had moved from one municipality to another. The lack of an accurate census during the 1905 elections had resulted in fraudulent voting, and therefore the Magoon administration, primarily in Cuba to hold honest elections, decided to count the voters and to secure other needed statistics on the age, race, sex, occupation, literacy, and conjugal status of the population.

On May 8, 1907, Governor Magoon issued a decree which called for the taking of a census, and provided for the appointment of a director, an assistant director, and six supervisors. The decree set forth in detail the data to be secured, the forms to be used, and the salaries to be paid. Victor H. Olmsted was appointed Director of the Census and he selected his assistants, instructed and drilled them, and then sent them into the provinces to select and train the district enumerators.[29] On September 6, 1907, the provisional governor issued a proclamation stating that the enumeration would begin on Monday, September 30, 1907, and that it was to be completed not later than November 14, 1907. Some eighteen hundred persons were employed in all provinces and the work was accomplished in a thorough and intelligent manner.[30] Census materials and messages were sent through the mails and by telegraph without charge. A large force of

---

[28] *Ibid.*, III, 28-29; *Decrees, passim.*

[29] *Decrees, 1907*, no. 520; Magoon, *Report*, I, 26.

[30] Martínez Ortiz, *Cuba*, II, 422. Some 6,000 applied for jobs as enumerators. *Havana Post*, May 28, 1907.

clerks checked the reports turned in by the enumerators and prepared alphabetical lists of the male citizens entitled to the privilege of suffrage. By March, 1908, most of the necessary clerical work was finished and the data which had been gathered was totaled and published.[31]

According to the completed census of 1907 the total population of Cuba including the Isle of Pines and the smaller islands was 2,048,980. This was an increase of 30 per cent since 1899. Of the total number, 1,074,822 were males and 974,098 were females; the white population was 1,428,176 and the colored 620,804; and the literate numbered 725,894 and the illiterate 643,615. The average age of all persons was 23.4 years. Some 1,820,239 of the persons counted or 88.8 per cent were native-born. Of the foreign-born population, 81.1 per cent came from Spain, 4.9 per cent from China and 3.5 per cent from the United States. Immigrants to Cuba during 1907 numbered 29,572. The census further showed that 37.7 per cent of the population was engaged in gainful occupations.[32] All data having been fully compiled and the register books having been turned over to the various municipalities, the Census Bureau was formally dissolved by a decree issued January 18, 1909.[33]

In addition to providing lists of qualified voters, the completed census supplied the government with valuable educational statistics. In 1907 children of school age, five to seventeen years, numbered 541,455; and of that number only 31.6 per cent had attended school the previous year.[34] To understand this poor showing it is necessary to review briefly the history and problems of Cuban education. Both generals

---

[31] *Decrees, 1907*, no. 520; Magoon, *Report*, II, 57.

[32] Olmsted and Gannett, *op. cit.*, pp. 131 *et seq.* This work contains valuable and interesting population tables. Comparisons are made with census figures of previous years and percentages are given.

[33] *Decrees, 1909*, no. 51.

[34] Olmsted and Gannett, *op. cit.*, p. 204.

Brooke and Wood had encouraged public education during the first intervention. However, the Brooke system had been abandoned in 1900 and it was the Wood public school system of primary instruction which was in force when the provisional government was established. Primary instruction was under the direction of the Department of Public Instruction, which also supervised the National University, the six institutes, the School of Arts and Trades, the School of Painting and Sculpture, and the National Library.[35] When Manuel Francisco Lamar, head of the Department of Public Instruction under Estrada Palma, resigned along with the other members of the cabinet in September, 1906, his duties developed upon Lincoln de Zayas, who continued as acting secretary of the department under Taft and Magoon.[36]

The August Resolution broke out just as the school term began. This disorganized the system and except in a few cities, public education was suspended. The provisional government authorized special agents to make a check on the condition and needs of schools throughout the island. Some were found to be without equipment and others were poorly constructed, unsanitary, and often inconveniently situated. To meet this situation equipment was purchased, schools were repaired, and several well located model schools were built. Law enforcement officers were ordered to arrest children between the ages of six and fourteen when they were found in the streets during school hours, and boards of education were instructed to file charges against factories and stores which employed children of school age during school hours. Charges were also ordered brought against parents and guardians who

---

[35] Aurelio Hevia, "General Leonard Wood and Public Instruction in Cuba," *Inter-America* IV (October, 1920), 3-16; Gonzalo de Quesada, *op. cit.*, pp. 274 *et seq.* For accounts of the Brooke and Wood school systems and the Frye-Hanna controversy see Chapman, *op. cit.*, pp. 111-14, and Robinson, *op. cit.*, pp. 141-49.

[36] Magoon, *Report*, I, 101. Guerra y Sánchez, *op. cit.*, pp. 86-92, gives a brief account of the Cuban educational system.

failed to send their children to school.[37] These methods were not effective in all cases, but by December, 1906, primary public school attendance was back to normal and some 122,214 pupils were being instructed by 3,649 teachers. By November 1, 1908, there were 195,975 pupils registered in public schools and 14,798 in private schools, and the number of public school teachers had increased to 4,326.[38]

The fact that school attendance was almost doubled and that 677 new teachers were employed, in spite of the effects of the August Revolution and the Panic of 1907, is a tribute to the Department of Public Instruction and the Magoon administration. However, the improvements made tended to be overshadowed by the fact that over 50 per cent of the children of school age were not in school. Also, friction developed within the public school system and members of the Department of Public Instruction were accused of padding the payroll and of awarding *botellas*.[39]

The friction in the public school system resulted from various causes. Many teachers and members of boards of education left their classes and residences to join the revolutionary movement in 1906. During their absence new schoolboard members and teachers were selected in various places. After the United States took charge the former teachers and board members demanded their jobs back and naturally friction ensued. Many cases were investigated and many teachers and board members had their jobs restored. Those who were not restored for alleged reasons of bad conduct, incompetence, failure to submit required reports, and for neglect of duty naturally claimed they were being persecuted for political

---

[37] Magoon, *Report*, I, 317-19; *ibid.*, II, 306.

[38] Olmsted and Gannett, *op. cit.*, p. 122; Magoon, *Report*, II, 304-9.

[39] The word *botella* means bottle. Political babies were supposed to be nursed by the government. One who received a *botella* drew a good salary and did little or no work.

reasons and that the government was going out of its way to favor particular individuals.[40] The race question was also a source of discord. As far as the students were concerned, mixed classes did not cause any special trouble, but when the question of appointing or dismissing a colored teacher was discussed the matter frequently caused dissatisfaction. The compulsory attendance law did not produce the desired results and its enforcement was a frequent cause of complaint against the Department of Public Instruction.[41] Discipline and corporal punishment in schools brought forth criticisms. Finally, the Ohio school law, transplanted to Cuba by Lieutenant Mathew E. Hanna during the first intervention, failed to meet Cuba's needs. This law permitted the people to elect their schoolboards with the result that many board members were illiterate, and few of them had had any experience. Local schoolboards not only fought over the appointment of teachers, but became centers of political activity. All of this caused friction with the central department and was the source of additional complaints against the Department of Public Instruction and its secretary.[42]

Complaints of a more serious nature concerned the padding of school payrolls and the awarding of *botellas*. One Gustave Escoto was discharged from the department for having his mother-in-law on the payroll.[43] Increased expenses for the office of the Secretary of Public Instruction met with just protests since most of the money went for personnel. The ex-

---

[40] Magoon, *Report*, I, 321.

[41] Trelles, *op. cit.*, p. 11, points out that the percentage of children attending public schools has been decreasing since 1900. In that year 75 per cent for every 1,000 inhabitants attended school. The attendance for 1902 was 72 per cent, for 1907 63, and for 1911 49 per cent.

[42] Magoon, *Report*, I, 340 *et seq.*; *The Cuban Review*, May, 1908, p. 9. *The Havana Daily Telegraph*, stated August 28, 1907, that Wood's school system had gone to pieces.

[43] *Havana Post*, August 22, 1908.

penses of that office rose from $43,526 in 1901–1902 to $101,-790 in 1907–1908.[44] However, the charge that teachers were employed just to provide *botellas* seems to be without foundation. In round numbers Cuba had 4,300 teachers, and some 200,000 registered pupils. One teacher for forty-six students would hardly be extravagant nor could a teacher with that many pupils be fairly accused of having a *botella*. It is probable that many of the criticisms directed against the Department of Public Instruction were enlarged and distorted, though undoubtedly a few employees held *botellas*.[45] It was unfortunate that the educational record of the provisional government should have been marred by the presence of graft and politics.

Higher education received due attention from the provisional administration and on the whole fared better than primary instruction. It has been noted that Secretary Taft attended the opening exercises of the National University on October 1, 1906. Under Magoon the faculty of sciences of that institution was divided into three sections: physical mathematical sciences, physical chemical sciences, and natural sciences.[46] In 1908 a school of veterinary medicine was added to the university. The course of dental surgery was made more comprehensive, new professors were added, and the university was authorized to grant the degree of Doctor of Dental Surgery in lieu of Surgeon Dentist.[47] The school of agronomy was enlarged, and in general the courses of instruction were made more practical and comprehensive. During the second intervention the National University was divided into faculties of literature and science, medicine and pharmacy,

---

[44] *El Comercio*, Havana, September 4, 1908.

[45] Trelles, *op. cit.*, pp. 11-12; Ortiz, "La decadencia cubana," *Revista bimestre cubana*, XIX (Enero-Febrero, 1924), 24-26.

[46] *Decrees, 1907*, no. 737; *Decrees, 1908*, no. 126.

[47] *Decrees, 1907*, no. 394.

and law. In addition to student fees the university received $357,385.00 per annum from the government.[48]

In capitals of each of the six provinces institutes were located to prepare students to enter the National University. During the provisional administration, courses in these schools were enlarged and harmonized, scientific laboratory equipment was supplied, and examinations were made less complicated. These schools received tuition from their students and $268,860.00 from the government during the school year of 1906–1907.[49]

The School of Arts (manual) and Trades was of great value to the poorer classes. During the second intervention courses were enlarged and improved and night classes were added. The night classes enabled many who worked during the day to receive instruction which would have been denied to them under the former system. Many skilled artisans and workmen secured their training at this school which received from the government an appropriation of $41,000.00 for the year 1906–1907.[50]

The School of Painting and Sculpture enrolled over 500 pupils during the 1906–1907 session. The government annually contributed $16,060 toward the support of this school.[51]

The National Library was founded by General Wood. During the second intervention its shelves contained some 40,000 volumes, and it received $11,660.00 per annum from the government. That amount, together with the sums allotted the various schools previously mentioned, was charged to the Department of Public Instruction. From September 29, 1906, to June 30, 1908, the total expenses of that department were $7,768,104.30.[52]

---

[48] Magoon, *Report*, I, 102.
[49] *Loc. cit.; Decrees, 1907*, no. 473.
[50] Magoon, *Report*, I, 103; *Decrees, 1909*, no. 115.
[51] Magoon, *Report*, I, 103.
[52] *Ibid.*, II, 172.

Another problem of the Magoon administration which was inherited from previous administrations and which aroused considerable interest was the Church property question. Between 1837 and 1841 the Spanish government confiscated a large amount of property belonging to the Catholic Church in Cuba.[53] That action led to a heated controversy between Spain and the Holy See. It was finally agreed in a concordat, published in 1861, that the properties which had been sold by Spain should be dropped from consideration, that those which were not needed by the government should be returned to the Church, and that Spain should pay a rental for those retained and used for secular purposes. From the date of the concordat until 1899 the payments made by the State to the Church in Cuba amounted to approximately $21,000,000.[54]

When rent payments ceased during the Spanish-American War, the Church claimed the property in question and demanded either that it be returned or that the military government pay the rentals heretofore paid by Spain. General Wood, acting on the report of a committee of distinguished Cubans, decided that the claims of the Church were valid and just and that steps should be taken to work out some satisfactory settlement of the question.[55] On October 23, 1901, the Bishop of Havana and General Wood signed a contract whereby the military government purchased certain property outright; upon the remainder the government secured options until June 30, 1906, by agreeing to pay an annual rental

---

[53] *Letter of Transmittal by the Secretary of War, with Inclosures, as to the Church Property in Habana, Cuba.* "Report of Charles E. Magoon, Provisional Governor of Cuba, on the Contract Dated October 23, 1901, Between the Military Government of Cuba and the Roman Catholic Church for the Purchase of Certain Properties Situate in the City of Havana, Republic of Cuba," p. 11. Hereafter cited as Magoon, *Church Report.*

[54] *Ibid.;* J. Lloyd Mecham, *Church and State in Latin America,* pp. 354-56. See also David A. Lockmiller, "The Settlement of the Church Property Question in Cuba," *The Hispanic American Historical Review,* XVII (November, 1937), 488-98. [55] Judge Otto Schoenrich to the author, July 13, 1936.

therefor. This contract covered the Church property in the province of Havana and included the Havana customhouse, Havana High School, Academy of Science building, and other lesser buildings. The property was appraised at approximately $1,499,550 and the government agreed to pay a rental of 5 per cent of that sum until the options expired. The contract provided that the rentals should be deducted from the purchase price in the event the government decided to buy the property.[56] On January 11, 1902, the military government entered into another contract with the Church, this time concerning its property in the province of Oriente. This property consisted chiefly of annuities and scattered rural estates and was valued at $535,000. The contract allowed the government an option for five years during which time 3 per cent of the purchase price was to be paid as rent.[57]

The military government did not purchase the Church property, but turned the contracts over to the Republic of Cuba on May 20, 1902. Estrada Palma called these contracts to the attention of the Cuban congress, but that body failed to act.[58] The options expired in 1906, but extensions were secured until June 30, 1907. There the matter stood when the provisional government was established on September 29, 1906.

Soon after Magoon took charge he received a call from Monsignor Aversa, Archbishop of Sardes and papal delegate for Cuba and Puerto Rico, who advised him that the Church would like to dispose of the matter of compliance with the contracts. Magoon made a thorough investigation of the subject and submitted a lengthy report to Secretary Taft in which he gave the history of the Church question, the terms of the contracts, the amounts remaining unpaid on the purchase

---

[56] Magoon, *Church Report*, pp. 12-13 and 47-54.
[57] Magoon, *Report*, II, 111; Robinson, *op. cit.*, p. 326.
[58] *Mensajes presidenciales*, pp. 108, 132, and 147.

prices, and the condition of the Cuban treasury. While the negotiations were pending Magoon secured an extension of the options on property in Oriente for another year, but was unable to secure extensions on the Havana property for other bids had been received by the Church. On February 26, 1907, Taft wrote Magoon that the Cuban government should either give up the buildings or purchase them and that since the government could not possibly dispense with the buildings it would be to its advantage to have a good fee title. Taft further stated that he thought the settlement an admirable one for the Church and the government, and authorized Magoon to issue the necessary decrees and to make payments to close the deal.[59] When it became known that the government was considering the purchase of the Church property in Havana, the people and the press of that city at once took sides and articles appeared which complained that the balance of $1,387,083.75 due under the contract was too high.[60] Some of the religious orders which had long since relinquished to the Church any rights they might have had to the property now claimed that the Church had no right to sell and that any sums paid should go to them.[61] In view of these considerations, Magoon ordered new appraisements made to list the property in terms of 1907 values. He also looked into the matter of titles and the authority of Monsignor Aversa to execute legal deeds for the Church.

An average of the appraisements submitted by various individuals and groups showed the property to be worth $1,-477,885.56 in June, 1908.[62] In the event the government

---

[59] Magoon, *Church Report,* pp. 13-15; Magoon, *Report,* I, 82.

[60] *El Mundo,* Havana, April 2, 1907; *Havana Post,* April 3, 1907. The *Post* and *El Mundo* opposed the purchase of the Church property and the *Telegraph* and *Diario de la Marina* favored the deal. *La Lucha* and *La Discusión,* by their silence, apparently approved the purchase.

[61] *Havana Post,* April 19, 1907.

[62] Magoon, *Church Report,* pp. 26-27.

did not exercise its option Sir William Redding, a wealthy resident of Havana, had offered to buy the property for himself and the United Fruit Company for $1,499,550.[63] Further investigation proved that the Bishop of Havana had absolute title to the property. President Roosevelt and Secretary Taft approved the purchase at the original contract figure and ordered Magoon to pay that sum. Accordingly, on July 12, 1907, the Bishop of Havana and Monsignor Aversa, the Pope's delegate, executed deeds for the Havana property to the Republic of Cuba and Magoon issued a decree which authorized the Acting Secretary of the Treasury to pay the Roman Catholic Church $1,387,083.75.[64]

With the purchase of the Havana property out of the way, Magoon turned his attention to the contract of January 11, 1902, which gave the government options on various tracts of land in and near the city of Santiago de Cuba. The Church had refused to extend these options a third time and accordingly an investigation was ordered to determine the advisability of either buying the property or returning it to the Church. The investigation, made by Judge Otto Schoenrich and a Cuban treasury official, revealed that the property consisted of town lots and rural estates. Many of the buildings had gone to ruin during the Ten Years' War, and the government had permitted veterans of the Cuban wars of liberation to settle on some of the estates. The investigation proved the property to be worth $360,900 and not $535,000, as stated in the contract of January 11, 1902.[65] The Church was given the choice of taking $360,900 for the property or of taking the property back and having the government condemn such portions as were needed by the State. The Church agreed to

---

[63] *Ibid.*, p. 26.
[64] *Decrees, 1907*, no. 768; *La Lucha*, Havana, July 13, 1907.
[65] Judge Otto Schoenrich to the author, July 13, 1936; Magoon, *Report*, II, 112.

accept the reduced price and the transaction was closed July 17, 1908. The purchase of the Church property completed the separation of Church and State in Cuba, and fairly and satisfactorily ended a long drawn out controversy.[66]

It was rumored in Cuba that Magoon and his associates had received bribes from the Church for purchasing the property for the State. It seems that when Estrada Palma had tried to get congress to take some action on the contracts a group of politicians fought the measure for the purpose of forcing the Church to pay $400,000 to end the opposition.[67] The Church would not and did not pay any such sum. After Magoon made the purchases for Cuba pursuant to Taft's order and with his and Roosevelt's approval, it was rumored that the $400,000 had been paid to Steinhart and that he had agreed to split with the provisional governor. As far as the rumor was concerned the money might better have been paid to Taft or Roosevelt as they and not Magoon had the final authority in the matter. The charge that the Church or its agents bribed Magoon, Steinhart or anyone else is without foundation in fact. It is a typical illustration of some of the rumors which have circulated concerning the provisional government.[68]

That the Church appreciated the provisional governor's courtesy and coöperation appears from the fact that Magoon received a letter of thanks and a photograph from the Bishop of Havana after the transactions concerning the Havana property had been closed.[69] He also received an oil portrait of Pope Pius X.[70] On October 4, 1907, Pope Pius X, on the

---

[66] *Decrees, 1908,* no. 762; *La Discusión,* Havana, July 19, 1908. Secretary Elihu Root, who had been consulted on this matter, opposed paying more than $360,900. Root to Taft, June 17, 1908. *Root Papers.*

[67] Magoon, *Church Report,* p. 31.

[68] *Ibid.* Conference with Frank Steinhart. Judge Otto Schoenrich to the author, July 13, 1936. The question of Magoon's honesty, fraudulent contracts, etc., will be treated fully in Chapter IX.

[69] Pedro González, Bishop of Havana, to Magoon, July 14, 1907.

[70] Conferences with General J. A. Ryan and Robert J. Flick.

recommendation of Monsignor Aversa, bestowed upon Magoon the title of Knight Commander of the Order of Saint Gregory the Great, of the civil class. This last recognition was openly made and it was not accepted by the provisional governor until he had been assured by Secretary of State Root that it would be legal and proper for him to accept the honor.[71]

If Magoon's mission in Cuba was merely to keep the island quiet, then it should be stated that the second intervention was a great success. Critics grant that the provisional government maintained law and order. Not only were the elections of 1908 peaceful, but chronic revolutionists, desperadoes, and brigands were brought to justice. The reorganized rural guard and the Cuban courts gave the island the best public order it had ever known.[72]

In July, 1907, one Masso Parra, a chronic troublemaker, returned to Cuba after an enforced absence of several years, and began to conspire against the provisional government. He and his companions held secret meetings, collected arms and ammunition, and planned to overthrow the government by destroying bridges, burning property, and killing United States citizens. The date set for the insurrection was September 27. On September 26, Masso Parra and other leaders were arrested, and Cuba was spared a serious outbreak.[73] News of the conspiracy made good copy for the Cuban press and the arrest, trial, and conviction of the ring leaders created

---

[71] Merry del Val, Secretary of State of the Holy See, to Magoon, October 4, 1907. *Magoon Papers*. Magoon was not an officer of the United States, but an agent of President Roosevelt and an officer of Cuba under Section Three of the appendix of the Cuban constitution (Platt Amendment), and thus the U. S. Constitution did not bar his accepting membership in the Order of St. Gregory the Great. Magoon wrote Secretary Root about the matter and Root assured him that it would be legal and proper for him to accept the honor. Root to Magoon, December 16, 1907. *Root Papers*.

[72] Martínez Ortiz, *Cuba*, II, 428; Barbarrosa, *op. cit.*, p. 81.

[73] Magoon, *Report*, I, 89-90.

a sensation.[74] The *Havana Post* stated that the revolt was backed by citizens of the United States who wished to discredit the Roosevelt administration.[75] There is no evidence to support this view and the blame must rest with Masso Parra who had been engaged in such activities in the Caribbean area on previous occasions.

Late in 1906, the rural guard put an end to a horse stealing expedition near Cienfuegos, and to the revolts in 1907 led by Arturo Mendoza in Santa Clara and Urbano Guerra in Oriente. In each case the leaders were captured, tried, and sentenced to long prison terms.[76] No reason can be given for these outbreaks except that certain restless Cubans considered it their privilege to take an outing in the mountains when moved by the spirit of lawlessness.

On the whole the conduct of the 6,000 United States soldiers and sailors stationed in Cuba during the second intervention was excellent. Only two instances of serious misconduct affecting Cubans were reported. On April 30, 1907, some intoxicated sailors on shore leave from the United States cruiser "Tacoma" had a clash with the police of Santiago de Cuba. Three policemen and seven sailors were injured. The affair was promptly investigated and those sailors found guilty were punished and three policemen were suspended from the force for exceeding their authority.[77] In March, 1908, three American soldiers stationed in Pinar del Río left their quarters and went to the harbor of Coloma where they hired a small fishing boat manned by two Cubans. Later the soldiers appeared in camp and stated that in a dispute with

---

[74] *Diario de la Marina*, Havana, September 27, 28, 1907; *La Lucha*, Havana, September 27, 28, 1907; *El Fígaro*, October 6, 1907, p. 496. Masso Parra and his imprisoned confederates were freed on March 5, 1909, by the general amnesty bill which was passed by the Cuban congress after the end of the second intervention. *Cámara de representantes. Curato período congresional . . . Memoria . . . 1909-1911*, IV, 131.

[75] *Havana Post*, September 27, 1907.

[76] Magoon, *Report*, II, 106-7; *Havana Post*, August 11, 1907.

[77] Magoon, *Report*, I, 88.

the boatmen concerning the amount to be paid for the use of the boat, they had been attacked with knives and that in self-defense they had shot the Cubans and thrown them overboard. There was strong evidence that the Americans were trying to desert and escape from the island. A special military court accepted the theory of self-defense and acquitted the accused.[78] The provisional governor dissented, on a review of the proceedings, from the findings of the court. The soldiers were released, but in view of Magoon's dissent they were discharged from the army without honor. Magoon had nothing to do with the trial and acquittal of these men, but as feeling ran high he was unjustly accused of having pardoned them.[79]

General Faustino Guerra, leader of the August Revolution, caused the provisional government some concern. On April 4, 1908, he was appointed Commander-in-Chief of the Cuban Army. This appointment was praised by Taft and acclaimed in Cuba. As Guerra was a Zayas Liberal, his promotion was considered a victory for that branch of the Liberal party and an indication that the provisional administration would support Alfredo Zayas instead of José Miguel Gómez for the presidency.[80] It was decided that it would be the best for the general to get his military training outside of Cuba, and accordingly he was sent to the United States and France to study military methods. Twenty-six years later General Guerra stated that he had enjoyed his travels, and added that there was little for a Cuban military man to do while United States troops and officials were in charge of his country.[81]

---

[78] *La Discusión*, Havana, May 28, 1908.

[79] Magoon, *Report*, II, 111; *The Nation*, LXXXVII (September 3, 1908), 199.

[80] *Decrees, 1908*, no. 366; *El Liberal*, Havana, April 5, 1908; *Havana Post*, May 1, 1908. On the evening of October 10, 1910, General Guerra was shot and wounded by supporters of President Gómez as he was leaving the President's Palace. It was asserted that Guerra planned to start a revolution in favor of Zayas. Some of the assassins were known, but no one was ever punished. Chapman, *op. cit.*, p. 299.

[81] *Havana Post*, April 21, 1908. Interview with General Faustino Guerra.

VII

The Work of the Advisory Law Commission

THE ADVISORY LAW COMMISSION, named by Governor Magoon on December 24, 1906, consisted of nine Cubans and three citizens of the United States.[1] Colonel Enoch H. Crowder of the United States Army, who was then adviser to the Acting Secretary of the Department of State and Justice and legal adviser to the provisional governor, was designated president of the commission. Crowder was a graduate of the Law School of the University of Missouri and was known to be an indefatigable worker. He had been active in the Judge-Advocate-General's department and had served as legal adviser to the military governor of the Philippines prior to his arrival in Cuba in 1906.[2]

---

[1] Cf. *supra*, p. 87; David A. Lockmiller, "The Advisory Law Commission of Cuba," *The Hispanic American Historical Review*, XVII (February, 1937), 2-29.

[2] *Monthly Bulletin of the International Bureau of the American Republics*, XXVI, Pt. 2 (April, 1908), 774. On September 25, 1906, Taft wired his staff in Washington to send Crowder to Havana "with all useful professional books." Wire of Taft to Staff, War Department, September 25, 1906, *Crowder Papers*. These papers are in the Library of the University of North Carolina at Chapel Hill. Crowder was Judge-Advocate-General when the United States entered the World War, and he drafted the Selective Service Act. Later he had the rank of Major-General and served as minister and as the first United States ambassador to Cuba.

146

The Cubans appointed to serve on this commission were Alfredo Zayas, candidate of the Zayista Liberals for president, a lawyer, orator, and member of the Cuban senate; Manuel M. Coronado, a leading member of the Conservative party and the owner and editor of *La Discusión;* Francisco Carrera Jústiz, an independent in politics, a lawyer, author, and professor of municipal government in the National University; Marío García Kohly, member of the Conservative party, a lawyer, and member of the house of representatives; Felipe González Sarraín, a Zayista Liberal, a lawyer, and member of the house of representatives; Rafael Montoro, an eminent statesman, orator, lawyer, and a member of the Conservative party, who had been minister to England and to Germany; Erasmo Regüeiferos Boudet, a Zayista Liberal and a prominent lawyer of Santiago de Cuba; Miguel F. Viondi, a Miguelista Liberal and a lawyer; and Juan Gualberto Gómez, secretary of the commission, a colored political leader, and editor of the Zayista organ *El Liberal.*[3]

The other United States members of the commission were Major Blanton Winship of the United States Army, and Judge Otto Schoenrich. Winship had served as Judge-Advocate and had had Philippine experience which fitted him for membership on this commission. Schoenrich was a member of Magoon's staff and had been a judge in Puerto Rico, where he had assisted in revising and compiling the laws of that island.[4]

The commission had hardly started its work of drafting the laws requested by the Liberals and approved by Taft and Bacon before it appeared that the whole body of Cuban law was in need of revision and codification. In 1907, Cuban law

---

[3] *Monthly Bulletin of the International Bureau of the American Republics,* XXVI, Pt. 2 (April, 1908), 774-775.

[4] *Ibid.,* p. 775. Winship later had the rank of Major-General and served as Judge-Advocate-General. He is now (1937) Governor of Puerto Rico. Schoenrich is a writer and international lawyer with offices in New York City.

147

was a mixture which made analysis, logical interpretation, and honest enforcement difficult. The main body of the law consisted of provisions moulded on monarchical and centralized lines for Spain which had been extended to Cuba. These provisions, some of them archaic, had been amended and modified at various times by many royal orders and decrees. Added to this body of law were the orders and decrees of the United States military government, the Cuban constitution, the laws enacted by the Cuban congress, and the decrees of the provisional governor. Laws designed by a monarchical government for its colony failed to meet the needs of an independent republic. The Cuban congress, hampered by lack of experience and by political dissensions, had failed to enact legislation required to give effect to the liberal and decentralizing constitution. To meet and remedy this condition, the scope of the Advisory Law Commission's activity was extended to cover other laws necessary to place the constitution in practice.[5]

The commission started its work on January 3, 1907. The twelve men were divided into four sub-committees to study existing laws and to propose new legislation. They had to draft all laws to conform to the Cuban constitution since it was deemed impracticable to amend the constitution during the life of the provisional government.[6] Crowder, Sarraín, and Montoro were on the electoral law committee; Zayas, Viondi, Carrera Jústiz, and Winship were on the municipal and provincial law committee; Winship, Kohly, and Regüeiferos Boudet were placed on the civil service committee; and Schoenrich, Coronado, and Gómez were named to the judicial committee.[7]

---

[5] Magoon, *Report*, I, 120 *et seq.*

[6] Letter of Crowder to Taft, January 13, 1907. *Crowder Papers.*

[7] *Diario de sesiónes de la comisión consultiva* (4 Vols. Habana, 1908 y 1916), Vol. I, no. 1. Hereafter cited as *Diario.* This journal gives the proceedings of the commission's meetings. Unfortunately no records were kept of the important

Most of the work of the commission was done by the sub-committee, which studied, debated, and drafted proposed laws. Usually one member of the respective sub-committee prepared the first draft, incorporated the suggestions made by the other members, explained the draft at the meetings of the commission, and in general took charge of the proposed law. In accordance with this procedure, Crowder prepared the first draft of the electoral law, Carrera Jústiz the first draft of the provincial and municipal laws, Winship the first draft of the civil service law, and Schoenrich the first draft of the judiciary law. The finished work was presented to the commission as a whole, and there, after discussion and at times heated debates, the proposed law was adopted, amended, or rejected. No project was sponsored by the commission unless it received a majority vote of all the commissioners.[8]

The general public was given a chance to pass on the proposed laws and to suggest changes before they were put into force. After being approved by the commission, the proposed laws were printed in pamphlet form in Spanish and English and copies were sent for criticism to political parties, newspapers, corporations, and indivduals throughout the island.[9] The commission later revised or modified a law in the light of such criticism and then submitted it to the provisional governor for approval. When approved, the new law was promulgated as a decree and as such it became a part of the permanent legislation of Cuba, subject to change only by the provisional governor or after his term by the duly elected Cuban congress. Public criticism of proposed laws was not a

---

proceedings and debates of the sub-committees. "These meetings were very informal, many of them at night and at the offices or homes of the members of the commission. Some of the Cuban members often missed meetings of the sub-committees, especially toward the latter part of the commission's work, when political aspirations took much time." Judge Schoenrich to the author, November 18, 1935.

[8] Judge Otto Schoenrich to the author, November 18, 1935.

[9] Magoon, *Report*, II, 77; *Decrees, 1909, passim.*

formal phrase, but criticisms were actually sought and considered by the commission on all projects. As a result of criticism and suggestions made by the public, minor changes were made in practically all projects. The new electoral and municipal laws were revised and the telephone law was not enacted because of such criticisms.[10]

Taft's proclamation establishing the provisional government had stated that when peace, order, and public confidence were restored elections would be held to determine those persons upon whom the permanent government of the Republic should devolve. Accordingly, the Advisory Law Commission first considered the framing of an electoral law as a preliminary to ending the intervention, and on December 30, 1907, a proposed electoral code was submitted to Governor Magoon. He directed that it be printed and distributed and fixed a period of thirty days within which suggestions or objections could be made in written or printed form. This requisite having been met, the proposed code was promulgated on April 1, 1908.[11] Following the provincial and municipal elections which were held in August, and as a result of further criticism, amendments were added and the law was promulgated in final form on September 11, 1908.[12]

The electoral law was an elaborate code based on the Australian system. It provided for a system of permanent electoral boards which would be in charge of elections. Each municipality was to have a board of three members, each province a board of five members, and over these was established a central board of five members in Havana. Under this law each board would have two political members representing

---

[10] *Decrees, 1908*, no. 699; *Diario*, Vol. I, nos. 16, 17, and 18.

[11] Magoon, *Report*, III, 16. Exhibit A of this report is the final report of the Advisory Law Commission. The proceedings of the commission relative to the electoral law are in *Diario*, Vol. I, *passim*.

[12] *Decrees, 1908*, nos. 331 and 899.

the two leading parties. The non-political members were to be delegates from the high schools, or the university, or officials of the judiciary. The law abolished voluntary registration and provided that each board should keep a registration list, based on the census of 1907, of all persons entitled to vote and gave the boards authority to correct the lists throughout the year.[13]

Article Thirty-nine of the constitution provided that minority parties should be represented in the house of representatives and in provincial and municipal councils. The electoral law of December 25, 1903, had complied with this provision by granting "to one minority party, whether large or small, an arbitrary one-third of the number of seats, providing that each voter could vote for only two-thirds of the number of persons to be selected." [14] The end desired was seldom attained since majority parties, by presenting different tickets and by instructing their voters, would elect candidates for all the seats. To remedy this the advisory commission made a thorough study of proportional representation as it existed in Belgium and Switzerland, and drafted articles which gave effect to the constitution by providing for representation according to the number of votes polled by each party.[15] According to this plan each voter expressed his choice by voting for several candidates in the order of his preference. The total of all valid votes cast for all candidates was then divided by the number of places to be filled, and the quotient obtained determined the number of votes required for election. Those candidates having votes equal to or above the quotient were declared elected. By transferring surplus votes from those candidates elected on the first count to second and third

---

[13] *Decrees, 1908,* no. 899, article 14 *et seq.*
[14] Magoon, *Report,* II, 78.
[15] *Official Gazette,* Havana, April 1, 1908.

choices, other candidates soon obtained sufficient votes to be elected to the remaining offices under the quotient figure required.[16]

Chapter Seven of the code provided that nominations should be made by official party conventions or by a fixed number of registered electors in the provinces. The numbers required for independent nominations ranged from eight hundred in the province of Havana to two hundred in Camagüey. All candidates, regardless of the method of nomination, were required to have nomination certificates which gave the name and emblem of the party or group supporting the candidate, the name and residence of the candidate, and the title and term of the office for which the nomination was made. The law further prescribed the methods whereby nominees might resign and vacancies could be filled.[17]

Eligibility for public office in general was restricted to Cubans who could read and write and were in the full enjoyment of all civil and political rights. Candidates for president and vice-president were required to have attained the age of forty years and to be citizens by birth or naturalization. In the latter case the candidate must have served Cuba under arms at least ten years in her wars for independence. To be a senator or delegate to a constitutional convention the candidate had to be thirty-five years of age and a Cuban by birth. Representatives were required to be twenty-five years of age and Cubans by birth or naturalization. In the latter case the candidate must have resided in Cuba eight years following his naturalization. The requirements for presidential and senatorial electors were similar to those for representatives.[18] Requirements for provincial and municipal offices were not prescribed

---

[16] *Decrees, 1908*, no. 899, article 192.

[17] *Ibid.*, no. 899, article 99 *et seq.*

[18] Most of the requirements listed above were based on articles 46, 49, and 65 of the Cuban constitution of 1901.

by the electoral law, but were fixed by the provincial and municipal codes.[19]

The new electoral law provided that all male Cubans over twenty-one years of age who were properly registered, except insane persons, those disqualified by reasons of crime, and members of the land and naval forces, had the right to vote for candidates for the various elective offices. It also defined electoral divisions, fixed the dates for the holding of elections, indicated forms of ballots, established rules of conduct for elections in great detail, and prescribed lighter penalties for election offences in the hope that the law would be more strictly enforced. Finally, the electoral law of December 25, 1903, including all amendments and other provisions was repealed.[20] The importance of the new electoral law lay in the great care and wealth of details with which the election machinery was set up—a contrast to the scanty and slipshod rules formerly prevailing. The new law provided for uniform elections throughout Cuba and greatly reduced the loopholes for fraud.

The Conservatives on the commission, in view of the large proportion of illiterates in Cuba and the large Negro element in the population, wished to establish a system of plural votes based on educational and property qualifications. The constitution prevented direct restriction of suffrage and accordingly a plan was proposed which would have deprived no one of his vote, but would have granted as many as three votes to the individual who could have met the additional requirements. The Liberals opposed plural votes for political reasons, but asserted that such a system would infringe Article Thirty-eight of the constitution which granted suffrage to all male Cubans over twenty-one years of age. They further stated that the evils complained of in previous elections could

---

[19] *Decrees, 1908,* no. 899, article 10 *et seq.*
[20] *Ibid.,* no. 899, *passim; La Discusión,* Havana, February 25, 1909.

not be attributed to universal suffrage but to dishonest and corrupt enforcement of the existing law. After much discussion, the Liberals with their pleas for universal manhood suffrage won, and the plan for plural votes was rejected.[21]

Another matter which provoked heated discussions within the commission and caused widespread discussion in Cuba was the question of granting the franchise to foreigners. It was proposed that aliens who had lived for more than five years in Cuba should be allowed to vote in municipal elections. The commission was flooded with letters and telegrams opposing any such extension of the franchise.[22] The Liberals on the commission opposed this plan, and a compromise was reached whereby foreigners, while not permitted to vote, were made eligible for election to municipal councils.[23] Having thus disposed of the troublesome matters of plural and foreign votes, the commission quickly completed the project of the electoral law and turned its attention to organic municipal and provincial laws.

Municipalities are highly regarded by the average Cuban because they affect his daily life more than any other governmental agency. Any attempt to meddle with a municipality meets with resentment, if not open opposition. It was the central government's interference with the municipalities in the election of 1905 more than any other factor that caused the August Revolution.

The municipal law of Cuba at the beginning of the second intervention was based on a Spanish law of 1877 which centralized control in the national authorities in Havana. The

---

[21] *Diario,* Vol. I, nos. 14 and 15. For information on this and other points in this chapter the writer is indebted to Dr. Francisco Carrera Jústiz and Dr. Francisco de Paula Coronado of Havana.

[22] *Ibid.,* nos. 16, 17, 18, 28, 29, 31.

[23] Magoon, *Report,* II, 78. The municipal law which was drafted later provided that qualified foreigners could be elected councilmen and could be appointed associate members of council committees.

Cuban constitution which went into force on May 20, 1902, granted liberal local self-government. Confusion resulted as the Cuban congress, under Estrada Palma, refused to enact legislation to give effect to the constitution. Thus the inconsistent Spanish law prevailed over the constitution, and the acts of the Moderates in removing Liberal municipal officials were legal but at the same time unconstitutional.[24] This legal problem was well known and every compromise plan following the August Revolution had provided for a reformed municipal law which would be in agreement with the constitution.

While the electoral law was being framed the advisory commission discussed an organic municipal law and at Magoon's suggestion kept in mind the drafting of a provincial law. These three laws were closely related and it was only natural that a discussion of one would bring out points relating to the other two. The proposed municipal and provincial laws were submitted to the provisional governor on January 24, 1906. Magoon ordered five thousand copies of each printed and distributed for study and criticism by the public. The organic municipal law was promulgated on May 29, and became effective on October 1, 1908.[25]

The municipal law organized the municipalities in harmony with the constitution, making them autonomous in purely local matters. The new law defined municipal districts and provided for their creation, fusion, segregation, and suppression. It divided municipalities into three classes determined by population: those above 100,000, those above 20,000, and those under 20,000. It also provided that the central govern-

---

[24] F. Carrera Jústiz, *El derecho público y la autonomía municipal; el fraude de un régime*, p. 50.

[25] Magoon, *Report*, III, 16. *Decrees, 1908*, nos. 568 and 907. For proceedings of the commission relative to these laws, see *Diario*, Vol. I, *passim*.

ment could supervise public work projects when it shared or paid the expenses of construction.[26]

The municipal code reorganized local government by reducing the number of councilmen from thirty to a number not to exceed twenty-six. It refused suffrage to foreigners, but provided that when otherwise qualified they could be elected councilmen. It provided for the election of a president and secretary of the council and did away with deputy mayors, syndics, and associate members. Departments of secretary, treasury, and accountancy were ordered established in all municipalities to provide uniformity, and councils were given the authority to establish *barrio* or ward mayors whenever they deemed it necessary. The code regulated the appointment and discharge of employees and prescribed the duties of the various offices. Amounts to be spent on personnel were limited according to total budget estimates. Where budgets did not exceed $10,000 a year, as much as 50 per cent could be spent for personnel, and in cases where the annual budget equalled or exceeded $1,000,000 only 9 per cent could be spent for personnel. These last provisions were undoubtedly designed to force the municipalities to live within their incomes and to check the custom of state aid relied upon for so long.

The municipal law outlined governmental functions and ordinance powers, and provided for municipal coöperation with the provinces and the central government. The mayor was made independent of the council and his powers and duties were defined. The new code required at least four annual meetings of the council in addition to special sessions.[27]

The eligibility requirements for the office of councilmen were designed to secure the best officials. A councilman had to be a Cuban by birth or naturalization, a resident of the

[26] *Decrees, 1908,* no. 568, article 1 *et seq.*
[27] *Ibid.,* article 42 *et seq.;* Carrera Jústiz, *op. cit.,* pp. 62-66.

municipality for one whole year prior to the election, twenty-three years of age, in the full enjoyment of political and civil rights, and able to read and write. Foreigners were required to prove a residence of five years in the country, one of which must have been spent in the municipality. They were also required to have a family, operate a commercial establishment or practice a profession, pay required taxes, and possess the regular suffrage qualifications. Those disqualified by judicial sentence, interest in contracts, or holding any other elective office could not serve as councilmen.[28]

The new code provided that municipal budgets should be effective without the approval of the Treasury Department of the central government as had been the custom in the past. It fixed tax rates, regulated loans, prescribed amounts of bonds to be given by treasuries, and limited special assessments to urban centers. Finally, it repealed the old municipal law of October 2, 1877, and all other legal provisions governing the organization and functions of municipalities.[29]

While the municipal law was being discussed it became evident that local taxation was in need of reform. Municipal tax laws and collection procedures were still regulated by a variety of old Spanish laws, military orders, and regulations. The new municipal law granted autonomy, yet the tax system of the country remained centralized. Consequently the municipalities lacked taxes of their own to carry on the usual functions of local self-government. It had long been the custom for the national government to collect the major portion of all taxes and to collect a surtax for the benefit of the municipalities or from time to time to make grants of various sums to the municipalities. It was to remedy this situation that the law of municipal taxation was drafted by the advisory

---

[28] *Decrees, 1908,* no. 568, article 45 *et seq.*
[29] *Ibid.,* article 186 *et seq.*

commission and decreed by Governor Magoon on September 21, 1908.[30]

The municipal law was the substantive law; the municipal tax law was a regulatory law which set forth rules to carry the organic municipal law into effect. The tax provisions of the municipal law and the provisions of the municipal tax law attempted to make the municipalities self-supporting by providing and clearly defining three sources of revenue:

(1) Land taxes, which the municipalities were authorized to collect on the income from real property within their territory. In the case of urban real property this tax might reach a maximum of 12 per cent of such income, and in the case of rural real property a maximum of eight per cent, six per cent, or four per cent depending on the crops or other uses to which the land was devoted. Land committees were provided for; these would register all rural or urban property, make appraisements and assist the various treasuries in effecting collections.

(2) Industrial taxes, on the exercise of industry, commerce, professions, arts and trades. The maximum tax was specified in most cases, but the taxpayers subject to any specific tax were authorized to distribute their quota of tax among themselves in proportion to their income from the business, thus lightening the burden of the small taxpayer.

(3) Miscellaneous taxes, including taxes on livestock transfers, slaughter of cattle, building permits, the inspection of weights and measures, and amusements.[31]

Most of these taxes had previously existed in one form or another, but the new law, by coördinating them, designating more equitable rates, and providing more thorough collection methods, made such former sources more bearable and more remunerative.

---

[30] *Official Gazette*, Havana, September 22, 1908; *Decrees, 1908*, no. 928.
[31] *Decrees, 1908*, no. 568, articles 216 to 220; and no. 928, *passim*.

The new tax law listed all exemptions, fixed penalties, and provided for appeals through the mayors to the *audiencias*. It gave all municipalities a uniform system of taxation and repealed the existing assortment of local tax laws. It was welcomed by taxpayers, courts, and lawyers alike because it gave the people "a fixed point from which to take their bearings, contrary to the existing chaos." [32]

The Advisory Law Commission also found municipal bookkeeping in a disorganized state and decided that if the organic municipal law was to be effective, a new regulatory law of municipal accounting would be needed to supplement the law of taxation. The laws which governed municipal finances were based on antiquated instructions, rules, regulations, and military orders of various dates. When the commission found that these could not be harmonized with the constitution, it proceeded to draft a new code based on experience and modern methods of accounting. The municipal accounting law, after having been criticized by the public, was submitted to Governor Magoon for his approval; and it was promulgated by him on September 21, 1908. This law and the tax law became effective on the same date as the municipal law, October 1, 1908. [33]

The accounting law specified how collections should be made and entered upon the books and how sums should be paid out of the treasury. The duties of mayors, auditors, treasurers, and other officials handling public funds were defined and penalties were fixed for violation of the law. The accounting law gave the municipalities a uniform system of budget making and bookkeeping. It repealed all old laws and regulations and brought municipal auditing into agreement with the municipal law and the constitution. [34]

---

[32] *Decrees, 1908*, no. 928; *Official Gazette*, Havana, September 23, 1908.
[33] *Decrees, 1908*, no. 927.
[34] *Ibid., passim.*

While the various municipal laws were being drafted, there was some talk of making Havana a national district. However, since complete nationalization of that city would have required a constitutional amendment, the matter was dropped. But the municipal law did provide that sanitation and public order in the capital city should be under the immediate control of the central government.[35]

The provincial law, which along with the municipal law was submitted to the provisional governor for consideration, was promulgated on June 2, 1908. It was planned to correct abuses which existed under the provisional law passed by the Cuban congress on March 10, 1903. The old law was a bare skeleton, but the new act reorganized provincial governments and harmonized provincial and municipal law.[36]

Under Spain the provinces were simply administrative divisions of the central government. Prior to the second intervention the Cuban congress had legislated generally and the municipalities locally. As the whole of Cuba was covered by national and municipal jurisdictions there was little for the provincial authorities to administer or legislate upon except public works.[37] As a matter of fact the provincial budgets allowed more for personnel than they did for public works.[38] Unnecessary employees drew good salaries for little or no work. Consequently, the municipalities and the Cuban people urged and approved the reform of provincial governments because of the enormous waste.[39]

The new organic provincial law equalized the budget by providing that expenses should not exceed the fixed revenues.

---

[35] Magoon, *Report,* II, 80.

[36] *Decrees, 1908,* no. 578.

[37] *American Journal of International Law,* III (January, 1909), 432.

[38] The total provincial budget for 1906–1907 allowed $316,308.00 for personnel and $243,529.45 for public works. Small sums were allowed for scholarships. Magoon, *Report,* II, 81.

[39] *Official Gazette,* Havana, May 8, 1908.

Expenses for personnel were limited by a per cent ratio. Provinces whose budgets did not exceed $50,000 could spend sums up to 35 per cent for personnel. Personnel expenses for provinces having budgets over $300,000 were limited to 20 per cent. The new law reduced the number of councilmen from twenty to eight, abolished salaries, and provided that councilmen's compensation should not exceed ten dollars a day for actual attendance and mileage. The qualifications for the provincial councilmen were practically the same as for those of the municipalities, except that the age limit was increased from twenty-three to twenty-five years. The minimum age for the governor also was fixed at twenty-five years.[40]

The provincial law prescribed the duties of the governor and gave him the veto power. It outlined the functions of the councils which were limited chiefly to the making of provincial laws and the supervision of public works. Tax rates, budget regulations, and auditing methods were fixed by this code. Bonded indebtedness was limited to a sum not to exceed 10 per cent of the total budgets of the province for the previous five years. Finally, the old provincial laws were repealed and the decree provided that the municipal law, the municipal tax law, and the municipal accounting law should be supplementary to this act. The legislative powers of the provinces were not changed because they were fixed by the constitution.[41] The new law prevented much waste, but Cuban provinces have been a disappointment to advocates both of federal and of unitary forms of government.

The advisory commission faced a difficult task in trying to draft a satisfactory judiciary law. The judicial system then in force was based on a Spanish law of 1891 which made the courts subordinate to the executive.[42] The Cuban constitution

---

[40] *Decrees, 1908,* no. 578.
[41] *Loc. cit.*
[42] *Official Gazette,* Havana, January 27, 1907.

stated that the courts should be independent, but congress had neglected to legislate on this matter and accordingly the Spanish law remained in force. Thus the primary work of the commission was to draft a law which would free and protect the courts from executive interference. Crowder pointed out the need for a thorough revision of the civil code, the code of civil procedure, the criminal code, the code of criminal procedure, and the commercial code, but the commission realized that the duration of the provisional government would not permit it to complete such a tremendous task.[43] Crowder considered these reforms "essential to the maintenance of orderly and stable government," and recommended that reestablishment of the Cuban government should be contingent upon guarantees that this work would be brought to a speedy conclusion.[44]

The Advisory Law Commission, lacking time to make a thorough revision of the laws of procedure, in drafting the organic judiciary law followed the general lines of the existing court system since they were the only ones compatible with the general legal system of the island. The new law brought the judicial system into agreement with the constitution by making the courts independent of other government departments. Decrees and laws inconsistent with the constitution were repealed and the various provisions of Spanish law, military orders, and acts of the Cuban congress dealing with judicial matters were compiled into one code.[45] Judicial districts were designated, and the membership and functions of the supreme court, the *audiencias,* the municipal courts, the

---

43 Magoon, *Report,* I, 134 *et seq.*; *La Discusión,* Havana, July 30, 1907; *Diario,* II, *passim.*

44 Magoon, *Report,* I, 139. Reforms were recommended but guarantees were not required when the United States withdrew on January 28, 1909, and little legal reform has taken place in Cuba since the second intervention. See Chapman, *op. cit.,* pp. 516-17.

45 *Official Gazette,* Havana, January 27, 1909.

courts of first instance, and the correctional courts were defined. The code specified that all judges should be Cuban citizens over twenty-three years of age, and excluded undischarged bankrupts, those guilty of crime, and those who were physically or mentally disqualified. All judges, except municipal judges of the third class, were required to be licensed attorneys.[46]

Under the new law the judges of the supreme court continued to be appointed by the president with the advice and consent of the senate, but other judges, except municipal judges, were to be appointed by the president from lists submitted by the supreme court. Judges thus appointed could be granted life terms by the supreme court if their services proved satisfactory. This law further provided that no judicial officer should be removed except by impeachment and conviction, and to cover such cases the law prescribed the proper procedure. It prescribed the oath of office, and fixed a scale of salaries for judges which ranged from $8,000 a year for the president of the supreme court to $1,500 a year from municipal judges of the second class. The office of municipal judge of the third class was declared to be gratuitous and honorary. The law also regulated suspensions, transfers, removals, and resignations of judges and court officials. Finally, it enacted provisions regulating admissions to the bar and provided for the establishment of bar associations.[47]

The proposed organic judiciary law was submitted to Governor Magoon on February 3, 1908, and by his order was printed and distributed for public consideration.[48] Criticisms were made and the commission, after considering the various suggestions, incorporated several changes and returned the law to Magoon for approval. Some felt that it went too far

---

[46] *Decrees, 1909*, no. 127.
[47] *Ibid., passim.*
[48] Magoon, *Report*, III, 17.

and others agreed with Crowder that it was only a belated beginning of necessary legal reform. The judiciary law was promulgated by the provisional governor on January 27, 1909.[49]

Much of the work of the advisory commission was taken for granted and viewed with indifference, but this was not the case with the civil service law. All who had public jobs and those who wanted such jobs, as well as their political chiefs and friends, became interested.[50] Hunger for jobs had done much to bring on the August Revolution and Taft and Bacon had agreed to the need of civil service reform.[51] The decree creating the advisory commission had called for legislation on this important topic and thus it was with much interest that the office holders and politicians awaited the publication of this new law.

On March 26, 1908, the project of the civil service law was submitted to the provisional governor.[52] Following his usual custom, Magoon ordered this law printed and distributed for public study and criticism. The new law, modeled after that of the United States, declared that its object was "to establish and maintain an efficient and honest civil service in all departments and dependencies of the central, provincial, and municipal governments of the Republic of Cuba." [53] The advisory commission expressed the hope that the law would be the means of creating a permanent service of civil administration and that it would, to a large degree, free the administration from political influence.[54]

The chief innovation of the civil service law was the section

---

[49] *Diario*, II, nos. 105, 107, and 113; *La Lucha*, Havana, January 27, 1909.

[50] *El Mundo*, Havana, April 17, 1907; *El Triunfo*, Havana, December 13, 1908.

[51] Taft and Bacon, *Report*, p. 461.

[52] Magoon, *Report*, III, 17.

[53] *Decrees, 1909*, no. 45, article 1.

[54] *Official Gazette*, Havana, January 18, 1909.

providing for the establishment of a civil service commission of three members which would serve as an examining board as well as classify personnel and determine appeals. In addition this section prescribed rules for examinations, distinguished between classified and unclassified services, gave a preference to veterans and their children, provided for pensions, and established rules governing dismissals, suspensions, and appeals. Most important of all, as far as the officeholders and politicians were concerned, was the provision that those holding jobs when the law went into effect were confirmed in their positions.[55] This provision naturally pleased those who held jobs and disappointed those who had hoped the new law would afford them immediate opportunity to get on the government payroll. The civil service law was promulgated on January 11, 1909, by Governor Magoon with the provision that it should go into effect at the beginning of the fiscal year, July 1, 1909.[56] This code supplied Cuba's need for a modern civil service law and provided the legal basis for a permanent civil service administration.

Prior to 1909 executive departments were operated largely by consent since there was little or no legal basis for their existence. Departments which had been established by Spain in 1897, when the new colonial system was put into operation, were continued and increased by the United States military government and the Estrada Palma administration. The constitution provided that the president should have a cabinet but it did not name the posts to be filled or prescribe the duties and powers of cabinet officials. Laws establishing executive departments and prescribing their functions had been considered by congress under Estrada Palma, but nothing had materialized in the way of a positive code.[57] There was nothing in the com-

---

[55] *Decrees, 1909*, no. 45, *passim*.
[56] *La Lucha*, Havana, January 12, 1909.
[57] *Official Gazette*, Havana, January 27, 1909.

promise plans advanced during the August Revolution that obligated the provisional government to consider the drafting of a law on this subject, but as it was urgently needed, Magoon on November 4, 1907, ordered the advisory commission to prepare a law of the executive power.[58]

On January 12, 1909, Governor Magoon promulgated the law of the executive power which had been prepared by the commission after a careful investigation had been made and after the bureau chiefs and others had given their views.[59] This law, the most extensive of all laws drafted by the commission, harmonized executive practice with the constitution, made legal provisions for cabinet posts, and rounded out the work started in the provincial and municipal laws. It contained detailed provisions concerning the powers and duties of the president, cabinet officials, and principal officers of the various departments and bureaus. It established eight executive departments, namely: State, Justice, Government, Treasury, Public Works, Public Instruction, Sanitation and Charities, and the combined department of Agriculture, Commerce, and Labor. It provided for the impeachment of the president or any cabinet member and gave the president the power to appoint and remove freely all secretaries.[60]

The new code fixed the salary of the president at $25,000 a year, that of the vice-president at $12,000 a year, and established a salary scale for all other grades of personnel connected with the executive branch of the government. Provisions of the law also regulated national budgets, appropriations, tax collections, auditing methods, and contracts for services and supplies. The law further provided that congress should proceed to elect a president in the case of vacancy, and it prescribed the oath to be sworn to by all presidential

---

[58] Magoon, *Report*, II, 85.

[59] *La Discusión*, Havana, January 13, 1909.

[60] *Decrees, 1909*, no. 78; *La Discusión*, Havana, February 25, 1909.

appointees. All orders, decrees, and laws inconsistent with the law of the executive power were repealed.[61] In addition to giving effect to the constitution, this code systematized the executive branch of the government and removed doubts as to duties and spheres of action; this latter defect had caused overlapping, inefficiency, and at times friction between various executive bureaus and secretaries.

The first law of the advisory commission to go into force was the law of armed forces which was promulgated by Magoon on April 4, 1908.[62] This law organized the armed forces of Cuba into the permanent army, the rural guards, and the militia. It provided that all male citizens between the ages of twenty-one and forty-five, unless physically disqualified or exempted by provisions of the law, should render military service in one branch of the armed forces in defense of the country. It also listed the number and rank of the various officers and prescribed pay schedules which allowed $6,000 a year for the major-general and $252 a year for privates. It was hoped that the creation of a sufficiently large body of trained forces would in the future prevent outbreaks similar to the August Revolution. The decree gave the president authority to unite all forces, if necessary, in defense of the country and its laws. Under this law General Faustino Guerra became commander-in-chief of the Cuban army and General Alejandro Rodríguez was placed in command of the rural guard.[63]

After drafting the law of armed forces, the advisory commission was charged with the duty of drawing up laws relating to military crimes and procedure. Such laws were prepared and submitted to Governor Magoon on January 15, 1909, and both were put into force by decrees issued on January 18,

---

[61] *Decrees, 1909*, no. 78.
[62] *La Lucha,* Havana, April 6, 1908.
[63] *Decrees, 1908*, nos. 365 and 366.

1909.[64] When the permanent army was organized it became necessary to have a penal code and a code of procedure which would define and punish the various offenses likely to be committed by members of armed forces. The military penal law and the military law of procedure were drafted to supply such needs. In preparing these laws the advisory commission attempted "to harmonize the exigencies of the strictest military duty and discipline, with respect to constitutional precepts. . . ." [65]

The military penal law stated that every military act or omission punished by it would be considered a crime, and that the violation of military police orders would be considered a misdemeanor. The law listed various offenses from treason to participation in politics, and prescribed penalties ranging from a reprimand to death by a firing squad. Treason as defined included desertion to the enemy, inducing a foreign power to declare war against Cuba, furnishing the enemy with information concerning military affairs, and instigating any plot or conspiracy to lower the national flag on the occasion of a battle without orders from the commander. The code also recognized international law and prohibited unnecessary devastation, plunder, and pillage. It forbade duels and provided severe penalties for the issuance or acceptance of challenges.[66] This code supplied the republic with necessary and up-to-date provisions for the regulation of all military crimes and offenses.

Inasmuch as the penal law failed to include methods of procedure it was essential that a code of military procedure should be drafted as a supplement. The law which was drafted by the advisory commission and promulgated by Governor Magoon provided for courts of inquiry to examine acts im-

---

[64] *Decrees, 1909*, nos. 125 and 126.
[65] *Official Gazette*, Havana, January 27, 1909.
[66] *Decrees, 1909*, no. 125, *passim*.

puted to officers and soldiers, and for courts-martial to try soldiers accused of offenses against the military penal law. It stated that questions of jurisdiction between military tribunals and civil courts should be determined by the supreme court. The law provided that the judge-advocate of the court should prosecute all cases in the name of the Republic of Cuba and required the commanding officer to detail a suitable officer as counsel for the defense. It also allowed those accused to employ civil counsel at their own expense. Courts-martial were required to keep a complete and correct record of all proceedings in case the accused decided to appeal his case to a court of review. Only the president could authorize such appeals. Finally, this law repealed all orders, decrees, and regulations inconsistent with its provisions.[67] It supplied rules of procedure essential to the enforcement of the military penal law. Both laws combined scattered material into definite codes and gave Cuba enlightened military legislation of the highest type.

While various laws were drafted by the advisory commission in addition to those already mentioned, only one other, the game law, was promulgated before the end of the provisional administration. The new game law was signed by the provisional governor on January 18, 1909.[68] It repealed the law of 1879 and all decrees and orders in so far as they were opposed to this law. The law declared all wild animals to be the property of the state and gave the state authority to regulate all forms of hunting. It guaranteed the ownership of tame and domestic animals so long as they remained under the dominion of the owner. Songbirds, woodpeckers, swallows, vultures, and other birds considered helpful to man were protected against destruction. An open season was allowed on animals, birds, and reptiles considered injurious to man; in-

---

[67] *Ibid.*, no. 126, *passim*.
[68] *Official Gazette*, Havana, January 22, 1909.

cluded in this classification were wild dogs, wild cats, wild boars, sparrow hawks, hornbills, alligators, and snakes. The law required all hunters to have licenses; it regulated the carrying of hunting arms, and prescribed penalties for infractions.[69] It recognized the right of the state to conserve and regulate its natural resources, and showed that the commission recognized the importance of animals, birds, reptiles, and insects in the daily life of man.

The advisory commission drafted several laws which were not promulgated by Magoon, but which were submitted by him to the newly elected Cuban congress for consideration on January 28, 1909. These dealt with a wide range of subjects, including telephones, juvenile courts, notaries, mortgages, drainage and irrigation, and property registration.[70] The project of the telephone law, which was based upon one that had been vetoed by President Estrada Palma, was submitted to the provisional governor on May 12, 1906. The law did not have the unanimous approval of the commission, and, as it met with much public opposition because of telephone complications of long standing, it was not put into force but was referred, with all records, to the Cuban congress on January 28, 1909.[71] In preparing a drainage and irrigation law, the advisory commission made extensive technical investigations. The final draft of this law was not complete when the commission terminated its work on January 15, 1909, and the provisional governor in his final message called this proposed law to the attention of congress for such action as that body deemed proper.[72] Proposed laws concerning notaries, juvenile courts and destitute children, the creation of a war and navy department, and the revision of mortgage laws with respect

[69] *Decrees, 1909*, no. 67.
[70] *Diario*, IV, *passim.*
[71] Magoon, *Report*, III, 30.
[72] *Ibid.*, II, 85; *ibid.*, III, 14.

to fees and registrations had been sponsored by one or more members of the advisory commission, but they were not favored by all and discussion of the same was not finished when the second intervention came to an end. Rough drafts of these laws together with all pertinent data were turned over to the Cuban congress.[73]

The laws thus far mentioned denote an enormous amount of work covering a wide field, but they do not constitute all the work done by the advisory commission. The provisional governor, from time to time, called on the commission to prepare special decrees and reports. Some of the more important decrees thus drafted, which became laws, related to the census, civil code, department of sanitation, law of estates held in common, and judicial salaries. Other subjects dealt with by the commission, but which were not decreed as laws, were trademarks, crop loans, and a land mortgage bank. The commission also served as an advisory body and aided Governor Magoon and the heads of the several executive departments in drafting decrees which dealt with the practice of pharmacy, tariff schedules, port regulations, civil registry, sanitary matters, and public instruction.[74]

The immense amount of work done by the Advisory Law Commission can only be briefly mentioned. From January 3, 1907, to January 15, 1909, the full commission held 330 sessions and the sub-committees held many more. Some 370 matters were started and finished by that body, and over 700 communications were received and some 1,171 were sent out. Some 3,000 petitions relating to proposed laws were received and all were acknowledged. The commission supervised the distribution of 19,000 copies of the electoral law, 12,000 copies of the municipal law, 6,500 copies of the provincial law, 2,000 copies of the judiciary law, 4,200 copies of the munici-

---

[73] Data furnished by Judge Otto Schoenrich of New York City.
[74] Magoon, *Report*, III, 18-19.

pal tax law, 3,200 copies of the municipal accounting law, 2,000 copies of the civil service law, and 1,000 copies of the telephone law.[75] When it is considered that all members of the commission had other duties to discharge at the same time they were industriously drafting laws—the Cubans their private law practice, political campaigns, and other interests, and the representatives of the United States their regular duties in connection with the provisional government—it will be apparent how seriously they devoted themselves to their task.

The Advisory Law Commission was officially dissolved on January 27, 1909. On the whole its work met with widespread approval.[76] However, some few felt that the commission had gone too far and that the provisional government had no authority to decree such important legislation without the approval of congress.[77] The fact that most of the laws decreed by Governor Magoon have lasted to the present date with few changes bespeaks a just praise of the work done by the Advisory Law Commission.[78]

---

[75] *Ibid.*, pp. 19-20.

[76] Martínez Ortiz, *Cuba*, II, 483; *La Discusión*, Havana, February 25, 1909; *American Journal of International Law*, III (April, 1909), 431-34.

[77] Barbarrosa, *op. cit.*, pp. 72-73; Hevia, *op. cit., passim; El Triunfo*, Havana, January 9, 1909.

In November 1907, after Magoon ordered the advisory commission to consider laws in addition to those recommended by the peace commissioners, members of the Cuban rump congress, which had been dissolved, claimed that they represented the Cuban people and that they should have the right to draft needed laws. The provisional governor ignored the claim and no further protests were made. *The Cuban Interpreter*, I (November 12, 1907), 50.

[78] Chapman, *op. cit.*, p. 517. A Cuban member of the commission well summarized its achievements as follows: "With those laws of Mr. Magoon, which are still in force, the Republic has made notable progress for a quarter of a century. It was truly a work of the greatest consequence, accomplished during Mr. Magoon's short stay of only two years in Cuba, and it gave great prestige to his reputation as a wise and honorable executive." Letter to the author from Carrera Jústiz, September 14, 1934.

The legislative program of the provisional government had not been completed when the intervention ended. Governor Magoon in his final message to the Cuban congress recommended that it create a commission similar to the advisory commission to revise the civil code, the law of civil procedure, the code of commerce, the law of public instruction, the law of eminent domain, the law of public works, the law of administrative contracts, the forestry law, the laws of mines and mining, and the patent law. Unfortunately Magoon's advice was not followed and most of the above laws are still in need of revision. A commission of prominent Cubans had been appointed by the provisional governor in 1908 to revise the penal code and the law of criminal procedure. This commission did not finish its work before the intervention ended, and receiving little encouragement from the new Cuban congress, its efforts came to naught.

VIII

The Restoration of the Cuban Government

AT THE OUTSET it was expected that the second United States intervention in Cuba would be a brief affair. There was talk of holding the elections in January, 1907, but to insure peace and quiet until the sugar crop could be harvested the election date, by general consent, was put off until May, 1907.[1] As the time advanced it became necessary to delay matters still more by the taking of a census and the drafting of additional laws. In April, 1907, Secretary Taft visited Cuba and assured the Cuban people that the terms of his proclamation would be faithfully kept and that he would recommend the restoration of Cuban government after the census had been completed.[2]

Taft's promise to the Cuban people was kept. The enumeration took place during the fall of 1907, and by the spring of 1908 most of the tabulation and clerical work had been finished.[3] On May 25, 1908, Governor Magoon issued a proclamation which provided that municipal and provincial elec-

---

[1] Chapman, *op. cit.*, p. 252.
[2] *Havana Post*, April 9, 1907.
[3] Ct. *supra*, pp. 131-32.

tions should be held on the first day of August.[4] It was generally understood that if these elections were held in an orderly and proper manner they would soon be followed by the presidential and congressional elections and the complete restoration of self-government.

Following Taft's visit in 1907, the provisional administration bent every effort to carry through its reforms in order that it could turn over to the new Cuban officials an improved and orderly state. Sanitation improvements, roads, and various public works were completed; the rural guard was reorganized and law and order were maintained; agriculture, industry, and commerce received aid and encouragement from the government; new schools were constructed and public education encouraged; the Church property question was settled; the census was completed; and most of the laws drafted by the Advisory Law Commission were approved and placed in operation.

In January, 1908, President Roosevelt and Secretary Root called Governor Magoon to Washington for a conference on Cuban affairs.[5] In August of 1908, Magoon made another trip to Washington. During this visit President Roosevelt and Governor Magoon selected November 14 as the date for the holding of the congressional and presidential elections and set January 28, 1909, the birthday of José Martí, as the date intervention should end.[6] During the early part of December, 1908, Magoon made his last trip to Washington while provisional governor. He had conferences with the President and the new Secretary of War, Luke E. Wright, at which the final plans for the restoration of the Cuban government were made.[7] During the short periods Magoon was out of Cuba

---

[4] *Decrees, 1908,* no. 538.
[5] *Washington Post,* January 25, 1908.
[6] *Havana Post,* August 26, 1908.
[7] *La Lucha,* Havana, December 4, 1908.

General Thomas H. Barry, commanding officer of the Army of Cuban Pacification, served in the capacity of acting provisional governor.

In June, 1908, Magoon's immediate superior, Secretary Taft, resigned from Roosevelt's Cabinet to become a candidate for the presidency of the United States as the nominee of the Republican party. Prior to Taft's resignation there were rumors to the effect that Magoon would succeed him as Secretary of War, but nothing came of them.[8] Luke E. Wright became the new Secretary of War in Roosevelt's Cabinet and the official responsible for Cuban affairs.[9] His appointment did not change the Roosevelt-Taft-Magoon program in Cuba. The promise to restore Cuban self-government was kept, and more important as far as Roosevelt was concerned was the fact that the intervention was to end before his term of office expired.

While Taft was running for the presidency and while Magoon was trying to solve various problems, the Cuban politicians were not idle. Candidates were being groomed for office, new parties were being organized, and Cuban voters were eagerly awaiting the chance to elect their favorites and to test the new electoral laws. The old Moderate party may be said to have passed away with the resignation of Estrada Palma, and Moderate leaders formally dissolved their organization on November 3, 1906.[10] During the same month Ríus Rivera made an attempt to organize the conservative elements against the Liberals, but his efforts proved to be premature.[11] However, by the summer of 1907 a Conservative party was organized which claimed that it had no connection with the old Moderate party, and by August, 1908, this party had be-

---

[8] *Havana Post*, March 10, 1908; *ibid.*, April 26, 1908.
[9] Mary L. Hinsdale, *A History of the President's Cabinet*, p. 274.
[10] Chapman, *op. cit.*, p. 258.
[11] Cf. *supra*, p. 80.

come so strong that it forced the factional Liberals to unite in self-defense.[12]

Soon after the provisional government took charge the Liberal party had split over the patronage into two groups, the Miguelistas and Zayistas.[13] Prior to the municipal and provincial elections José Miguel Gómez was the leader and candidate of the Miguelista Liberals for president, and in like manner Alfredo Zayas was supported ardently by all Zayista Liberals. Both factions were especially active in the municipal and provincial elections, and speeches were made and huge parades were held, those in Havana being most notable.[14] The Liberal split gave the Conservatives an advantage which was promptly used to the dismay and disappointment of many Liberals. The Conservatives did not name a presidential candidate until after the municipal and provincial elections.

As the elections approached new political groups appeared in the field. During the early part of 1908, a political group composed largely of patriot leaders organized *La Junta Patriótica*. That body named a committee to select candidates "for the good of Cuba." [15] More important was the Independent Party of Color which was formed in 1907 by Evaristo Estenoz.[16] Estenoz, a Negro, had been an insurrectionist general in the August Revolution, was a likable leader, and advocated political justice for the Cuban people of color. Many colored men, such as Senator Morúa Delgado, opposed the colored movement, and pointed out that foreign nations would not permit another black republic in the Caribbean and that the Negroes had nothing to gain by a race war.[17] Nothing came of the Independent party at this time, but later under

---

[12] Magoon, *Report*, II, 65.
[13] Cf. *supra*, p. 80.
[14] *La Discusión*, Havana, July 27, 1908; *El Mundo*, Havana, July 30, 1908.
[15] *El Triunfo*, Havana, May 8, 1908.
[16] *La Discusión*, Havana, August 11, 1907.
[17] Martínez Ortiz, *Cuba*, II, 422-23.

President Gómez a law was passed to prevent parties organizing along color lines. Estenoz led a revolt against this law and the movement was put down with difficulty after the loss of several lives.[18]

The political campaigns of all factions were carried on in an orderly manner. There was little discussion of political issues, but the merits and demerits of the various candidates were widely and at times forcefully discussed. "In individual cases there were offensive personal attacks and bombastic utterances as to what would be done if Cuban independence was not restored," but generally speaking the campaign speeches were moderate.[19]

The Conservatives, Miguelistas, and Zayistas named tickets for all provincial offices while the Independents named provincial candidates in three provinces only. Municipal elections were held in a total of eighty-two municipalities. The Conservatives nominated tickets in eighty of these, the Miguelistas had tickets in sixty-nine, the Zayistas made nominations in sixty-seven, and the Independent party entered the race in twenty-four municipalities.[20]

The elections of 1908 were held in accordance with the new electoral law and Colonel E. H. Crowder, the president of the advisory commission which had drafted the law, was named by Governor Magoon as head of the central election board.[21] Crowder and his assistants on the board supervised the provincial, municipal, presidential, and congressional elections. They furnished all electoral supplies, alloted election appropriations, and gave advice to all the electoral boards throughout the island. In this work, the board issued numerous instructions and circulars, answered thousands of queries,

[18] Chapman, *op. cit.*, pp. 308-13.
[19] Magoon, *Report*, II, 67.
[20] *Ibid.*, p. 66.
[21] *Havana Post*, April 18, 1908.

distributed some 8,000 voting booths and 1,650 ballot boxes, and suggested and drafted decrees facilitating the execution of the new law.[22] The successful conduct of the elections was in a great degree due to the efficient and careful manner in which these arduous and exacting tasks were performed.

The provisional administration took every precaution to insure honest registration lists and fair elections. Registration frauds in 1905 had caused the defeat of the Liberals and had done much to bring on the August Revolution. Accordingly, electoral boards carefully checked registration lists furnished by the census office and passed upon thousands of appeals for the inclusion and exclusion of names. The census showed the total population of Cuba to be 2,048,980. Of that number some 419,342 were in the preliminary lists of qualified voters. By the August elections that number had been increased to 451,677 and by the time the presidential elections were held in November the party managers had names included until qualified voters of Cuba numbered 466,745. This appears to have been a large increase over the original list, but it was evidently justified and shared in by all parties for no protests were made.[23]

Soon after Taft took charge in Cuba, congress was suspended and the seats of those members elected in 1905 were vacated.[24] No action had been taken with regard to the provincial governors and councilmen elected in 1905. As the elections approached the Liberals asked that these be dismissed in view of the illegalities with which their election was tainted. On April 8, 1908, the terms of those councilmen elected in 1904 expired, and only those elected in 1905 remained in office. These did not constitute a quorum and Magoon on April 6, 1908, in the interest of a fair election de-

---

[22] Magoon, *Report*, II, 64.
[23] *Ibid.*, pp. 62-63.
[24] Cf. *supra*, p. 84.

clared the offices of the remaining councilmen vacant. The provisional governor also requested and received the resignations of the provincial governors.[25] The power of the provincial councils was temporarily vested in the provisional governor. The six provincial governors were replaced by United States Army officers. Colonel Indalecio Sobrado, Governor of Pinar del Río, was replaced by Captain George W. Read; General Emilio Núñez, Governor of Havana, was succeeded by Major Frederick S. Foltz; Colonel Domingo Lecuona, Governor of Matanzas, was followed by Captain Edmund Wittenmyer; Manuel Ramón Silva, Governor of Camagüey, was replaced by Major Wallis O. Clark; and in Oriente Governor Frederico Pérez Carbó was succeeded by Captain Andrew J. Dougherty. The governor's office in Santa Clara was vacant and that was filled by Major William D. Beach. The United States officers held these posts until October 1, 1908, when they were succeeded by the newly elected Cuban officials.[26]

On August 1, 1908, some 269,132 voters, about 60 per cent of the total registered, cast their ballots for local officials.[27] The Conservatives elected governors in the provinces of Pinar del Río, Matanzas, and Santa Clara, the Miguelistas in Camagüey and Oriente, and the Zayistas in the province of Havana. In the municipal elections these parties elected twenty-eight, thirty-five and eighteen mayors respectively. In the town of Pedro Betancourt a Liberal fusion mayor was elected. The split in the Liberal party allowed the Conservatives to win more offices than would have been the case had the Liberals been united. Had a united Liberal party secured the vote cast for the two factions, the Liberals would have

---

[25] *Decrees, 1908,* no. 373; *Havana Post,* April 6, 1908.

[26] *Decrees, 1908,* no. 374; *Havana Post,* October 2, 1906. Magoon would have appointed Cuban governors instead of the army officers, but the various parties could not agree on proposed appointments. Magoon, *Report,* II, 61.

[27] *Ibid.,* p. 67; *La Lucha,* Havana, August 2, 1908.

elected all six provincial governors and sixty-one out of the eighty-two mayors.[28] The elections were quiet and orderly and were accepted as fair by all parties. President Roosevelt and Governor Magoon congratulated Cuba on the way the elections were conducted. No party left the polls as is often the case in Hispanic American countries, and the elections proved to be real tests of party strength.[29] The vote in Santa Clara Province and in a few municipalities was close enough to give rise to appeals against the canvass, but in all save one or two minor cases the canvassing boards were sustained.[30]

The August elections convinced both factions of the Liberal party that they would have to unite before the national elections if they expected to defeat the Conservatives. An agreement was finally reached whereby General José Miguel Gómez became the joint candidate of the two factions for the presidency and Alfredo Zayas for the vice-presidency. The agreement further provided that each group should keep its own organization, but that congressional offices should be proportionately distributed.[31] Gómez, aside from his personal qualifications, seems to have been selected for first honors because his faction polled the larger vote in August and because many Cubans felt he had unjustly been deprived of the presidency in 1905.[32]

On August 24, 1908, the Conservatives met and nominated General Mario García Menocal and Rafael Montoro as their

---

[28] Magoon, *Report*, II, 68-69; *La Discusión*, Havana, August 3, 1908.

[29] Chapman, *op. cit.*, p. 262; *Havana Post*, August 2, 1908; Magoon, *Report*, II, 66.

[30] T. B. Steels (Captain, Coast Artillery Corps), "Abstract and Review of the Decisions of the Audiencias and of the Supreme Court on Electoral Appeals," *passim.* Manuscript in *Crowder Papers*; *El Comercio*, Havana, August 30, 1908.

[31] *Havana Post*, September 3, 1908; Magoon, *Report*, II, 71.

[32] The followers of Gómez, Miguelistas, were also known as the Historical Liberals. They claimed that inasmuch as there had been no legal election in 1905, Gómez was still the official nominee of the Liberal party. Johnson, *op. cit.*, IV, 289.

candidates for president and vice-president.[33] The Conservatives with fresh candidates in the field did not think the united Liberal party would secure all the votes of its factions. The Liberals relied on the combined majority they had obtained in the August elections. Following the nomination of the Conservative candidates and the fusion of the Liberals a heated and enthusiastic campaign ensued.

On September 12, 1908, Governor Magoon decreed that a general election should be held on November 14 for the selection of presidential, vice-presidential, and senatorial electors, and for the election of members to the lower house of congress. In general the machinery and the safeguards for fair and honest elections were the same for the general as for the local elections. It was determined in advance that the new representatives should draw lots for the four year or full terms and the half terms to make the elections harmonize with the constitution.[34] With the details attended to the Cuban electorate, stirred by speeches, bands, and great parades, marched to the polls.

Liberal presidential and vice-presidential electors secured majorities in all provinces, ranging from 1,726 in Camagüey to 26,031 in Havana. Their total majority was 70,943. Thus Gómez and Zayas were elected, receiving the entire 107 electoral votes. The Liberals elected all the senatorial electors, assuring their control of the upper house. Under the law of proportional representation the Conservatives secured thirty-two representatives and the Liberals fifty-one. Out of a possible 466,745 votes a total of 331,455 votes were cast—the Liberals receiving 61 per cent of the total vote.[35]

Opinion was almost unanimous that the elections held by

---

[33] *La Discusión,* Havana, August 25, 1908.

[34] Magoon, *Report,* II, 70.

[35] Pardo Suárez, *op. cit.,* p. 118. Magoon, *Report,* II, 73. This work contains tables of the votes by provinces.

the provisional government were orderly, fair, and honest.[36]
Roosevelt, Taft, and Wright cabled their congratulations to
Gómez and the Cuban people and to Governor Magoon.[37]
One writer while admitting the honesty of the elections made
the point that the Liberals had the advantage because the
United States had recognized their party and placed many
of them in office.[38] In other words, Cubans naturally wanted
to be on the winning side. Considering the admitted fairness
of the election officials and the Liberal majorities the point
seems to have no special merit. The Liberal historian, Martínez Ortiz, stated that the elections were orderly and honest,
but added that they were supervised by the United States and
that success in 1908 was no proof that the Cubans could hold
honest elections in the future.[39]

In 1908 as in 1902 there were those who doubted the wisdom of granting self-government to Cuba. The various uprisings in 1907 had caused many to lose faith in the political
stability of the Cuban people.[40] By and large the Cuban press
favored self-government. The *Havana Post* was friendly to
Cuban independence, but the *Havana Daily Telegraph*, which
had done much to secure intervention, frankly advocated
that Cuba be annexed to the United States.[41] President Roosevelt may have doubted the ability of the Cubans to govern
themselves, but he was determined to carry out his Cuban
policy in good faith and to give the Cubans another chance.

---

[36] *La Discusión,* Havana, November 15, 1908; *El Mundo,* Havana, November
15, 1908; *La Lucha,* Havana, November 15, 1908. General Menocal, who
served Cuba as president from 1913 to 1921, in an interview granted the writer,
stated that he felt that the United States and the provisional government were
biased in favor of the Liberals.

[37] *Havana Post,* November 16, 1908.

[38] Johnson, *op. cit.,* IV, 285.

[39] Martínez Ortiz, *Cuba,* II, 455. Chapman in his book, *A History of the Cuban
Republic,* p. 263, states that "it is probable that Cuba has never had such well conducted elections either before or since."

[40] Cf. *supra,* pp. 143-44.

[41] *Havana Post,* January 28, 1909; *Havana Daily Telegraph,* July 13, 1908.

In his annual message to Congress in December, 1908, President Roosevelt made the following statement concerning the second intervention:

In Cuba our occupancy will cease in about two months' time; the Cubans have in orderly manner elected their own governmental authorities, and the island will be turned over to them. Our occupation on this occasion has lasted a little over two years, and Cuba has thriven and prospered under it. Our earnest hope and one desire is that the people of the island shall now govern themselves with justice, so that peace and order may be secure. We will gladly help them to this end; but I would solemnly warn them to remember the great truth that the only way a people can permanently avoid being governed from without is to show that they both can and will govern themselves from within.[42]

The rejoicing of the Cuban people over the fact that self-government would soon be restored was greatly dampened on November 4, 1908, by the death of former President Estrada Palma.[43] While many still harbored bitterness against the old patriot, the nation at large seemed to realize that Cuba had lost a great and noble man. Governor Magoon recognized his services to his country and the condition of his family when he awarded his widow a pension of $5,000 a year. National mourning was declared and the mortal remains of Cuba's first president, after lying in state in the Provincial Council Hall of Oriente, were buried with all national honors.[44]

The president elect, General José Miguel Gómez, was no stranger in Cuba. In the War for Liberation against Spain he had attained the rank of Major-General. He was a member of the Cuban constitutional convention and had served as governor of the province of Santa Clara. In 1905, Gómez was

---

[42] Roosevelt, *op. cit.*, p. 539.
[43] Cf. *supra*, p. 62; *La Lucha*, Havana, November 5, 1908.
[44] *Decrees, 1908*, nos. 1065 and 1067; *La Discusión*, November 8, 1908.

the presidential candidate of the Liberal party against Estrada Palma, and his defeat did much to bring on the August Revolution. He continued active in political affairs under Magoon and when the Liberal party split over patronage he became the chief of the Miguelista faction. Gómez was a man of considerable ability; he possessed an agreeable personality and in addition to the strength of his personal following, played a shrewd game of politics. He secured jobs and pardons for his friends, surrounded himself with able young men, and ruled his followers with an iron hand.[45]

General Gómez was not so well known outside of Cuba. Citizens of the United States and other foreigners who had stakes in the island did not know just what to expect from the new administration. The Liberals had denounced the Platt Amendment, but that was nothing new in Cuban politics. Aside from having the most popular candidate they had promised the people legal cockfighting, less work, and a lottery.[46] They had discussed personalities, but little had been said about governmental policies. It is doubtful if the Liberals themselves knew just what they would do when they got in office other than that they planned to pardon their friends and run the country. Much doubt created by the election of the Liberals was dispelled when Gómez sent a cordial reply to President Roosevelt's congratulatory message and addressed a good will message to the people of the United States.[47]

---

[45] Miguel Lozano Casado, *La personalidad del general José Miguel Gómez, passim.* The author eulogizes Gómez. For a good brief account of Gómez see Chapman, *op. cit.*, pp. 270-73. The *Havana Post*, May 20, 1906, contains good character sketches of contemporary Cubans. See also William B. Parker, *Cubans of Today.*

[46] Johnson, *op. cit.*, IV., 291. A national lottery was urged by the *Havana Daily Telegraph*, December 22, 1908, on the theory that Cubans were bound to gamble and that it would be better for the money to be kept at home than for it to be spent on European lotteries as was then the case.

[47] Martínez Ortiz, *Cuba*, II, 458-59.

Before the electoral college met in December, General Gómez had selected his cabinet. The following men were named for the various posts: Justo García Vélez, Secretary of State; Marcelius de Villergas, Secretary of the Treasury; Octavio Diviño, Secretary of Justice; Nicolas Alberdi, Secretary of Interior; Ortelio Foyo, Secretary of Agriculture; Ramón Meza, Secretary of Public Instruction; Matais Duque, Secretary of Sanitation; and Benito Lagueruela, Secretary of Public Works.[48] The president-elect and his advisors frequently consulted Governor Magoon and leading United States officers about Cuban affairs. After the election the old and new officials coöperated to wind up the intervention in good order and to launch the new government with well laid plans.

On New Year's Day a great reception was held in the President's Palace. Governor Magoon invited Gómez, Zayas, and other prominent Cubans to help him receive the guests. This was the beginning of a round of festivities which, mixed with serious work, continued until the end of the second intervention. Early in January the provisional governor made a final tour of the Republic. Cienfuegos gave him a big reception and held a parade in his honor. Santa Clara, Camagüey, and Santiago de Cuba also gave Magoon enthusiastic welcomes.[49]

In recent years it has been the habit of many Cubans to refer to Governor Magoon as an unworthy representative of the United States and as a man who was very unpopular in Cuba. The evidence does not support such charges. Magoon's work speaks for itself. He at all times commanded the support of Roosevelt, Root, and Taft, and the better elements of the Cuban people. His popularity may have suffered an eclipse because of a great deal of criticism after he left Cuba, but from October, 1906, until the end of the intervention in 1909,

---

[48] *Havana Post*, November 19, 1908.
[49] *Ibid.*, 1-10, 1909.

Charles E. Magoon was a respected and popular governor. The city of Havana made him an adopted son.[50] He was made an honorary president of the fire department of that city and one of its streets was named in his honor.[51] Pinar del Río and other towns honored Magoon by making him an adopted son.[52] Each time he left for the United States the wharves and shore lines were crowded to bid him *adios,* and when he returned the people thronged the harbor to welcome him back. The merchants and business men of Havana on January 15 gave a big banquet honoring Magoon and the new Cuban president and vice-president. On January 27 a farewell banquet was held in Havana's city hall for Magoon and his fellow officers. Many speakers praised him and his administration and the sentiment was expressed that the provisional governor could continue as president if he would become a Cuban citizen.[53]

Magoon's last days as provisional governor were strenuous. Social demands required much of his time; important laws, drafted by the advisory commission, had to be considered; applications for pardons were studied; and a host of official and personal matters required time and attention.

One of the provisional governor's acts which met with acclaim in Cuba and abroad was the signing on January 1, 1909, of a decree which retired the aged physician and scientist, Dr. Carlos J. Finlay, as honorary president of the National Board of Sanitation and Charities at a salary of $2,500 a year for life. The decree also provided that Dr. Finlay could collect and edit his writings and have them published at the expense of the state.[54] Dr. Finlay had served as chief sanitation officer during the provisional administration, and both

---

[50] *La Lucha,* Havana, December 10, 1908.
[51] *Havana Post,* May 21, 1908; *ibid.,* August 11, 1908.
[52] *Ibid.,* June 2, 1908.
[53] Conference with Robert J. Flick; *El Fígaro,* January, 1909, p. 54.
[54] *Decrees, 1908,* no. 1130.

Magoon and Wood owe much of their success to this Cuban who discovered the means by which yellow fever was transmitted and led the successful fight against that scourge on the island.

Another matter of more immediate concern to Cubans had to do with the Army of Pacification. Some of the United States troops left Cuba early in January, 1909, but following an agreement with President Gómez, the remaining troops stayed at Camp Columbia until April. It was alleged that the troops would keep the camp in a good state of repair until General Faustino Guerra could organize a Cuban army and take charge. However, it seems that both the United States authorities and General Gómez wanted to be sure that the new government would get under way without any trouble. No trouble was apparent or expected, but the available United States troops were symbols of order.[55]

From military matters the provisional governor turned to consider the complaints growing out of the embezzlement of $195,000 by Miguel de La Torre, late treasurer of the fiscal zone of Havana.[56] The money taken by the trusted official who had served his government for thirty-six years was in several packages and consisted largely of cash deposits which had been made in lieu of bonds required in judicial proceedings. The accounts of the treasurer had been inspected in June, 1908, and were found to be correct. Miguel de La Torre probably thought that would be the last inspection made by the provisional government, but another general inspection was ordered in October, 1908, and his shortage was discovered. Promptly arrested, he admitted his guilt, but refused to return any of the money or to disclose what he had done with it. When it became apparent that none of the money would be recovered those who had sustained losses de-

---

[55] *The Cuba Review*, January, 1908, p. 8; *Havana Post*, November 29, 1908.
[56] Cf. *supra*, p. 94. *El Comercio*, Havana, October 20, 1908.

manded that the government reimburse them.[57] They contended that the government and its agents were obligated to keep the deposits safe, and that the matter involved not only a dishonest official, but also the honesty and good faith of the government. After considering the equities of the claims, Governor Magoon, upon the recommendation of the Acting Secretary of the Treasury, issued a decree on January 16, 1909, which provided that those persons and corporations which had sustained losses should be reimbursed from the national treasury.[58]

As the time approached for the provisional administration to withdraw, the Havana sewering and paving projects and the Cienfuegos water and sewer systems were not yet finished.[59] To prevent further trouble and litigation over these projects Governor Magoon on January 25, 1909, with the approval of President Roosevelt, secretaries Root and Wright, and acting under orders from Secretary Wright, issued a decree which authorized the president of the Republic of Cuba to issue bonds for a foreign loan for an amount not to exceed $16,500,000.[60]

Another matter involving future expenditures by the Cuban government was the settlement of Spanish claims for war materials left in Cuba in 1898. On January 29, 1909, the day after Magoon left Cuba, a convention negotiated by the provisional government with Spain over these materials was signed in Madrid. By the terms of this treaty Cuba agreed to pay Spain $300,000 in installments for cannons on the Havana forts and for other war supplies.[61] In July, 1909, when the first payment became due, uninformed persons attacked the convention and the provisional government. García Vélez,

---

[57] Magoon, *Report*, II, 117; *La Discusión*, Havana, January 17, 1909.
[58] *Decrees, 1909*, no. 47.
[59] Cf. *supra*, pp. 118-21.
[60] *Decrees, 1909*, no. 114; cf. *supra*, p. 121 n.
[61] *The Cuba Review*, February, 1909, p. 8.

who had handled the negotiations, promptly explained the matter and the payment was made and the incident closed.[62]

On January 2, 1909, Magoon issued a call for the newly elected congress to assemble in Havana on January 13. The decree convoking congress into session was designed to prevent a few members from breaking a quorum and thus making legislation impossible under the constitution. Under Estrada Palma it had been the frequent practice for small groups of congressmen to block or delay legislation by refusing to attend sessions which for a quorum required the attendance of two-thirds of the members of each house. Magoon's decree provided that after congress was organized, a majority of the members of each house should constitute a quorum. The decree further provided that no member of either house should, without the express consent of the house to which he belonged, absent himself from any session, and further that neither house should grant absence leave at the same time to more than one-sixth of its members. The decree provided that in the absence of a quorum five or more members should by majority vote compel the attendance of all absentees. More important than the above provisions was the one which allowed no pay to those who absented themselves without permission.[63] While most of these provisions had been advocated by General Gómez, they were bitterly denounced by members of congress and others as contrary to the rights and dignity of congress.[64] Although good legislation for Cuba, the objectionable quorum-forcing provisions were repealed by congress toward the end of the Gómez administration.[65]

On December 19, 1908, the senatorial electors had met in the provincial capitals and elected the full number of four

---

[62] *El Triunfo*, Havana, July 2, 1909; *La Discusión*, Havana, July 12, 1909.
[63] *Decrees, 1909*, no. 7.
[64] *The Cuba Review*, January, 1909, p. 7.
[65] Chapman, *op. cit.*, p. 512.

senators from each province. On December 24, 1908, the presidential and vice-presidential electors met and cast unanimous votes for Gómez and Zayas.[66] Congress assembled on January 13, 1909, and passed on the certificates of election of its members. On January 18, Senator Martín Morúa Delgado was elected president of the senate and Orestes Ferrara was selected speaker of the house.[67] At a session of the congress on January 20, the presidential and vice-presidential votes were canvassed and Gómez and Zayas were respectively proclaimed elected president and vice-president of the Republic of Cuba.[68] On the morning of January 28 Alfredo Zayas was inducted into office at a joint session of the house and senate.[69] With these matters out of the way the country turned its attention to the inauguration of General Gómez and the departure of the United States officials.

Following the inauguration of Vice-President Zayas, President-elect Gómez and Governor Magoon arrived at the Palace. Assembled there were the leading United States officials in Cuba, members of the diplomatic corps accredited to the Cuban Republic, a number of diplomats accredited to the government of the United States who visited Havana to represent their governments, the supreme court of Cuba, the consular corps, members of the Cuban congress, and other dignitaries and prominent citizens. At twelve o'clock noon General Gómez, accompanied by Governor Magoon, the chief justice, and associate justices of the supreme court, stepped onto the balcony of the Palace and in the presence of a great gathering of citizens assembled in the Plaza de Armas took the oath of office administered by the chief justice.[70]

---

[66] Magoon, *Report*, III, 7; *La Lucha*, Havana, December 24, 1908.
[67] *La Discusión*, Havana, January 19, 1909.
[68] *Official Gazette*, Havana, January 28, 1909.
[69] Magoon, *Report*, III, 8.
[70] *Havana Post*, January 29, 1909; *La Lucha*, Havana, January 29, 1909.

Immediately after taking the oath of office President Gómez addressed the assembly of citizens, saying:

It is customary for the oath of office to be administered within the palace, but, at the suggestion of the provisional governor, which suggestion I most heartily approve, I take the oath in your presence that it may be an evidence to you and all the people of Cuba that every act of my administration will conform to the constitution and to the laws.[71]

Following these brief remarks President Gómez, the provisional governor, and the members of the supreme court retired within the Palace to the reception room where the formal acts terminating the provisional government took place without delay. Governor Magoon read the following message which had been approved by President Roosevelt and his Cabinet:

To the President and Congress of the Republic of Cuba.

Sirs:

Under the direction of the President of the United States, I now relinquish to you as the duly elected representatives of the people of Cuba, to be held and exercised by you under the general provisions of the constitution of the Republic, the power and authority for some time held and exercised by me under the provisions of the third article of the appendix to the constitution pursuant to the appointment of the President of the United States; and I hereby declare the provisional administration of the Republic of Cuba, established by the United States pursuant to the treaty between the United States of America and the Republic of Cuba, concluded May 22, 1903, and the said third article of the appendix to the constitution of Cuba, to be ended.

It is the understanding of the Government of the United States and, as a part of its final act in the exercise of the rights and powers conferred upon it as aforesaid, it now declares that all the executive and legislative decrees, regulations, and rulings of the

---

[71] Magoon, *Report,* III, 8.

provisional government now in force are to continue in force and effect until such time as the same shall be legally revoked by the Government of Cuba duly constituted in accordance with the general provisions of the constitution.

All money obligations of the provisional government down to this date have been paid as far as practicable. Such claims and obligations of the provisional government, however, as may remain unpaid are to be regarded as claims and obligations of the Republic of Cuba, and the Government of the United States understands that these claims and obligations will be so treated.

The Republic of Cuba under the provisional administration of the United States has executed the provisions of Article V of the appendix to the constitution of the Republic of Cuba to the extent of construction of other works of sanitation contemplated by said article, and the government and control of the island are transferred to you, as the duly elected representatives of the people of Cuba under the constitution, with the express understanding that said contracts and all contracts entered into by the Republic of Cuba under the provisional administration of the United States relating to sanitation or for other public purposes shall be held inviolate and that they will be executed in accordance with their terms, and all rights acquired thereunder shall be maintained and protected.

I am also directed by the President of the United States to declare that the United States considers that the second article of the appendix to the constitution of Cuba forbids the Government of Cuba to assume or contract any public debt in excess of, or in addition to, the debt already contracted or authorized by now existing laws and now existing decrees of the provisional government; and that the Government of the United States will not recognize or concede to be a valid obligation of the Government of Cuba any bond or evidence of debt which may be issued in violation of this understanding. I am further directed by the President of the United States to declare that it is the final and conclusive determination and decision of the provisional government of Cuba that all claims of the soldiers of the war of liberation have been fully satisfied and discharged by the execution of existing laws, and the Republic of Cuba remains under no further obligations or indebtedness in respect thereof; and that the declaration hereinbefore contained in respect to the increase of the Cuban debt specifically and especially applies to any attempt to create an indebtedness for the discharge of such alleged or pretended obligations.

On behalf of the President, the Government, and the people of the United States, the retiring provisional governor extends to the officials of the Republic now to assume control of the island, heartiest felicitations and good wishes for the success of the new administration, and to the people of Cuba the sincere friendship and good wishes of the United States and the most earnest hope for the stability and success of the reestablished government, for the blessings of peace, justice, prosperity, and well-regulated freedom throughout the island, and for enduring friendship between the Republic of the United States and the Republic of Cuba.[72]

President Gómez replied as follows:

To the Honorable the Provisional Governor of Cuba.
Sir:

We receive from you the government of the Republic of Cuba with which you have been charged up to the present time, and which you turn over to us as the duly elected representatives of the people, in compliance with the instructions of the President of the United States. We have heard your statements made in accordance with the appendix to the Cuban constitution and the treaty between the Republic of Cuba and the United States of America, and take note of the document which you deliver us.

All acquired rights shall be respected in harmony with the principles of international law, the principles of our constitution, and the provisions of the appendix of the constitution.

Our government will find its inspiration in an adherence to the principles dictated by modern civilization, protecting the individual in his relations with the State and with his fellow-citizens.

---

[72] *Ibid.*, pp. 9-10.

The constitution—which is the solemn pact between those who govern and those who are governed—shall be upheld in all its integrity, because our chief concern will be to preserve it inviolate. With its strict application shall come the satisfaction born of justice, the blessings of peace, the enjoyment of great prosperity, and all the privileges which grow out of free institutions.

We shall faithfully adhere to the treaty between the United States of America and the Republic of Cuba, as this is our duty while the same remains in force, and we shall endeavor through good government and vigilant administration to obviate that at any time it shall be found necessary to apply any of its clauses.

The United States of America will always find a friendly nation in the Republic of Cuba. The promptings of the hearts of our people remain the same as they were in the trying times when friendly arms from the North hastened to assist them in maintaining their ideals; and these sentiments will not change so long as these ideals form a common bond of love between the two countries.

We are indebted to your nation for its generous aid in the maintenance of our institutions, and the cordial relations existing will never grow less through any act of ours.

To-day we are again completely free, and for us it is an hour of rejoicing. Once again we are masters of our fate, and there is not a Cuban heart but swears to maintain for all time the newly acquired integrity of the nation and who does not at the same time feel the profoundest gratitude toward those who after governing them have faithfully performed their agreement and now leave us in the full enjoyment of our sovereignty.

We deeply appreciate the congratulations and well wishes of the President, Government, and people of the United States, and our people are also grateful for the avowed assurances of sincere and cordial friendship.

Convey to President Roosevelt, whom Cuba admires and respects, to the Government, and to the people of the United States the kindly feeling of the Cuban nation for them and their hope that the friendship existing between the two countries shall be permanent; and you, personally, receive our best wishes for your happiness and prosperity and our gratitude for the wisdom, impartiality, and sincere desire to promote the welfare of this Republic and its people with which you have administered the government during your term of office.[73]

President Gómez and other leaders of the new Cuban government received the congratulations of those present and numerous greetings were received by wire from all parts of the world.[74]

Governor Magoon and the United States supervisors and assistants left the Palace shortly after the ceremonies were over. They were accompanied to the pier by President Gómez, Vice-President Zayas, the resident and visiting diplomats, the consular corps, members of the Cuban congress and other dignitaries. They made their way through the throngs along the street amid volleys of *adios*. Governor Magoon and his aid, Captain James A. Ryan, embarked on board the United States battleship "Maine." The United States officials and employees embarked on the army transport "McClellan." The United States battleship "Mississippi" acted as escort and the three ships amid the firing of salutes left the harbor accompanied by many small crafts and cheered by a large crowd assembled along the waterfront.[75]

---

[73] *Ibid.*, p. 10.

[74] *Havana Post*, January 29, 1909.

[75] Vivid accounts of the inauguration of Gómez and the departure of the provisional governor and his assistants are given in *La Lucha*, Havana, January 29, 1909; *Diario de la Marina*, Havana, January 29, 1909; *Havana Post*, January 29, 1909, and in most of the other Cuban papers of the same date. See also the *Washington Post*, January 29, 1909.

IX

An Evaluation of the Second Intervention

GOVERNOR MAGOON and the United States officials who had conducted the provisional government were not out of Cuba before judgments were being passed on their work. Immediate reactions showed a diversity of opinion. *El Mundo*, a leading independent newspaper of Havana, in an editorial entitled "Long Live the Republic" made the following comment on the provisional governor:

Mr. Magoon has governed our country well. On his return trip he carries the affection of the Cubans. He has performed with discretion the difficult task of governing and administering, without previous experience, a country with laws, customs, and language very different from his, and this in a country disturbed with the passion of unrestrained politics. Mr. Magoon has not signed a single death sentence and he has been very kind in all his dealings. We have to thank the United States for its good work in intervening, but if this work has been carried out well it is due to the efforts of Mr. Magoon.[1]

The editor of the *Havana Post*, a newspaper owned by citizens of the United States and one which frequently criticized the provisional administration, stated:

---

[1] *El Mundo*, Havana, January 28, 1909.

War has been stopped, commercial activity has been revived, industry has started anew, business and financial confidence has been restored. Peace has been brought out of political chaos. Harmony reigns where a few years ago all was strife.[2]

The United States journalist, Henry Watterson, who was in Cuba during January, 1909, said:

Magoon, the Magician, is the proper name for him. His work here has been far-reaching. He has caused two blades of grass to grow where but one grew before.[3]

La Lucha, a Liberal paper which usually sided with the provisional government, praised Magoon and his work as outlined in the official report as follows:

To have brought matters up to date so satisfactorily, surrounded by the various economic and political difficulties which have existed, Governor Magoon has accomplished a stupendous task, but it is a fact that his greatest merit has not been in his constant industry, but rather in his capacious understanding. It is surprising with what facility and rapidity he has been able to study our multitudinous problems, with which he was not familiar, and the manner in which he grasped and determined them, as demonstrated by his report, which reflects both credit and honor upon him.[4]

Some of the Cuban newspapers, apparently indifferent concerning the success or failure of the provisional government, published only news accounts of the departure of the United States officials and made no editorial comment either for or against the Magoon administration.[5] *El Comercio,* an independent paper with conservative leanings, mixed praise with blame. It spoke highly of Magoon as an individual, but criti-

---

[2] *Havana Post,* January 28, 1909.
[3] *Ibid.,* January 29, 1909.
[4] *La Lucha,* Havana, January 16, 1909.
[5] *La Discusión,* Havana, January 28, 1909; *Diario de la Marina,* Havana, January 28, 1909.

cized his management of the patronage. It indicated, without mentioning names or giving details, that the Cuban Republic had been ruled by sinister elements during the second intervention and stated that these elements would not depart when Magoon left the country. It expressed the hope that the "evil influences," no longer aided by Taft and Magoon, would die.[6]

Manuel Secades, writing in *Cuba*, praised Magoon as a private citizen and gave him credit for holding fair elections, but condemned him for granting too many pardons.[7] The *Diario Español* criticized the United States for having endangered Cuban liberty and advised the people to forget the governor who left amid general indifference. It urged the Cubans to conduct their government in the future so that another intervention would never be required.[8]

Generally speaking, the press of the United States viewed the results of the second intervention in Cuba with pride and satisfaction. An occasional note was sounded to the effect that a third intervention would mean annexation.[9] Perhaps the best balanced criticism of the provisional administration was that appearing in *The Nation* under the title of "Our Trusteeship in Cuba." The writer stated:

Americans may take solid satisfaction in reviewing their guardianship of the island of Cuba. It would, of course, be idle to deny that mistakes have been made. The general policy of the American Administration has too often smacked of compromise, of a desire to conciliate where a vigorous grappling with discordant elements would have been wiser. Thus the retention of one-third of the Congressmen on the insular payroll for doing nothing during the interregnum has seemed an injustice and a bad example

---

[6] *El Comercio*, Havana, January 28, 1909.

[7] *Cuba*, Havana, January 27, 1909.

[8] *Diario Español*, Havana, January 28, 1909.

[9] For digest of United States newspaper comment see *The Cuba Review*, VII (January, 1909), 10.

to set to the community; again Mr. Taft's inclusion with his amnesty proclamation of the men who killed innocent rural guards at Guanabacoa, nearly a year before the revolution, was a tactical error, as was the payment of the insurgents for the horses they stole while "in the woods." But on these minor details we do not desire to dwell to-day. Moreover, it would be unjust to hold Mr. Magoon wholly responsible for the mistakes; Havana is too near Washington to make it always clear whether a given policy was Mr. Magoon's or a superior's at the Federal Capital.[10]

The weight of contemporary opinion in Cuba and the United States was favorable to the Magoon administration. Subsequently plaudits accorded Magoon by Cubans were forgotten and the faults attributed to his administration enlarged.[11] The chief complaints advanced against the provisional government may be listed as follows: extravagance and the creation of a bonded debt, patronage discrimination and the awarding of *botellas*, too many pardons, favoritism to United States contractors who produced poor work, and a policy which temporized and compromised when it should have been firm and determined. These charges, as well as those involving the personal honesty of Governor Magoon, merit special attention.

Just before the August Revolution there was $26,000,000 in the national treasury. Within a month the Estrada Palma government and its partisans reduced this sum by half in attempting to suppress the rebellion.[12] When Taft took charge in Cuba there was in the treasury a balance of $13,500,000, over a million dollars of which was in Cuban bonds.[13] It is customary for Cuban writers to tell of the twelve or thirteen million or the twenty-five or twenty-six million that Estrada

---

[10] *The Nation*, LXXXVIII (February 4, 1909), 102.

[11] Barbarrosa, *op. cit.*, pp. 71-89; Trelles, *op. cit.*, pp. 8-12.

[12] Trelles, *op. cit.*, pp. 7-8. Unless otherwise indicated figures are given in round numbers.

[13] Taft and Bacon, *Report*, p. 536.

Palma had saved, and then to accuse the provisional government of wasting that sum.[14] In fact the money left by Estrada Palma was not sufficient to cover the obligations created by his government, and Magoon, instead of having a surplus, was faced with a deficit of approximately $4,000,000.[15]

On October 26, 1906, Lieutenant Colonel E. F. Ladd, military supervisor of the treasury, submitted a report to the provisional governor which gave the balance required to meet budget obligations as $17,500,000. The balance required to meet war expenses, the increase of the rural guard, the expenses of the military occupation, and the damage claims incident to the war were estimated to be $4,500,000. An additional $9,000,000 was required to meet special appropriations for various public works which had been authorized by the Estrada Palma government. However, by the end of the fiscal year, June 30, 1907, the total disbursements had only reached $25,500,000 and consequently the expected deficit of $4,000,000 was converted into a temporary surplus of approximately $17,000,000.[16]

Unfavorable crops, the Panic of 1907, and large government expenditures reduced the balance in the treasury to $6,500,000 by July 1, 1908.[17] On January 27, 1909, the day before Magoon left Cuba, the cash balance in the treasury, with all obligations of the provisional government as fully paid to date "as practicable," was $2,860,668.47. In addition to this sum the treasury held $1,000,000 in Cuban bonds which had been purchased by the Estrada Palma government and which were carried on the books as cash. After deducting

---

[14] Barbarrosa, *op. cit.*, pp. 71-87; Trelles, *op. cit.*, p. 9; Martínez Ortiz, *Cuba*, II, 391; Emilio Roig de Leuchsenring, *El intervencionismo, mal de males de Cuba republicana*, p. 13.

[15] Magoon, *Report*, II, 167-68; see also Chapman, *op. cit.*, pp. 237-38. The figures compiled by Lieutenant Colonel E. F. Ladd and listed in the Magoon *Reports* are the most accurate to be had.

[16] Cf. *supra*, pp. 88-89. Magoon, *Report*, II, 156-69.

[17] *Ibid.*, p. 169.

all credits from the outstanding obligations the deficit of the provisional government amounted to approximately $6,447,-117.[18]

Such figures do not lend color to the charges of waste and extravagance. In addition to the usual government expenditures, large emergency sums were spent to settle the cost and claims of the August Revolution, to finance the extensive public improvement program, to purchase Church property, to improve public health and sanitation, and to maintain law and order. When all these factors are considered in connection with the economic chaos prevailing in the fall of 1906, the Panic of 1907, the cyclones, the drouths, and the labor troubles which plagued the Magoon administration, it will be seen that the financial affairs of the provisional government were well managed. An accurate record was kept of all receipts and expenditures, and Colonel Ladd's ability and honesty as supervisor of the treasury has never been questioned.

On January 25, 1909, Governor Magoon, following orders from Washington, gave the new Cuban government authority to issue improvement bonds to the extent of $16,500,000 at 4½ per cent for forty years.[19] For this act he has been severely criticized for burdening Cuba with a large bonded debt.[20] The money secured from the sale of the bonds was to be used exclusively for the completion of the Cienfuegos water and sewer systems and the Havana paving and sewer projects. The Cienfuegos improvements had their origin in

---

[18] *Ibid.*, III, 13. The figures given by Magoon are at variance with those submitted by President Gómez to the Cuban congress on April 5, 1909. Gómez gave the cash balance on January 27 as $1,809,479 plus the $1,000,000 in Cuban bonds, and he included with the debts left by the provisional government an item of $1,613,019, on credits granted by previous governments. This last item when added to the deficit of the provisional government made the Cuban debt total approximately $8,060,136. *Mensajes presidenciales*, I, 201.

[19] Cf. *supra*, p. 121 n.

[20] Roig de Leuchsenring, *El intervencionismo*, p. 13; Trelles, *op. cit.*, p. 22; Barbarrosa, *op. cit.*, p. 77.

the Estrada Palma administration, and the Havana projects dated back to contracts made during the Wood administration in 1902. The Havana and Cienfuegos improvements had caused much trouble and to adjust these matters and prevent further litigation, Roosevelt and Taft ordered Magoon to make settlements by having the improvements made and by providing for payment through a foreign loan if necessary.[21] The bonds, when finally issued and sold, purchased necessary public services for the people of the two cities. It hardly seems that there was cause to criticize Magoon, but if so, the blame must be shared by Roosevelt, Taft, Wright, Wood, Estrada Palma, and a host of other good men.

The $16,500,000 loan was actually contracted by President Gómez, who had assured congress that he would not resort to a loan but would set aside part of the revenues to discharge the Havana and Cienfuegos contracts.[22] The forty-year 4½ per cent bond issue was purchased by Speyer & Company of New York at a discount of 12 per cent. The cash yield, less incidental costs of issue and transfer, was approximately $14,-500,000.[23] The loan was guaranteed by 10 per cent of customs collections of the port of Havana.[24] Some Cubans professed to see evil in the loan because Frank Steinhart, former United States consul-general and adviser to Taft and Magoon, and Henry W. Taft, brother of Secretary Taft, successfully negotiated the loan as the duly authorized agents of Speyer & Company.[25] No evidence has been adduced to show that Steinhart, Taft, or anyone else connected with the loan negotia-

---

[21] Cf. *supra*, p. 120.

[22] *Mensajes presidenciales*, p. 202.

[23] *The Import and Industrial Record of Cuba*, IX (April, 1934), 30. The $35,000,000 forty-year 5 per cent bonds issued in 1904 by the Estrada Palma government to placate the veterans had been purchased by Speyer & Company at a discount of 10 per cent. *Ibid.*, p. 29.

[24] *Decrees*, 1909, no. 114.

[25] *La Opinión Cubana*, I (September 1, 1909), 52; Roig de Leuchsenring, *La enmienda platt*, p. 413; *Cuba*, Havana, December 3, 1908.

tions was guilty of any impropriety. As would have been the case with any other agents, they received commissions to which they were entitled.

Aside from the increased cost of conducting a bilingual government, the Magoon administration, with its original deficit and extraordinary expenses, compares favorably with that of Estrada Palma. In matters of national finance and economy it surpasses all Cuban administrations which have followed.[26] The complaints made against the financial policies of the provisional government do not seem to be well founded. The fact of a small cash balance with limited future obligations at the end of the intervention is of little importance when it is recalled that conditions in 1909 were much better than those which had existed in September, 1906, and that the Gómez administration enjoyed a prosperity which resulted to a large degree from the expenditures and the achievements of the Magoon administration.

Further criticism of the provisional government arose over its use of the patronage. Following the August Revolution the political principles of all parties were forgotten in the scramble for jobs. The Liberals wanted all Moderates removed from office and the Moderates and later the Conservatives accused the provisional governor of appointing unworthy Liberals to posts of trust and honor. Taft early announced the policy, which Magoon followed, that worthy Moderates would not be discharged for political reasons, but that as

---

[26] The total expenditures of various governments were summarized in 1924 by Trelles as follows:

Brooke	$14,000,000	(1 year)
Wood	40,000,000	(2 years)
Estrada Palma	88,000,000	(4 years)
Magoon	83,000,000	(2 years)
Gómez	140,000,000	(4 years)
Menocal	560,000,000	(8 years)

Carlos Manuel Trelles, *Biblioteca histórica cubana*, II, 43. See also Chapman, *op. cit.*, pp. 450 *et seq.*

vacancies occurred, Liberals would be preferred until an equality was restored.[27] The Liberals named a committee to advise Magoon in making his appointments. This plan was soon abandoned since the Liberals, failing to agree on a proper distribution of jobs among themselves, split into Zayistas and Miguelistas.[28] Later another patronage committee was named which gave equal representation to the three principal parties which supported candidates in the 1908 elections. This committee followed the policy of naming the party to receive the appointment and the party selected the man to be appointed by the provisional governor.[29]

It was impossible for Magoon to know the qualifications and political affiliations of the hundreds of applicants for jobs. He undoubtedly placed too much reliance on the patronage committees and the party leaders who advised him concerning the honesty and fitness of the many office-seekers. The system used resulted in some dishonesty and inefficiency, but it seems to have been the only practicable solution.[30] The provisional government, like all governments before and since, did not have sufficient jobs to satisfy all demands. The patronage charge is one that can be made against practically all governments and in this case the responsibility must be shared by some of the most prominent Cubans of that day, who as party chiefs and national leaders advised the provisional governor and sought jobs for themselves and their friends.

More serious charges were those which alleged that the provisional administration created the *botella* and granted too

---

[27] Cf. *supra*, p. 68.

[28] Cf. *supra*, p. 79.

[29] Chapman, *op. cit.*, p. 253.

[30] Several inefficient and dishonest officials and employees, chiefly from the revenue and education departments, were discharged from time to time. Cf. *supra*, pp. 93-94. The audits made by the provisional government provided checks on fiscal matters, but no similar check was made on efficiency and it is probable that only flagrant cases of inefficiency were reported.

many soft jobs. One Cuban writer in discussing this aspect of the second intervention stated:

> . . . the greatest evil which Mr. Magoon brought to our country was the creation of the damned *botella*, which has been one of the principal sources of administrative corruption and of the retrocession and disorganization which we are witnessing in almost all the Departments of the Public Administration.[31]

The Liberal historian Martínez Ortiz in discussing the patronage problem of the provisional government said:

> The government opened its hands and let loose the purse strings without any regard. It had no idea other than pleasing the committee on jobs . . . Mr. Magoon didn't know how to say "No," he always said "Amen" and signed the papers, and in this way the money so carefully saved by D. Tomás Estrada Palma gradually disappeared.
>
> The governor defended himself from his critics saying he was doing nothing but granting the requests of the great Cuban politicians. His kindness in granting *botellas* became a public shame. With the establishment of this system the chiefs of the Administrative Departments lost their moral strength, . . . and the administration in general returned to the corrupt practices of Colonial times.[32]

Although this account is biased, it shows clearly that the Cuban politicians provided the original impulse for the alleged evil system. Antonio San Miguel, former owner and editor of *La Lucha*, in discussing *botellas* stated:

---

[31] Trelles, *El progreso y el retroceso de la república de Cuba*, p. 9. Dr. Trelles, in an interview granted the writer, admitted that this statement was too strong. He agreed that the evil of *botellas* had existed from the early Colonial period, but contended that the earlier *botellas* were small ones and that Magoon had introduced the five-gallon variety.

[32] Martínez Ortiz, *Cuba*, II, 487-88.

I have no knowledge of the existence of the *botella* during the administration of President Palma, nor was it known during the governorship of Mr. Magoon. The *botella* came into existence just as soon as General Gómez became President. It was then that the *botella* was created to pay off political favours promised to his associate workers.[33]

It seems clear that *botellas* or sinecures existed in Cuba under Spanish rule, and the custom of awarding easy or soft jobs has not been limited to that country. Magoon awarded *botellas*, but data do not exist to show the number granted or the persons holding such positions. He found that the easiest and quickest way to quiet a revolutionary spirit or to get a prominent undesirable person out of the country was to give him a *botella*. It will be recalled that General Faustino Guerra was appointed Major-General of the army and sent to the United States and France to secure his military training.[34] The granting of *botellas* may have been essential to the policy of keeping Cuba quiet, but it was a mistake. It has enabled Cuban politicians in recent years to excuse inefficiency and corruption on the ground that Magoon introduced and used the *botella*. Magoon and the United States officials in Washington should have known that Cuban memory of any United States administrative impropriety would not soon be forgotten.

The charge that the provisional governor granted entirely too many pardons has been briefly discussed.[35] On this score one of the ablest and most severe critics of the Magoon administration said, "the industry of pardons had its beginning then, 1140 being granted during his two years of government, the greater part for common crimes."[36] Martínez Ortiz criticized Magoon for granting too many pardons, and stated that as a

[33] Antonio San Miguel to the author, July 17, 1934.
[34] Cf. *supra*, p. 145.
[35] Cf. *supra*, pp. 94-96.
[36] Trelles, *El progreso y el retroceso de la república de Cuba*, p. 9.

result crime increased and Cuba presented a poor record of law enforcement to the world. Manuel Secades and Fernando Ortiz also took the Magoon administration to task for granting too many pardons.[37] Magoon in defending his record pointed out that an average of 2092 persons a year had benefited from amnesty decrees and pardons under the United States military government, while only 648 persons a year received executive clemency during the first two years of the Estrada Palma government, and that during his two years in office the annual average was reduced to 555.[38] The figures given by Magoon and his critics do not distinguish between pardons and commutations nor do they draw a line between those pardoned and those freed under amnesty laws. Regardless of previous averages and distinctions between pardons and amnesties, the evidence indicates that Magoon was probably too generous with his pardoning power for the welfare of Cuba.[39]

The fact that Magoon may have granted too many pardons does not admit that he or other governmental officials sold pardons or accepted bribes. However, it does indicate that he and his assistants did not thoroughly investigate all applications. Some of the Cuban attorneys and political chiefs conducted pardon "rackets" and the chances are that they were well paid for their services. On this point Antonio San Miguel stated:

---

[37] Martínez Ortiz, *Cuba*, II, 399; *Cuba*, Havana, January 27, 1909; Ortiz, "La decadencia cubana," *Revista bimestre cubana*, XIX (Enero-Febrero, 1924), 94.

Special pardon pleas were made for veterans, but they received no consideration as a class. Manuel Secades and Horacio Díaz Pardo, *La justicia en Cuba; los veteranos y los indultos, passim*.

[38] Magoon, *Report*, II, 89-94.

[39] Apparently Magoon's kindness served as a precedent or else he did not issue enough pardons or grant them to the right people. On March 6, 1909, President Gómez signed the "jail delivery bill" which released some 800 prisoners, including Masso Parra who had planned the revolt of 1907. This bill covered practically all crimes except those which involved rape or the death penalty. Chapman, *op. cit.*, pp. 529-30; *The Cuba Review*, March 1909, p. 10.

It is possible that many of the promoters of those pardons received money as an expression of appreciation from the people pardoned. Everybody in Cuba knew of political offices which were dedicated to the securing of amnesties by exerting their political influence in favor of the members of their own party or their friends. We suppose that such offices collected professional fees for their services.[40]

Had the provisional government investigated these "political offices" and carefully inquired into every application for pardon, it seems likely that fewer pardons would have been granted.

Pardon applications were investigated by the Department of Justice, headed by Manuel Landa, who was advised by Colonel E. H. Crowder. These men prepared all necessary papers for the provisional governor to sign. They may have failed to investigate thoroughly the hundreds of pardon applications, but this neglect does not convict them or Magoon of accepting bribes or of being accomplices of the Cuban politicians. The honesty and reputation of Crowder and Landa have not been questioned. The blame for issuing too many pardons, as in the case of the patronage, should not be directed entirely at the provisional administration, but in part to those Cuban leaders who recommended clemency and to the policy of the United States which temporized and compromised while keeping Cuba quiet.

Criticisms have also been made with reference to the construction and repair projects of the provisional government. This work was carried on by the Department of Public Works and through contracts awarded to Cuban and United States firms. Complaints were made that the contracts were not honestly awarded and that United States firms were unduly

---

[40] San Miguel to the author, July 17, 1934.

favored.[41] On April 17, 1908, the *Havana Post* voiced the criticism by asking Governor Magoon if he was going to award the big road contract in Pinar del Río to Cuban or United States contractors. This paper advocated that road contracts be given to Cubans and to citizens of the United States resident in Cuba and opposed their award to non-resident profiteers. In the case in question Cuban contractors had submitted the lowest bids on some sections, but Oliver & Company of Knoxville, Tennessee, had submitted the lowest average bid on all sections. Accordingly, Governor Magoon awarded the job to Oliver & Company and saved the Republic of Cuba $49,000.[42]

A typical criticism of "Mr. Magoon's contracts" is the following extract from an editorial by Luis M. Pérez, editor of *La Opinión Cubana:*

> Many of these contracts were made in the most informal not to say immoral manner, and gave rise to much scandal and to the complete discredit of the Provisional Administration. They cost the Cuban Treasury vast sums, and it is the general impression that in many cases the execution of the work was deficient.[43]

In this case the author was referring to the Havana and Cienfuegos contracts which have been fully discussed. He neglected to state that the contracts originated with Wood and Estrada Palma and not with Magoon, and he offers no proof in support of the statement that there was so much scandal that the provisional administration was completely discredited.

Some critics have made much of the fact that several United States firms cancelled their contracts after the provisional government withdrew. The inference was that the

---

41 *Havana Post,* April 17, 1908; *La Opinión Cubana,* August 1, 1909.

42 *Havana Post,* April 24, 1908.

43 *La Opinión Cubana,* August 1, 1909.

contracts were based on "profound immoralities" which the Gómez government would not tolerate.[44] Now that we can compare the Gómez and Magoon administrations the reasoning seems false. The reason for the cancellation of the contracts probably was that United States business men would not put their money into foreign projects unless they were certain of their pay and assured of peaceful working conditions. They no doubt recalled the experiences of McGivney and Rokeby with the Estrada Palma government.[45] San Miguel in discussing this matter states, "We should suppose that the contracts were given honorably and [that] almost all of them went to Cuban contractors who for some years had had experience in that kind of work." [46] In the absence of proof the assumption must be that the contracts were fairly awarded and that there was no discrimination against Cubans. The historian Martínez Ortiz states that there was talk of fraud, but admits that there is no proof.[47]

The quality of the roads constructed by the provisional government was also questioned. Trelles seems to class all roads built by Magoon as "waste." [48] On the other hand Martínez Ortiz admits that Magoon should be congratulated on his public works program.[49] Another writer stated that Magoon's greatest accomplishment in Cuba was the construction of "macadamized roads built on the most approved modern principles." [50] Chapman in discussing this point noted that "precise evidence" was lacking and then he quoted a strong statement made to him by a citizen of the United States

---

[44] *La Discusión*, Havana, June 9, 1909.
[45] Cf. *supra*, 117. See also Chapman, *op. cit.*, pp. 270 *et seq.*
[46] San Miguel, letter to writer, July 17, 1934.
[47] Martínez Ortiz, *Cuba*, II, 487.
[48] Trelles, *El progreso y el retroceso de la república de Cuba*, p. 9.
[49] Martínez Ortiz, *Cuba*, II, 487.
[50] DuPuy, "Road Building by the United States in Cuba," *Scientific American*, C-CI (February 13, 1909), 136.

who built one of the roads to the effect that the charges of corruption were untrue.[51]

Magoon knew that roads in Cuba would not last unless kept in repair and while he was provisional governor "flying gangs" were stationed at fifteen-mile intervals to make the necessary repairs from time to time. Gómez did not make the necessary repairs, and politics, rain, and the heavy *carretas* destroyed much of the provisional government's work.[52]

W. F. Johnson, author of *The History of Cuba,* summarily disposed of the whole question of contract frauds and poor roads when he stated that the roads were needed, that they were built, and that the results, generally speaking, were excellent.[53]

In closing this matter it should be said that most Cubans admit the achievements of the provisional administration in the field of public works. Evidences of work well done during the second intervention can be seen in Cuba today.

That the Magoon administration had its faults cannot be questioned. However, the faults have grown and have been magnified while the achievements have frequently been forgotten or obscured by prejudice and rumor. It is especially unfortunate that biased charges have been printed in Cuban school books and are taught as truths to innocent minds. One account describes the provisional government as follows:

The government of Mr. Magoon was very wasteful. He not only expended the whole public income each year, but he also spent twelve million dollars which he found in the treasury that had been economized by Don Tomás. Mr. Magoon was prodigal with pardons, and although he attended to the development of public works these were often not completed in due form. The

[51] Chapman, *op. cit.,* p. 244.
[52] *Ibid.,* p. 245.
[53] Johnson, *op. cit.,* IV, 286.

administration of Mr. Magoon left a bad memory and bad example in the country.[54]

A review of the evidence and the charges made against the provisional government shows that the criticisms concerning fiscal matters and public works are largely without merit. Some of the patronage and pardon charges are valid, but they have been exaggerated. The most serious charge and the one which underlies all others is the fact that the United States temporized and compromised in Cuba from the beginning and thus gave tone to the provisional government which followed.[55] On this point, most of the criticisms have been directed at Secretary Taft, Magoon's immediate superior. Taft had recommended that the insurgents be allowed to keep the horses they had stolen and that the government indemnify any owner who could produce a registered title. This action was construed by many Cubans to mean that the United States sanctioned horse stealing.[56] Luis M. Pérez, a bitter critic of the United States, blamed Taft for all the faults of the second intervention, stating that he legalized the theft of horses, violated the constitution and laws of Cuba, and ordered the awarding of illegal contracts.[57] The provisional government's policy of temporization and compromise gained order and contentment, but at the expense of future welfare and respect. No one person can fairly be blamed for this policy of temporization and compromise. The responsibility belongs to all who had a part in bringing on and conducting the second intervention.

The personal attacks made on Governor Magoon are

---

[54] Chapman, *op. cit.*, p. 231, quoting Ramiro Guerra, *Historia elemental de Cuba*, pp. 243-44.
[55] Irene A. Wright, *op. cit.*, pp. 181-82.
[56] Cf. *supra*, pp. 66-67.
[57] *La Opinión Cubana*, September 1, 1909.

varied and include venal corruption and dishonesty. Trelles stated that:

> The American Governor . . . profoundly corrupted the Cuban nation, and on account of his venality was looked upon with contempt by the honorable element of the Great North American Confederation, where he died a short time ago completely obscured and repudiated.[58]

This opinion is obviously biased, but it is typical of the views held by some Cubans today. Magoon's reputation in Cuba is further proof of the statement that the truth is often not as important as what people believe to be the truth. Another Cuban critic said that Magoon was "pliant" and a "man of wax." [59] This charge was probably based on the fact that Magoon was agreeable, easy-going, and kind. He tried to placate all factions and, as is usually the case, failed to win the wholehearted support of any. That he had independence and determination is clear from the way he dealt with the telephone companies and the Cienfuegos contractors, yet he reversed his own decree and appeared to Cubans to have meekly followed orders from Washington.[60]

In judging Magoon's record as provisional governor it should be remembered that he was placed in the difficult and at times impossible position of administering a civil government satisfactory to both Cubans and officials in Washington.[61] He continued the Taft policy of keeping Cuba quiet and in so doing subjected himself to all the criticisms of the

---

[58] Trelles, *El progreso y el retroceso de la república de Cuba*, p. 9. Many Cubans criticize Magoon because he was a foreigner who used foreign methods.

[59] Barbarrosa, *op. cit.*, p. 88.

[60] Many Cubans felt that Magoon as head of the Cuban government should have championed Cuban rights and should have resigned in protest when forced to take orders from Washington. Interviews with Dr. Francisco de Paula Coronado and Dr. Emilio Roig de Leuchsenring.

[61] The provisional governor was under the supervision of the United States War Department. Cf. *supra*, p. 78.

system with which he was associated. Martínez Ortiz admitted that Magoon has been judged too severely and stated that his bad points have been overemphasized while his good ones have been ignored.[62]

Some Cubans profess to believe that Magoon was a poor obscure law clerk before he arrived in Havana and state that he left Cuba a wealthy man. It is intimated that he secured a commission when he purchased the Church property for Cuba. He is supposed to have received "rake-offs" for granting a franchise for the extension of the Havana Electric Railway lines, and for authorizing the $16,500,000 loan.[63] Such accusations must be mentioned, but it should be noted that those who make and entertain such charges fail to offer any evidence to substantiate them.

When Magoon left Lincoln, Nebraska, in 1899 for Washington he was worth approximately $100,000.[64] In 1904 before going to Panama, Magoon made a will in which he listed property to the value of $100,000.[65] His private fortune upon his arrival in Cuba was about the same as it had been in 1904.[66] As governor of Cuba, Magoon saved about $10,000 on a salary of $1,400 a month. This saving was in part effected through the loyal and efficient services of his aid, Captain J. A. Ryan. Captain Ryan, now Brigadier-General Ryan, wrote of Magoon's honesty and finances as follows:

I handled all his money while I was his aide and for four months after we returned to the United States. I had charge of his bank account, knew where every dollar came from and how it was expended. Had there been any graft money I would have known it. There was none. Governor Magoon was so careful

[62] Martínez Ortiz, *Cuba*, II, 481.
[63] Cf. *supra*, pp. 74, 142, 106-7, 203.
[64] John T. Dorgan to the author, September 6, 1934.
[65] Interview with R. J. Flick, executor of Magoon's estate.
[66] *Ibid.*

that he would not take as a souvenir from the old palace an old piece of Sheffield plate which was afterwards thrown out as unfit for a palace. Magoon was honesty personified. He was loyal to his friends and to his principles and he never sacrificed either.[67]

While in Cuba Magoon purchased two hundred shares of Havana Electric Railway common stock then selling at about fifteen dollars a share. That was a legitimate purchase and with his salary was all Magoon ever acquired in Cuba.[68]

Magoon's income in retirement was less than $5,000 per year. He worried about expenses for he did not feel that he could return to the practice of law.[69] Robert J. Flick of Beverly Hills, California, a man Magoon and his mother had aided as a boy in Nebraska, gave Magoon some $31,500 worth of preferred stock and $12,500 worth of common stock in his company. The preferred stock paid 8 per cent interest but the common stock paid no dividends. During the last three or four years of his life Magoon received $300 a month from Flick. When Magoon died on January 14, 1920, he left an estate of $86,595.04, approximately $15,000 less than he had when he went to Cuba.[70]

There is nothing to support the charge that Magoon was discredited in the United States and abandoned by Roosevelt and Taft because of his poor record in Cuba. Roosevelt's opinion of Magoon and his service is clearly stated in the following letter:

Now that your term of service under me has come to an end, I wish to thank you for all that you have done in the different

[67] General J. A. Ryan to the author, September 4, 1934.

[68] Chapman, *op. cit.*, p. 233.

[69] Magoon's robust health had been impaired by tropical service in Panama and Cuba. Interviews with Robert J. Flick and Archibald Runner.

[70] Conference with Robert J. Flick. Magoon and his mother took care of Flick as a boy for more than fifteen years and gave him his start in life. Flick proved worthy and grateful. He served as executor of Magoon's estate. About $60,000 was paid to Magoon's relatives. The balance, less debts and funeral expenses, went to Flick to repay him for sums he had advanced.

positions of the highest responsibility and importance which you have filled while I was President. You are one of the men to whom this country owes much for the work that has been done during the past seven years. You have filled with singular credit positions where the work was as delicate and difficult as it was useful and honorable. I thank you and congratulate you. I can not too highly state the service you have rendered.[71]

On June 5, 1909, President Taft, who had been Magoon's superior during the greater part of his stay in Cuba, submitted the provisional governor's final report to the Senate and House of Representatives. In his letter of transmittal he said:

I think it only proper to take this opportunity to say that the administration by Governor Magoon of the government of Cuba from 1906 to 1909 involved the disposition and settlement of many very difficult questions and required on his part the exercise of ability and tact of the highest order. It gives me much pleasure to note in this public record the credit due to Governor Magoon for his distinguished service.[72]

It is true that Taft and Magoon disagreed about certain Cuban policies and that Taft did not make him Secretary of War in his Cabinet, but that does not prove that Magoon was "discredited" by the United States or by Taft. Taft may not have had a free hand in the selection of his Cabinet and aside from this it is doubtful if Magoon was physically fit to accept a Cabinet post in March, 1909, had one been offered. Furthermore, it appears that Mrs. Taft, who greatly influenced her husband's decisions, did not like Magoon. It seems that she felt that Magoon should have gone to the Philippines in 1906, where he had been ordered by Taft before Roosevelt

[71] Theodore Roosevelt to Magoon, February 4, 1909. *Magoon Papers.*
[72] Magoon, *Report*, III, 3.

and Root sent him to Cuba, and that Taft's former private secretary and choice for provisional governor, Beekman Winthrop, should have gone to Cuba. Regardless of this, Taft offered to give Magoon a Philippine appointment in 1909, but Magoon, who preferred service in the United States to the tropics, declined for reasons of health.[73] It should be remembered that Magoon was not an army officer or a member of the diplomatic corps. He was a special type of executive agent and when his duties in Cuba under Roosevelt were finished there was no reason for the new President to employ him unless his services were needed.

In the late spring of 1909 Magoon sailed for Europe to secure rest and medical treatment. Before he left the United States President Taft gave him a letter of introduction addressed to all Diplomatic and Consular offices of the United States. In this letter Taft stated that Magoon was "his warm personal friend." [74] Magoon spent several months in Europe where he was received by the president of France and other notables. He consulted physicians in France and Germany and took a series of bath treatments in the latter country. On his visit to England he was greatly impressed by the debates in the House of Commons.[75] Late in 1909 he returned to the United States and after visiting in Lincoln, Nebraska, made his home in Washington, D. C., where he first lived at the Marlborough and then at the Metropolitan Club. In Washington Magoon led a quiet life and enjoyed the friendship of a large group of prominent people. He frequently visited the Roosevelts at Oyster Bay, and when Woodrow Wilson became President, Magoon was among those in Washington who were usually invited to the various White House re-

---

[73] Interviews with Robert J. Flick and Archibald Runner.

[74] Taft to Diplomatic and Consular offices of the United States, May 11, 1909. *Magoon Papers.*

[75] Interview with Robert J. Flick; Dr. Charles E. Magoun to the author, September 30, 1934.

ceptions.[76] On January 12, 1920, he underwent an operation for acute appendicitis; this resulted in his death two days later.[77]

A host of tributes to Magoon's honesty and integrity could be given.[78] Manuel Landa, president of the civil section of the *audiencia* of Havana, wrote in defense of his former chief as follows:

> I became acquainted with Mr. Magoon upon his first arrival in Cuba and was, during all his stay in this Island, in most cordial and intimate relations with him, both socially and officially, at all times and under all circumstances finding him correct and upright in all his actions and the soul of honor. It gives me great pleasure to assure you of the absolute falsity of any and all rumors to the contrary. His actions were always open and above reproach, as far as his personal honesty was concerned.
>
> Immediately following a revolution Mr. Magoon occupied a very difficult position, treating most successfully with many different elements and divergent interests, and his memory should be honored by all Americans as well as all Cuban citizens.
>
> After leaving Cuba, I had the pleasure of meeting Mr. Magoon in Washington on various occasions, and found him living in a most simple way, apparently lacking many of the comforts and some necessities of life. This I mention as bearing out my intimate knowledge of the man's absolute honesty and straightforwardness.[79]

Another prominent Cuban stated:

> I repeat that Governor Magoon lived in the *Palacio de la Plaza de Armas* in a simple and honest manner. The "Palacio" was open

---

[76] Dr. Charles E. Magoun to the author, September 30, 1934. Invitations from President and Mrs. Roosevelt and President and Mrs. Wilson to Judge Charles E. Magoon. *Magoon Papers.*

[77] *Washington Post,* January 14, 1920; *New York Times,* January 15, 1920.

[78] For an account of Magoon's early life, his work as Law Officer, and his services in Panama, cf. *supra,* pp. 73-77.

[79] Manuel Landa to Ambassador E. H. Crowder, March 25, 1925. *Crowder Papers.*

to everybody; the Governor could be seen at all hours . . . Magoon left Cuba as clean of soul as when he arrived on the Island. A man without vice, modest, extremely modest; he returned to Washington and there he lived as poorly as before being Provisional Governor of Cuba. He died poor and therefore all the calumnies of which he has been accused are absolutely false. His life in Washington is known by every body there. In Cuba he had no social life; he never visited the theatres nor recreation places. All of his luxury was reduced to a modest automobile in which he rode two hours daily outside of the city.[80]

A tribute to Magoon and to Enoch H. Crowder by a co-worker, Judge Otto Schoenrich, an eminent lawyer and writer, reads as follows:

During the entire intervention I was next to Magoon as Secretary and Chief of Office and I certainly would have noticed if anything improper had been going on. Nothing ever happened which could have raised the slightest suspicion. Moreover, all his more important decrees were passed on by Colonel Crowder who was also the soul of honesty.[81]

One of Magoon's best friends in the United States was General John J. Pershing. The men grew up together and Magoon was best man at Pershing's wedding. If any man knew Magoon's private and personal life, Pershing did. In 1924 General Pershing heard that Magoon's honesty had been questioned and at once defended the name of his deceased friend in the following vigorous terms:

. . . I am horrified at what you say with reference to these insinuations about Magoon. I do not believe one solitary word of it. In fact, I suppose I knew Charlie about as well as did any of his friends, and I know as well as I know anything that he was as honest as the day is long.

---

[80] Antonio San Miguel to the author, July 17, 1934.
[81] Otto Schoenrich to the author, July 13, 1936.

So far as his having a fortune upon retirement from the Governorship is concerned, he accumulated what-ever he had long before he went to Cuba and, as I remember it, before he came to Washington. He was always thrifty and dealt to a certain extent in real estate, and I know that on one occasion he made something between $80,000 and $100,000 on one deal with a friend of his who is now dead. So all of this is unfair, unjust, and untrue, I believe, in every detail.

The whole thing makes me very furious as I know of no man who was a more sincere friend and patriot, or more devoted to the service of his country than was Governor Magoon, and I do not believe that he was ever capable of doing a dishonest thing.[82]

In another letter at a later date General Pershing said of Magoon:

He was a man of strong character and great ability and throughout his distinguished career in public life rendered efficient and devoted service to his country. I could not speak too highly of him.[83]

A study of Magoon's life and work and a consideration of the many statements made about him will convince one that he was neither dishonest nor discredited.

Magoon did not claim all the credit for the accomplishments of the provisional government. In his second annual report he devoted six pages to thanking and commending those who had assisted him in administering the government of Cuba. He gave special commendation to the supervisors of the executive departments and mentioned in detail the services of Colonel Enoch H. Crowder, Major Frederick S. Foltz, Major Blanton Winship, Captain J. A. Ryan, Judge Otto Schoenrich, and Frank Steinhart.[84] On numerous occa-

---

[82] John J. Pershing to Ambassador E. H. Crowder, September 16, 1924. *Crowder Papers.*

[83] John J. Pershing to Robert J. Flick, May 18, 1934.

[84] Magoon, *Report*, II, 147-53.

sions, at Palace gatherings, at banquets, at dedications, and through the press he expressed his sincere appreciation to the many patriotic Cubans who coöperated with him in discharging his difficult duties as provisional governor.

It is impossible to pass a final judgment on the second United States intervention in Cuba. The success or failure of the provisional government cannot be judged by the record made by the military government nor can Magoon be compared with Wood. The two men were opposite types. Wood was a soldier and administered a military government in Cuba under the United States flag. Magoon was a civilian charged with governing Cuba under its own flag and constitution.

Considering the historical background and the traits of the Cubans and their lack of experience in self-government it is safe to say that a military government could ordinarily accomplish more and command greater respect than a civil government. Cubans today have a greater respect for Wood than for Magoon. Wood is associated with their struggle for independence. He wrought great improvements in Cuba, was stern, and ruled with an iron hand. His achievements were praised by Estrada Palma, who attempted to carry on where Wood left off. Magoon was not a military hero, and he was kind and easy with the Cubans. Where Wood ordered something done, Magoon made requests.[85] Magoon's achievements were belittled by Gómez, and many of his roads, bridges, and other improvements were allowed to fall into decay. Both Wood and Magoon failed to teach the Cubans how to govern themselves, both have their critics, and both deserve credit for their accomplishments in the fields of public order, sanitation, education, and public works.

In retrospect it is clear that President Roosevelt was reluctant to intervene in Cuba in September, 1906. In fact

---

[85] Irene A. Wright, *op. cit.*, pp. 191-92.

intervention was not granted when requested by Estrada Palma, but was delayed until compromise plans had failed and the Cuban government had resigned. It is a matter of opinion, but the author is inclined to the view that the Taft and Bacon Peace Commission made a mistake by not supporting the Estrada Palma government, thereby avoiding formal intervention. Estrada Palma was an able and sincere patriot and he had a statesmanlike program under way when circumstances forced his resignation. What he could and would have done had he been maintained in office by the United States will always be a matter of conjecture. It is interesting to note that in 1917, during the February Revolution which was very similar to the August Revolution of 1906, the United States supported President Menocal and refused to take over the Cuban government.[86]

When Roosevelt became convinced that intervention in Cuba was the only practicable solution, the provisional government was established and in the face of many obstacles the affairs of the island were administered in an able manner for twenty-eight months. Peace was restored, order was maintained, all kinds of public improvements were made, and new laws were drafted and put into force. Most important of all, however, was the fact that the Cuban people, who had lost their government through corruption and rebellion, received it back on a working basis. The United States, by withdrawing from the island in 1909, lived up to the original meaning of the Platt Amendment and kept faith with a sister republic.[87]

---

[86] Cf. *supra,* pp. 60-61; Chapman, *op. cit.,* pp. 362 *et seq.*

[87] On May 5, 1910, Roosevelt in making a speech in Christiania, Norway, stated that he had been told by many European diplomats that the United States would not withdraw from Cuba in 1902, and after having withdrawn then, the same diplomats told him that the promise of withdrawal made in September 1906 would not be kept. Roosevelt said that he had told them that the promise would be kept and he emphasized to his audience that the promise had been kept in the letter and in the spirit. Lawrence F. Abbott, *Impressions of Theodore Roosevelt,* pp. 128-30.

Selected Bibliography

Cuban and United States works are listed separately under the following headings: Bibliographies, Government Publications, Manuscripts, Histories and Monographs, Pamphlets, Newspapers, Magazines, and Special Articles.

I. BIBLIOGRAPHIES

A. CUBAN

TRELLES, CARLOS MANUEL, *Biblioteca histórica cubana.* 3 Vols. (Contains illustrations and critical notes.) Matanzas, Cuba. I: 1922; II: 1924; and III: Habana, 1926.

B. UNITED STATES

GRIFFIN, A. P. C., Compiler, "Books Relating to Cuba," in Quesada, Gonzalo de, *Cuba* (Handbook of the International Bureau of the American Republics). Washington: Government Printing Office, 1905.

II. GOVERNMENT PUBLICATIONS

A. CUBAN

BEVANS, JAMES L., and CERICE, LUCAS ALVAREZ, *Report of the Hospitals and the National Insane Asylum of the Republic of Cuba, 1909.* Havana: Seoane y Alvarez, 1909.

Cámara de representantes. Memoria de los trabajos realizados (tercer período congresional, 1906–1908). Habana: Rambla y Bouza, 1902–.

SELECTED BIBLIOGRAPHY

Cámara de representantes. Mensajes presidenciales, remitidos al congreso, durante los siete períodos congresionales, transcunidos desde el veinte de mayo de mil novecientos dos, hasta el primero de abril de mil novecientos diez y siete, e indice correlative y por materias de los mismos. Vol. I, Habana.

Censo de la república de Cuba bajo la administración provisional de los Estados Unidos 1907 (Victor H. Olmsted, Director). Washington: Oficino del censo de los Estados Unidos, 1908.

Comisión consultiva agraria: memoria de sus trabajos. Habana: Manuel Ruiz S. en C., 1908.

Constitución de la república de Cuba. Habana: Rambla y Bouza, 1910.

Diario de sesiónes de la convención constituyente de la isla de Cuba. Habana: 1901.

Diario de sesiónes de la comisión consultiva. 4 Vols. Habana: 1908 y 1916.

Gaceta oficial de la república. Habana: 1902–.

MAGOON, CHARLES E., *Report of Provisional Administration: From October 13th, 1906 to December 1st, 1907.* (Also contains the reports of the secretaries of the various executive departments.) Havana: Rambla and Bouza, 1908. See also *Senate Document No. 155.*

————, *Report of Provisional Administration: From December 1st, 1907 to December 1st, 1908.* (Also contains the reports of the secretaries of the various executive departments.) Havana: Rambla and Bouza, 1909. See also *House Document No. 1457.*

————, *Report of Provisional Administration: From December 1st, 1908 to January 29th, 1909.* See *Senate Document No. 80.*

Memoria de la administración del presidente de la república de Cuba, Mayor General José Miguel Gómez, durante el período comprendido entre el 28 de enero y el 31 de diciembre de 1909. Habana: Rambla y Bouza, 1910.

Report of the Hospitals and the National Insane Asylum of the Republic of Cuba, 1909. (Contains Reports of James L. Bevans and Lucas Alvarez Cerice.) Havana: Seoane y Alvarez, 1909.

Republic of Cuba, Under the Provisional Government of the United States, Decrees, 1906–1909. 9 Vols. Havana: Rambla and Bouza. (The official laws, decrees, and proclamations of the provisional governor selected from the *Gaceta oficial de la república,* and printed in English and Spanish.)

226

Senado. Memoria de los trabajos realizados durante las cuarto legis-laturas y sesión extraordinaria del primer período congresional, 1902–1904. Habana: Rambla y Bouza, 1918.

B. UNITED STATES

Congressional Record: Containing the Proceedings and Debates of . . . Congress of the United States of America. Washington: Government Printing Office, 1874–.

House Document No. 2 (Fifty-sixth Congress, second session). "Civil Report of Major General Leonard Wood, Military Governor of Cuba, 1900." 8 Vols. Washington. [Wood's report for 1901, 9 Vols., n. p., n. d.; and the report for 1902, 6 Vols., was published privately in Baltimore, n. d.]

House Document No. 2 (Fifty-seventh Congress, first session). "Annual Reports of the War Department for the Fiscal Year Ended June 30, 1901." Vol. II. Washington: Government Printing Office, 1901.

House Document No. 2 (Fifty-seventh Congress, second session). "Report of the Secretary of War and Reports of Bureau Chiefs." Vol. I. Washington: Government Printing Office, 1903.

House Document No. 2 (Fifty-ninth Congress, second session). "Annual Reports of the War Department for the Fiscal Year Ended June 30, 1906." Vol. I. Washington: Government Printing Office, 1907.

House Document No. 1457 (Sixtieth Congress, second session). "Annual Report of Charles E. Magoon, Provisional Governor of Cuba, to the Secretary of War 1908." Washington: Government Printing Office, 1909.

Letter of Transmittal By the Secretary of War, With Inclosures, as to the Church Property in Habana, Cuba. "Report of Charles E. Magoon, Provisional Governor of Cuba, on the Contract Dated October 23, 1901, Between the Military Government of Cuba and the Roman Catholic Church for the Purchase of Certain Properties Situate in the City of Havana, Republic of Cuba." Washington: Government Printing Office, 1907.

MAGOON, CHARLES E., *Report on the Law of Civil Government in Territory Subject to Military Occupation by the Military Forces of the United States.* Washington: Government Printing Office, 1902.

MALLOY, WILLIAM M., "Treaties, Conventions, International Acts, Protocols, and Agreements between the United States of America and Other Powers, 1776–1909," *Senate Document No. 357* (Sixty-first

Congress, second session), 2 Vols. Washington: Government Printing Office, 1910.

Monthly Consular and Trade Reports, 1906–1909 (Published by Department of Commerce and Labor, Bureau of Manufactures). Washington: Government Printing Office, 1906–1909.

MOORE, JOHN BASSETT, *A Digest of International Law as Embodied in Diplomatic Discussions, Treaties and other International Agreements, International Awards, the Decisions of Municipal Courts, and the Writings of Jurists, and Especially in Documents, Published and Unpublished. Issued by the Presidents and Secretaries of State of the United States, the Opinions of the Attorneys-General, and the Decisions of Courts, Federal and State.* 8 Vols. Washington: Government Printing Office, 1906.

OLMSTED, VICTOR H., and GANNETT, HENRY, Compilers, *Cuba: Population, History, and Resources, 1907.* Washington: United States Bureau of the Census, 1909.

Papers Relating to the Foreign Relations of the United States, 1906–1907. Pt. 1. Washington: Government Printing Office, 1909.

Papers Relating to the Foreign Relations of the United States, 1907. Washington: Government Printing Office, 1910.

Papers Relating to the Foreign Relations of the United States, 1908. Washington: Government Printing Office, 1912.

QUESADA, GONZALO DE, *Cuba.* (Handbook of the International Bureau of the American Republics). Washington: Government Printing Office, 1905.

RICHARDSON, J. D., *A Compilation of the Messages and Papers of the Presidents, 1789–1908.* 11 Vols. Washington: Government Printing Office, 1908.

Senate Document No. 105 (Fifty-eighth Congress, second session). "Compilation of the Acts of Congress, Treaties and Proclamations, Relating to Insular and Military Affairs, from March 4, 1897 to March 3, 1903." Washington: Government Printing Office, 1904.

Senate Document No. 155 (Sixtieth Congress, first session). "Annual Report of Charles E. Magoon, Provisional Governor of Cuba to the Secretary of War, 1907." Washington: Government Printing Office, 1908.

Senate Document No. 80 (Sixty-first Congress, first session). "Message from the President of the United States Transmitting a Communication from the Acting Secretary of War, Submitting a Supplemental Report, with Accompanying Papers, of Honorable Charles E. Magoon, Provisional Governor of Cuba for the Period from December 1, 1908 to January 29, 1909." Washington: Government Printing Office, 1909.

Senate Document No. 822 (Sixty-first Congress, third session). "Yellow Fever." Washington: Government Printing Office, 1911.

Statutes at Large of the United States, Concurrent Resolutions of the Two Houses of Congress, and Recent Treaties, Conventions, and Executive Proclamations. (Published by Authority of the Secretary of State.) Washington: Government Printing Office, 1856–.

TAFT, W. H., and BACON, ROBERT, *Cuban Pacification.* (Excerpt from the Report of the Secretary of War, 1906.) Washington: Government Printing Office, 1907.

The Establishment of Free Government in Cuba. (Compiled by the Bureau of Insular Affairs, War Department.) Washington: Government Printing Office, 1904.

III. MANUSCRIPTS

Many government files of Cuban and United States bureaus covering the period of the second intervention are not yet open to investigators. Much of the private correspondence of the period has been lost or destroyed and the remainder is widely scattered.

Crowder Papers. The letters, papers, and books of Major General Enoch H. Crowder are in the Library of the University of North Carolina at Chapel Hill, N. C. This collection has not yet been classified and is restricted. For the period of this study it contains the Taft and Bacon and the Magoon reports, the *Decrees*, the R. Floyd Clarke, "Brief on the Havana Paving and Sewer Contract," and the T. B. Steele, "Abstract and Review of the Decisions on the 1908 Electoral Appeals." There are a few letters relating to Crowder's work as a member of the Advisory Law Commission and letters from General John J. Pershing, Brigadier General J. A. Ryan, Robert J. Flick, and others which discuss the character and reputation of Governor Magoon. The great bulk of the unpublished material in the collection concerning Cuba relates to United States-Cuban relations from 1919 to 1929.

Magoon Papers. Most of Charles E. Magoon's papers were destroyed shortly after his death. His Cuban reports, decrees, a scrapbook relating to his life as a lawyer in Lincoln, Nebraska, some photographs, decorations, commissions, and a few letters, chiefly of commendation, from Roosevelt, Taft, and others are in the possession of Robert J. Flick of Beverly Hills, California.

Roosevelt Papers. The collection in the Manuscript Division of the Library of Congress in Washington contains important letters, telegrams, and memorandums which deal with Cuban affairs during the period of the second intervention. The letters from Magoon to Roosevelt give the provisional governor's views and recommendations on Cuban problems. The telegrams deal chiefly with work of the Peace Commission and the establishment of the provisional government. The memorandums prepared by General George B. Davis and J. Will Charlton make the point that the President had the right to intervene in Cuba under the Platt Amendment without any action by Congress. These papers show that Roosevelt was forced to intervene in Cuba and that he was well informed on Cuban affairs.

Root Papers. Most of the letters, letter-books, and papers of Elihu Root, Sr., are in the Manuscript Division of the Library of Congress in Washington, D. C. This collection contains only a few letters relating to the second intervention, but they are significant as they give Mr. Root's views on the status of the provisional governor as a constitutional officer of Cuba, and show that he was consulted about the purchase of the Church property in Cuba.

Taft Papers. These papers are in the Manuscript Division of the Library of Congress in Washington, D. C. The collection does not contain the material one would expect by virtue of the fact that Taft was Magoon's immediate superior during practically all of the second intervention. However, there is ample data on the Peace Commission, and Taft's preference of Beekman Winthrop instead of Magoon for the post of provisional governor. Personal letters indicate that the Secretary of War and the provisional governor were quite friendly and that Magoon was in constant touch with Taft personally. The personal conferences between Taft, Magoon, Root, and others may explain the absence of written material dealing with the administration of Cuba.

IV. HISTORIES AND MONOGRAPHS

A. CUBAN

Barbarrosa, Enrique, *El proceso de la república, análisis de la situación política y económica de Cuba bajo el gobierno presidencial de Tomás Estrada Palma y José Miguel Gómez.* Habana: Imp. "Militar," 1911.

Cararallo Setelengo, F., *El imperialismo Norte Americano.* Habana: Imprenta "el Siglo XX," 1914.

Carrera Jústiz, F., *El derecho público y la autonomía municipal, el fraude de un régimen.* Habana: Imp. y Librería "La Moderna Poesía," 1913.

COLLAZO, ENRIQUE, *Cuba: intervenida*. Habana: C. Martínez y Ca., 1910.

————, *La revolución de agosto de 1906*. Habana: C. Martínez y Ca., 1907.

————, *Los Americanos en Cuba*. 2 Vols. Habana: C. Martínez y Ca., 1905.

CONTE, RAFAEL y JOSÉ M. CAPMANY, *Guerra de Razas*. Habana: Imp. Militar, 1912.

FIGUERAS, FRANCISCO, *La intervención y su política*. Habana: Avisador Commercial, 1906.

GARRIGO, ROQUE E., *La convulsión cubana*. Habana: Imprenta la Razón, 1906.

GUERRA Y SÁNCHEZ, RAMIRO, *Un cuarto de siglo de evolución cubana*. Habana: Librería "Cervantes" de R. Veloso, 1924.

HEVIA, AURELIO, *Colección de artículos y documentos referentes a la condición actual de Cuba*. Habana: 1909.

IZNAGA, R., *Tres años de república, 1902–1905*. Habana: Rambla y Bouza, 1905.

LEISCEA, JUAN M., *Historia de Cuba*, Habana: Librería "Cervantes" de R. Veloso, 1925.

LÓPEZ-HIDALGO, A. V., *Cuba y la enmienda Platt: relaciones políticas entre Cuba y los Estados Unidos da la América del Norte, derivadas del tratado permanente celebrado entre ambos pueblos*. Habana: Imprenta "El Siglo XX," 1921.

LOZANO CASADO, MIGUEL, *La personalidad del general José Miguel Gómez*. Habana: 1913.

MACHADO Y ORTEGA, LUIS, *La enmienda Platt: estudio de su alcance e interpretación y doctrina sobre su aplicación*. Habana: Imprenta "El Siglo XX," 1922.

MARTÍ, JOSÉ, *Obras completas*. 8 Vols. Habana: "La Prensa," 1918–1920.

MARTÍNEZ ORTIZ, RAFAEL, *Cuba: los primeros años de independencia*. 2 Vols. Tercera Edición. Paris: Le Livre Libre, 1924.

MEDEL, JOSÉ ANTONIO, *The Spanish-American War and Its Results*. Havana: P. Fernandez y Ca., 1932.

NAVAS, JOSÉ, *Cuba y los Estados Unidos boceto histórico sobre el eco de la causa cubana en la gran nación vecina*. Habana: P. Fernandez y Ca., 1916.

231

PARDO SUÁREZ, VICENTE, *La elección presidencial en Cuba.* Habana: Rambla, Bouza y Ca., 1923.

PÉREZ, MARINO LUIS (Compiler), *Newspaper Clippings Relative to the Period of the Administration of Cuba by the United States, September, 1906, to January, 1909.* 15 Vols. (In the Library of Congress, Washington.)

PURI, MANUEL C. (Editor), *La revolución de agosto: historia de un corresponsal por Arture F. Sainz de la Peña.* Habana: Imprenta "La Prueba," 1909.

RANDÍN, AMADO, *Cuba: reivindicada.* Habana: Imp. "Bolivar," 1907.

ROIG DE LEUCHSENRING, EMILIO, *El intervencionismo, mal de males de Cuba republicana.* San José de Costa Rica, A. C., Ediciones del "Repertorio Americano," 1931.

————, *La enmienda Platt: su interpretación primitiva y sus aplicaciones posteriores* (Anuario de 1922, Sociedad Cubana de Derecho Internacional). Habana: Imprenta "El Siglo XX," 1922.

SANTOVENIA, EMETERIO S., *Los presidentes de Cuba libre.* Habana: Seoane y Fernandez, 1930.

SECADES, MANUEL, *Patriotas y traidores.* 2 Vols. Habana: 1914.

————, and DÍAZ PARDO, HORACIO, *La justicia en Cuba; los veteranos y los indultos.* Habana: Imprenta "La Prueba," 1908.

SUÁREZ VERA, LUIS, *General Emilio Núñez: su historia revoluconaria y su actuacion en la vide publica.* Habana: 1915.

Tres años de Cuba libre; paz, prosperidad, y progreso, 1902–1905. Habana: Selama y Ca., 1905.

VARONA, ENRIQUE JOSÉ, *De la colonia a la república: selección de trabajos políticos ordenada por sus autor.* Habana: Sociedad Editoral Cuba Contemporánea, 1919.

————, *Mirando en torno.* Habana: Rambla y Bouza, 1910.

VELASCO, CARLOS DE, *Aspectos nacionales.* Habana: Librería "Studium," 1915.

————, *Estrada Palma: contribución historica.* Habana: "La Universal," 1911.

B. UNITED STATES

ABBOTT, LAWRENCE F., *Impressions of Theodore Roosevelt.* Garden City: Doubleday, Page and Company, 1923.

ALGER, R. A., *The Spanish-American War.* New York and London: Harper and Brothers, 1901.

SELECTED BIBLIOGRAPHY

ATKINS, EDWIN FARNSWORTH, *Sixty Years in Cuba*. Cambridge, Massachusetts: Riverside Press, 1926.

BEALS, CARLETON, *The Crime of Cuba*. Philadelphia and London: J. B. Lippincott Company, 1933.

BEMIS, SAMUEL FLAGG (Editor), *The American Secretaries of State and Their Diplomacy*. 10 Vols. New York: Alfred A. Knopf, 1927–1929.

BISHOP, JOSEPH BUCKLIN, *Theodore Roosevelt and His Time Shown in His Own Letters*. 2 Vols. New York: Charles Scribner's Sons, 1919, 1920.

BUELL, RAYMOND LESLIE, *et al.*, *Problems of the New Cuba: Report of the Commission on Cuban Affairs*. New York: Foreign Policy Association, Incorporated, 1935.

CALLAHAN, JAMES M., *Cuba and International Relations: A Historical Study in American Diplomacy*. Baltimore: The Johns Hopkins Press, 1899.

CHADWICK, FRENCH ENSOR, *The Relations of the United States and Spain: Diplomacy*. New York: Charles Scribner's Sons, 1909.

———, *The Relations of the United States and Spain: the Spanish-American War*. 2 Vols. New York: Charles Scribner's Sons, 1911.

CHAPMAN, CHARLES E., *A History of the Cuban Republic: A Study in Hispanic American Politics*. New York: The Macmillan Company, 1927.

CLARK, WILLIAM J., *Commercial Cuba: A Book for Business Men*. New York: Charles Scribner's Sons, 1898.

COOLIDGE, LOUIS A., *An Old-Fashioned Senator, Orville H. Platt, of Connecticut: The Story of a Life Unselfishly Devoted to the Public Service*. New York: G. P. Putnam's Sons, 1910.

Dictionary of American Biography. 20 Vols. Malone, Dumas, Editor (Under the Auspices of the American Council of Learned Societies). New York: Charles Scribner's Sons, 1928–1936.

DUFFY, HERBERT S., *William Howard Taft*. New York: Minton, Balch and Company, 1930.

FITZGIBBON, RUSSELL H., *Cuba and the United States: 1900–1935*. Menasha, Wisconsin: George Banta Publishing Company, 1936.

FORAKER, JOSEPH B., *Notes on a Busy Life*. 2 Vols. Cincinnati: Steward and Kidd Company, 1917.

GUGGENHEIM, HARRY F., *The United States and Cuba: A Study in International Relations*. New York: The Macmillan Company, 1934.

233

HAGEDORN, HERMANN, *Leonard Wood: A Biography.* 2 Vols. New York: Harper and Brothers, 1931.

HILL, HOWARD C., *Roosevelt and the Caribbean.* Chicago: The University of Chicago Press, 1927.

HINSDALE, MARY L., *A History of the President's Cabinet.* Ann Arbor: George Wahr, 1911.

JENKS, L. H., *Our Cuban Colony: A Study in Sugar.* New York: Vanguard Press, 1928.

JOHNSON, W. F., *The History of Cuba.* 5 Vols. New York: B. F. Buck and Company, Inc., 1920.

JONES, CHESTER LLOYD, *Caribbean Interests of the United States.* New York: D. Appleton and Company, 1916.

————, *The Caribbean Since 1900.* New York: Prentice-Hall, Inc., 1936.

LATANE, JOHN H., *America as a World Power, 1897–1907* (*The American Nation: A History*, Vol. XXV, edited by A. B. Hart). New York and London: Harper and Brothers, 1907.

LODGE, HENRY C., *Selections from the Correspondence of Theodore Roosevelt and Henry Cabot Lodge.* 2 Vols. New York: Charles Scribner's Sons, 1925.

MECHAM, J. LLOYD, *Church and State in Latin America: A History of Politico-Ecclesiastical Relations.* Chapel Hill: The University of North Carolina Press, 1934.

MUNRO, D. G., *The United States and the Caribbean Area.* Boston: World Peace Foundation, 1934.

NEARING, SCOTT and FREEMAN, JOSEPH, *Dollar Diplomacy: A Study in American Imperialism.* New York: The Viking Press, 1925.

PARKER, WILLIAM B. (Editor), *Cubans of To-day.* (Hispanic Society of America.) New York and London: G. P. Putnam's Sons, 1919.

PORTER, ROBERT P., *Industrial Cuba: Being a Study of Present Commercial and Industrial Conditions, with Suggestions as to the Opportunities Presented in the Island for American Capital, Enterprise, and Labor.* New York and London: G. P. Putnam's Sons, 1899.

ROBINSON, ALBERT G., *Cuba and the Intervention.* New York: Longmans, Green, and Company, 1905.

ROOSEVELT, THEODORE, *Autobiography* (Vol. XX of complete works). New York: Charles Scribner's Sons, 1926.

————, *The Rough Riders.* New York: Charles Scribner's Sons, 1899.

————————, *State Papers as Governor and President* (Vol. XV of complete works). New York: Charles Scribner's Sons, 1926.

Root Elihu, *The Military and Colonial Policy of the United States.* (Robert Bacon and James Brown Scott, Editors.) Cambridge, Massachusetts: 1916.

Rubens, Horatio S., *Liberty: The Story of Cuba.* New York: Brewer, Warren, and Putnam, Inc., 1932.

Scott, James Brown, *Robert Bacon: Life and Letters.* New York: Doubleday, Page and Company, 1923.

Stowell, Ellery C., *Intervention in International Law.* Washington: John Byrne and Company, 1921.

Strode, Hudson, *The Pageant of Cuba.* New York: Harrison Smith and Robert Haas, 1934.

Terry, Thomas P., *Terry's Guide to Cuba, Including the Isle of Pines.* Boston: Houghton Mifflin Company, 1929.

Wright, Irene A., *Cuba.* New York: The Macmillan Company, 1910.

Wright, Philip G., *The Cuban Situation and Our Treaty Relations.* Washington: The Brookings Institution, 1931.

Wright, Quincy, *The Control of American Foreign Relations.* New York: The Macmillan Company, 1922.

Wriston, Henry Merritt, *Executive Agents in American Foreign Relations.* Baltimore: Johns Hopkins Press, 1929.

V. PAMPHLETS

A. CUBAN

Carballal, Rodolfo Z., *El General José Miguel Gómez.* Habana: 1913.

Collazo, Enrique, *Cosas de Cuba: cuentas claras.* Habana: "La Universal" de Ruiz y Ca., 1913.

Coronado, Tomás, *Biografía del Dr. Carlos Finlay.* Habana: 1902.

Cuba Under the Presidential Administration of Major General José Miguel Gómez. (In English and Spanish.) Habana: Rambla y Bouza, 1911.

Hernández, Cartaya, Enrique, *La reforma del derecho público cubano.* Habana: Imprenta "El Siglo XX," 1919.

Hevia, Aurelio, *Discurso leído sobre la tumba del Coronel Manuel Sanguily, al conmemoratse el segundo aniversario de su muerte, el 23 de enero de 1927.* Habana: Impreso por la Asociacion Patriótica "Columna de Defensa Nacional," 1926.

ROIG DE LEUCHSENRING, EMILIO, *La colonia superviva: Cuba a los veintidós años de república.* Habana: Imprenta "El Siglo XX," 1925.

The Republic of Cuba in 1909: September. (In English and Spanish.) Habana: Rambla y Bouza, 1909.

TRELLES, CARLOS MANUEL, *El progreso (1902 a 1905) y el retroceso (1906 a 1922) de la república de Cuba.* Habana: Imprenta el Score, 1923.

VARELA ZEQUEIRA, EDUARDO, *La política en 1905.* Habana: Rambla y Bouza, 1905.

VARONA, ENRIQUE JOSÉ, *Mirando en torno.* Habana: Rambla y Bouza, 1910.

B. UNITED STATES

BUELL, RAYMOND LESLIE, *Cuba and the Platt Amendment.* Foreign Policy Association Information Service, New York: Vol. 5, No. 3 (April 17, 1929).

CLARKE, R. FLOYD, "The Havana Paving and Sewering Contract: Being the Documents Relating to the Contract between the Republic of Cuba and McGivney and Rokeby Construction Company" (Confidential brief by Counsel for the Company), *Crowder Papers.*

VI. NEWSPAPERS

A. CUBAN

Cuba (Havana)

Diario Español (Havana)

Diario de la Marina (Havana)

El Comercio (Havana)

El Liberal (Havana)

El Mundo (Havana)

El Triunfo (Havana)

Havana Daily Telegraph (Havana)

Havana Post (Havana)

La Discusion (Havana)

La Lucha (Havana)

SELECTED BIBLIOGRAPHY

B. UNITED STATES

New York Times (New York City)
New York World (New York City)
The Sun (New York City)
Washington Post (Washington, D. C.)

C. FOREIGN

The Star and Herald (Panama)
The Times (London)

VII. MAGAZINES

A. CUBAN

Cuba contemporánea
Cuban Interpreter
Cuba y América
El Fígaro
Import and Industrial Record of Cuba
La opinión cubana
Letras
Reforma Social
Revista bimestre cubana

B. UNITED STATES

Agricultural History
American Journal of International Law
Annals of the American Academy of Political and Social Science
Cuba Review
Harper's Weekly
Independent
Inter-America
Literary Digest
Lippincott's Magazine
McClure's Magazine
Monthly Bulletin of the International Bureau of the American Republics

237

SELECTED BIBLIOGRAPHY

The Nation
North American Review
Outlook
Review of Reviews
Scientific American
Scribner's Magazine
The Hispanic American Historical Review
World To-day

VIII. SPECIAL ARTICLES

A. CUBAN

Gómez, Juan Gualberto, "William McKinley, impresiones sobre su vida y su obras," *La Discusión*, Habana: September 19, 1901.

Guiral Moreno, Mario, "Nuestros problemas políticos, económicos y sociales," *Cuba contemporánea*, V (August, 1914), 401-24.

Hevia, Aurelio, "General Leonard Wood and Public Instruction in Cuba," *Inter-America*, IV (October, 1920), 3-16.

Lagomasino, Luis, "Mayor General Bartólomé Masó," *La Discusión*, Habana: February 24, 1915.

Lockmiller, David A., "La base legal de la intervención de los Estados Unidos en Cuba en 1906," *Revista bimestre cubana*, XXXVIII (Septiembre-Diciembre, 1936), 268-81.

"Mision en Cuba de los secretarios Taft y Bacon." *La Discusión*, Habana: December 18, 1906.

Ortiz, Fernando, "La decadencia cubana," *Revista bimestre cubana*, XIX (Enero-Febrero, 1924), 17-45.

Ríus Rivera, Juan, "Cuba y los Estados Unidos," *La Discusión*, Habana: November 19, 1901.

Sanguily, Manuel, "Estrada Palma y sus detractores," *La Discusión*, Habana: November 19, 1901.

Valdés Rodríguez, Manuel, "Epocs de la fundación de las principales instruciones de educación de Cuba," *Cuba y América*, April 22, 25, and 29, and May 2, 1908.

Varona, Enrique José, "El talon de Aquiles," *El Fígaro*, XXII (September 30, 1906), 490.

B. UNITED STATES

Bullard, Robert Lee, "The Cuban Negro," *North American Review*, CLXXXIV (March 15, 1907), 623-30.
238

SELECTED BIBLIOGRAPHY

CONANT, CHARLES ARTHUR, "Our Duty in Cuba," *North American Review*, CLXXXV (May 17, 1907), 141-46.

DuPUY, WILLIAM A., "Road Building by the United States in Cuba," *Scientific American*, C-CI (February 13, 1909), 136-37.

EARLE, F. S., "Agricultural Cuba," *The World To-day*, XI (November, 1906), 1175-84.

HEMMINGWAY, WILLIAM, "To-morrow in Cuba," *Harper's Weekly*, LIII (March 20, 1909), 25-28.

JOHNSON, SIR HARRY, "An Englishman's Impressions of American Rule in Cuba," *McClure's*, XXXIII (September, 1909), 496-504.

LOCKMILLER, DAVID A., "Agriculture in Cuba During the Second United States Intervention, 1906–1909," *Agricultural History*, XI (July, 1937), 181-88.

————, "The Advisory Law Commission of Cuba," *The Hispanic American Historical Review*, XVII (February, 1937), 2-29.

————, "The Settlement of the Church Property Question in Cuba," *The Hispanic American Historical Review*, XVII (November, 1937), 488-98.

MAGOON, CHARLES E., "The War Department: Administration of Civil Government," *Scribner's Magazine*, XXXIV (July, 1903), 85-95.

NIETO DE DURLAND, CARMELA, "Home Rule in Cuba Once More," *The World To-day*, XVI (March, 1909), 285-88.

ROWE, LEO STANTON, "The Reorganization of Local Government in Cuba," *Annals of the American Academy of Political and Social Science*, XXV (March, 1905), 311-21.

"The Restoration of the Cuban Government," Editorial, *American Journal of International Law*, III (April, 1909), 431-34.

WARD, L. B., "The Economical Surface Mining Operations of Cuba," *Scientific American*, XCVII (July 6, 1907), 11-13.

WEIGHTMAN, RICHARD C., "Cuba's American Governor," *Review of Reviews*, XXXIV (November, 1905), 556-59.

WOOD, LEONARD, "The Military Government of Cuba," *Annals of the American Academy of Political and Social Science*, XXI (March, 1903), 153-82.

WRIGHT, IRENE A., "The Cart-Roads of Mister Magoon," *The World To-day*, XVI (June, 1909), 641-46.

Index

Acosta, Angel José, 93.
Advisory Law Commission, 87, 98, 110, 146-73, 175.
Agramonte, J. Agustin, 93.
Agricultural League, 87, 125.
Agriculture, 6, 20, 80, 99, 122-25. See also Sugar.
Aguacate, 78.
Ainsworth, General, 46.
Alberdi, Nicolas, 186.
Alquízar, 78.
Annexation, Estrada Palma's views on, 18-19; Isle of Pines and, 22 n., 81; desired by Americans and Cubans, 36; various opinions on, 69; opposed by Roosevelt, 70; desired by foreigners in Cuba, 81; Roosevelt keeps promise concerning, 223 n. See also Platt Amendment, and Permanent Treaty.
Armed Forces, Law of, 167.
Army. See Army of Pacification, Rural Guard, Militia, and Insurgents.
Army of Pacification, 46, 65, 84, 144, 188.
Asbert, Ernesto, 37, 60, 67 n., 79, 95.
August Revolution, discussed, 33-63; standard of revolt raised in Pinar del Río, 34; progress of described by Peace Commission, 36-37; property of foreigners damaged by, 37; Estrada Palma refuses to compromise with leaders of, 39; denounced by Roosevelt, 44; leaders of negotiate with Peace Commissioners, 52-53; occasions intervention, 57; denounced by Cuban writers, 59-60; compared with February Revolution, 61, 223; men-

tioned by Roosevelt to Congress, 63; forces of surrender and disband, 64-68; disturbed economic conditions, 80-81, 126; expenses of, 89, 202; road program abandoned because of, 101; agriculture hurt by, 124; unemployment caused by, 129; disrupts school system, 133; caused by interference with municipalities, 154; occasions legal reform, 155, 164, 166, 167; caused by election frauds, 179, 185; political principles forgotten after, 204. See also Estrada Palma, Insurgents, and Liberal Party.
Aversa, Archbishop, 139, 140, 141, 143.

Bacon, A. O., 50.
Bacon, Robert, wire to Steinhart, 40; sent to Cuba as Peace Commissioner, 45; leaves Oyster Bay with Taft, 46; arrives in Havana, 51; suggests rules for truce, 52; confers with Cuban leaders, 53; conference with Estrada Palma, 55; aids Taft when Cuban government resigns, 56-57; in favor of upholding Estrada Palma, 60; returns to United States, 72; he and Taft thanked by Americans in Havana, 73. See also Taft, Root, and Roosevelt.
Bahía Honda, 24, 25 n.
Banks. See Finances and Treasury Department.
Baracoa, 111, 116.
Barber, Henry A., 82.
Barnet, Enrique B., 112.
Barnhardt, George C., 82.

241

Gómez, José Miguel (*Continued*)
member of patronage committee, 79;
pardons granted by, 95; Magoon
leaves obligations to, 111, 202; mentioned for presidency, 145; supporters
of wound Faustino Guerra, 145 n.;
leader and candidate of Miguelista
Liberals, 177; reaches agreement with
Zayas, 181; elected president, 182;
brief history of, 184-85; selects cabinet, 186; attends reception, 187;
makes agreement concerning U. S.
troops, 188; inaugurated as president,
191-92; replies to Magoon's address,
194-96; escorts Magoon to pier, 196;
contracts loan, 203; expenditures of,
204 n.; contracts cancelled under,
210-11; fails to repair roads, 212;
belittles Magoon's administration,
222. *See also* Estrada Palma, Miguelistas, and Zayas.

Gómez, Juan Gualberto, 35, 79, 147,
148.

Gómez, Máximo, 5, 9, 16, 25.

González Llorente, Pedro, 13.

González Sarraín, Felipe, 147, 148.

Great Britain and England, proposed
commercial treaty with Cuba mentioned, 25; property of nationals damaged, 37; claims filed by nationals of,
83; secures iron ore in Cuba, 126;
trades with Cuba, 128; visited by Magoon, 218.

Greble, E. St. J., 97, 115, 127.

Guanabacoa, 33, 68, 78, 117, 200.

Guanajay, 78, 116.

Guane, 78.

Guantánamo, 24, 116.

Guardiola, Santos, 17.

Guerra, Faustino, leaves congress, 34;
starts revolt in Pinar del Río, 34;
states purpose of insurgents, 35; in-
vades province of Havana, 36-37;
states rebels would not fight U. S.
troops, 60; member commission on
surrender, 65; president of patronage
committee, 79; appointed Commander-
in-Chief Cuban army, 145, 167;
wounded by supporters of Gómez,
145 n.; to take charge at Camp Columbia, 188; visits the United States
and France, 207. *See also* August Revolution and Insurgents.

Guerra, Urbano, 144.

Güines, 78.

Guira de Macuriges, 117.

Guiteras, Juan, 112, 115.

Guzmán, Eduardo, 37, 79.

Hanna, Mark, 7.

Hanna, Mathew E., 135.

Harbors and Rivers, 104-6. *See also*
Ships and Commerce.

Havana, City of, naval station lease
signed at, 24; threatened by rebels,
41-42; troops from "Denver" landed
to protect, 42; Peace Commissioners
sent to, 45; Peace Commissioners arrive in, 51; Liberals held prisoners in,
52-53; Estrada Palma leaves, 60, 62;
Camp Columbia near, 65; Magoon arrives in, 71; Americans in thank
Peace Commissioners, 74; troubled by
strikes, 91-92; improvement board for
named, 105; telephone companies in,
108-9; health services of, 114; nurses'
home built in, 116; contract for
sewers and pavements, 117-18; Vedado suburb of, 118; bond issue for
improvements in, 221 n., 189, 202;
Church property in purchased, 139-41;
Crowder sent to, 146 n.; national district proposed for, 160; political
parades in, 177; honors Magoon, 187;
Magoon leaves, 196.

Havana, Province of, 33, 36, 37, 41,
122, 139, 180.

Havana Bay, 65, 81.

Havana Bond and Loan Company, 119.

Havana Daily Telegraph, 34, 183.

Havana Electric Railway Company, 106,
215, 216.

Havana Post, 46, 59, 83, 144, 183, 197,
210.

Havana Telephone Company, 109.

Havana University. *See* University of
Havana, National.

Hawley, Roberto B., 88.

Hay, John, 23.

Health, 6, 23, 86, 112-16. *See also*
Yellow fever and sanitation.

Hernández, Carlos, 65, 107.

Historical Liberals. *See* Miguelistas.

Holguín-Santiago Mine Company, 126.

Holy See, 138.

Honduras, 17.

Horse certificates, 66, 67, 83.

House of Commons, 218.

House of Representatives. *See* Congress.